GETTYSBURG

ALSO BY RICHARD A. SAUERS

Advance the Colors!
Pennsylvania Civil War Battle Flags

The Civil War Journal of Colonel William J. Bolton:
51st Pennsylvania, April 20, 1861–August 2, 1865

How to Do Civil War Research

GETTYSBURG

THE MEADE-SICKLES CONTROVERSY

Richard A. Sauers

BRASSEY'S, INC.
WASHINGTON, D.C.

Library of Congress Cataloging-in-Publication Data
Sauers, Richard Allen.
   Gettysburg : the Meade-Sickles controversy / Richard A. Sauers.
      p. cm.—(Military controversies)
Includes bibliographical references and index.
   ISBN 1-57488-488-3 (hardcover : alk. paper)
   1. Gettysburg, Battle of, Gettysburg, Pa., 1863. 2. Gettysburg, Battle of, Gettysburg, Pa., 1863—Historiography. 3. Meade, George Gordon, 1815–1872. 4. Sickles, Daniel Edgar, 1819–1914—Military leadership. 5. Strategy—History—19th century. 6. Generals—United States—Biography. I. Title. II. Series.
   E475.53 .S355 2003
   973.7'349—dc21

                            2002012064

Brassey's, Inc.
22841 Quicksilver Drive
Dulles, Virginia 20166

First Edition

10 9 8 7 6 5 4 3 2 1

CONTENTS

MAPS

PREFACE AND ACKNOWLEDGMENTS

Gettysburg is the most written-about battle in American history. Yet the very abundance of material on this epic engagement has also served to shroud it in controversy. For almost every statement written about it, at least one contradictory statement exists. The importance of this American Civil War battle and the ensuing mass of both published and unpublished literature have created a nightmare for historians. Already in 1886, a New York editor commenting on the battle wrote that "a Caspian Sea of ink has been shed in descriptions of its various details and monuments have been set up by the different states to indicate the spot where everybody stood, and these are covered with legends to show what everybody did."[1]

However, in spite of the general accessibility of most of this literature, many twentieth-century historians have either neglected much of it or allowed the veracity of unreliable sources to go without challenge. These factors, combined with great general interest in the Gettysburg battle, have often resulted in shoddy scholarship. Many historians—both amateur and professional—have relied too heavily upon published works written in the period from 1863 to about 1920. Most of these books were by writers who did not acknowledge their sources. A close examination of these battle narratives reveals many flagrant errors. Thus, stories that began as a slight stretching of the truth blossomed into outright falsehoods over the years, and many modern writers did not check and recheck the validity of what, by the turn of the nineteenth century, was taken as the "truth" of Gettysburg.

Another problem associated with Gettysburg historiography is the emotional nature of much of the literature. Many of the participants in the Meade-Sickles controversy resorted to passionate defenses of their chiefs' records at Gettysburg. One of the outstanding students of the battle has written the following about this particular type of source: "An abundance of polemical tracts furiously attacking and defending Meade's record at Gettysburg have cluttered up the literature of the battle."[2] Obviously, these writings must be used with caution, for, on the whole, they combine truths, half-truths, and lies. In this study, although I was forced to use this type of source, I also relied on other sources in an attempt to corroborate what others have written and produce as accurate an analysis of the controversy as possible. In some cases, I have quoted the exact words of the participants. However, in many instances I have paraphrased or summarized the writings of others, fully realizing that such paraphrasing can lead to unintentional misinterpretation of someone else's words.

The Meade-Sickles controversy is one of the major historiographical problems of the Battle of Gettysburg. I became interested in the topic in the late 1970s while gathering material for a Gettysburg bibliography. At that time, I noticed the lack of any coherent, exhaustive study of the controversy. My initial research yielded an article in the September 1980 issue of *Civil War History* and later my master's thesis.

This book is the first exhaustive treatment of a complicated historiographical problem. The lack of a logically consistent narrative of the Meade-Sickles feud was of prime concern to me when I originally organized the material. Accordingly, the first two chapters set the stage for the controversy by describing the actions of the major protagonists on the second day at Gettysburg. Chapters 3 and 4 continue the story during the postbattle years, using primarily the writings of the two generals and their respective supporters. Chapter 5 surveys the interpretations of the controversy by historians and biographers.

Chapters 6 through 9 organize General Sickles' defense of his actions at Gettysburg into four major points. Each point is carefully examined and then shown to be a product of Sickles' skillful blend of reality and fiction. These chapters illustrate how Sickles and his henchmen perverted the history of the battle and also describe the unusual success his story has maintained over the past century. A concluding chapter provides a summary of the controversy and ties together some loose ends.

In writing this book, I have presupposed of the reader a general knowledge of both the Battle of Gettysburg and the American Civil War. I do not consider the book to be the definitive history of the battle's second day. Harry Pfanz's tactical study of the fighting on Sickles' front, followed by his account of Cemetery and Culp's Hills, form a perfect companion to this work.[3]

What I have attempted is an examination of the written battle that was one of the results of the actual battlefield confrontation on July 2, 1863. When I began working on the controversy in the early 1980s, I had few preconceptions about where my research would take me. By the time I was finished with my work, what I found had made me very biased in favor of General Meade's point of view. Thus, I structured the book's thesis on a scrutiny of Sickles' writings and a comparison of his statements with those of others. While I could also have taken Sickles' side of the argument and defended his position, I felt that the argument against doing so was too strong. Thus, if part of the challenge of writing good analytical history is taking as unbiased a course as possible, I must confess that I may not have done so. By passionately defending Meade's record at Gettysburg, I have written what may well prove to be a controversial book that Sickles supporters will disdain. If so, I have succeeded in renewing fresh interest in an old controversy. One man's history is merely how he has interpreted the past; discovering alternative interpretations is part of the fun of this discipline.

The feud between Generals Meade and Sickles was not an isolated case of strained relations. Personality conflicts and quarrels occurred far too often during the Civil War. Examples range from the noncooperation between George B. McClellan and John Pope during the Second Manassas Campaign to the shady dealings behind Ambrose E. Burnside's back after Fredericksburg. On the Confederate side, Braxton Bragg and his subordinates feuded after the battle of Chickamauga, and after the war, supporters of Robert E. Lee looked for a scapegoat for the defeat at Gettysburg. Such controversies remain fresh topics for future civil warriors to examine in detail. I hope that this study of one such controversy will spark similar analyses of other equally important military relationships during one of America's most well-known wars.

At the Pennsylvania State University graduate school where I completed my master's on the Meade-Sickles controversy, I had the enthusiastic backing and guidance of Dr. Warren W. Hassler, Jr. I owe a great debt to Professor Hassler, an outstanding teacher as well as a genuinely kind human being who has spawned a generation of historians, of which I am proud to be a part.

A number of people generously aided me at times during the course of my research into this topic. Chief among these friends are: Dr. Gary W. Gallagher, then of Penn State University, for his helpful comments and the use of part of his typescript of E. P. Alexander's memoirs; Kathleen Georg Harrison, chief historian, Gettysburg National Military Park, for answering my questions about topography and place names; John Heiser, Gettysburg, cartographer extraordinaire; the late Dick Lemal, Plainfield, N.J., for his help in obtaining copies of manuscripts from New York repositories, for his hospitality when I visited New York, and for his criticism of my original manuscript; Brian Pohanka, Alexandria, Va., for helping me with questions about some of the individuals involved in the controversy; Bill Styple, Kearny, N.J., for alerting me to the memoirs of H. A. Johnson, 3d Maine; Dr. Sergei V. Utechin, professor emeritus at Penn State, for training me in source criticism; and Stuart Vogt, Springfield, Mass., for introducing me to the treasure trove of Hiram Berdan material in the National Archives.

Also, my thanks to the following repositories for allowing me to quote from manuscripts: the Alabama Department of Archives and History, Duke University, the Historical Society of Pennsylvania, the New Hampshire Historical Society, the New York Public Library, the New York State Library, the Virginia Historical Society, and Yale University. Kent State University Press, publisher of *Civil War History*, has permitted me to quote extensively from my 1980 article in that journal. The United States Army Military History Institute, Carlisle Barracks, Pa., has allowed me to use photographs from the Massachusetts Commandery Collection, Military Order of the Loyal Legion of the United States, housed in that repository.

Chapter One

BACKGROUND: THE GETTYSBURG CAMPAIGN THROUGH JULY 1

The Gettysburg Campaign began on June 3, 1863, as units of Gen. Robert E. Lee's Army of Northern Virginia began to leave their positions near Fredericksburg, Virginia, and march toward the Shenandoah Valley. After the victory at Chancellorsville, Pennsylvania, in May, General Lee, after consultations with President Jefferson Davis, decided to attempt a second invasion of Northern soil. The major reason for doing so was the hope that a successful strike into the North would loosen Federal Maj. Gen. Ulysses S. Grant's siege of Vicksburg, which, together with Port Hudson, was the Confederacy's last outpost on the Mississippi River. A Southern foray north of the Mason-Dixon line might prevent more reinforcements from reaching Grant, while a military victory on enemy ground might lead to the foreign recognition that the Confederacy so desperately needed to continue the war effort. In addition, Lee wanted to spare the Virginia countryside the effects of yet another campaign; the invasion would also enable his soldiers to gather supplies from a countryside much more able to provide such necessities than the depleted Virginia farms could.[1]

And so, throughout the month of May, Lee reorganized his army and drew up his invasion plans. The death of Stonewall Jackson, his most trusted subordinate, left Lee with no alternative but to reorganize his troops. The Army of Northern Virginia had consisted of two large corps, one led by Jackson and one by Lt. Gen. James Longstreet, also an outstanding corps commander. But beyond these two officers, there was no one capable of commanding such a large number of troops, so Lee decided to divide the army into three corps, each smaller than the previous two. Longstreet retained his position as chief of the 1st Corps, while two new lieutenant generals, Richard S. Ewell and Ambrose P. Hill, were placed in command of the 2d and 3d Corps, respectively. The cavalry, led by the dashing Gen. James E. B. "Jeb" Stuart, received new regiments that almost doubled its previous strength. This revamped army contained about eighty thousand soldiers, most of them seasoned veterans.[2]

Across the Rappahannock River from Fredericksburg lay the Federal Army of the Potomac, commanded by Maj. Gen. Joseph Hooker. This massive force of one hundred-twenty thousand men had been defeated at Chancellorsville by a Confederate force half its size, through a combination of Lee's superior generalship and some key mistakes by Hooker. The campaign had begun with Hooker's brilliant flanking maneuver designed to force Lee out of his fortifications at Fredericksburg. However, when Lee did the unexpected by fighting instead of running, Hooker lost his nerve and failed to use much of his army in the ensuing battle. Hooker's abject failure as army commander had already aroused severe hostility from the government in Washington. As the Gettysburg Campaign unfolded, President Lincoln and his General in Chief, Maj. Gen. Henry W. Halleck, initiated a search for a replacement. Maj. Gen. John F. Reynolds, commanding the 1st Corps, was offered the position, but turned it down when he was refused an absolute free hand in regard to strategy.[3]

As Lee's troops began the evacuation of their positions at Fredericksburg and marched off toward the Shenandoah Valley, Union intelligence began to notice some of the telltale signs presaging this movement. Hooker at first believed that the intelligence reports indicated a large-scale cavalry raid into Federal territory, so he determined to preempt the raid before it could begin. At dawn on June 9, the Union Cavalry Corps, led by Maj. Gen. Alfred Pleasonton, stormed across the Rappahannock to strike at Stuart's horsemen near Brandy Station. After a day-long series of engagements, Pleasonton withdrew to report the presence of the enemy in strong force at this point. Shortly afterward, other intelligence information corroborated the fact that Lee's men were indeed on the march north, so Hooker began to shift units of his army northward to stay between Lee and Washington.[4]

However, by the time Hooker started to move his army northward, Lee had had a good head start. When Hooker realized this, he proposed a southward advance toward Richmond in an effort to force Lee to halt his invasion because of the Federal threat to his capital. Lincoln and Halleck vetoed this suggestion and ordered Hooker to stay between Washington and the enemy.[5]

Disgruntled with his superiors, Hooker began to exhibit evidence of his dissatisfaction by asking for more and more men for the army, arguing that Lee's army was stronger than his own. While this statement of Hooker's was not true—if indeed Hooker actually believed it himself—his calls for reinforcements were justified: the government's faulty recruiting procedures had become very evident. As the Army of the Potomac moved north, many two-year and nine-month regiments began mustering out and going home, thereby reducing the army by at least twenty thousand men. This came at a time when the Army of Northern Virginia was the largest it had been since mid-1862. So, even with reinforcements from Washington, Hooker's command would not be much stronger than Lee's.[6]

As the Federal troops slowly moved north, Lee's veterans were already crossing the Potomac River into Maryland. Ewell's 2d Corps, in the lead, had smashed Maj. Gen. Robert H. Milroy's defense of Winchester, Virginia, capturing or scattering the garrison of some eight thousand troops.[7] Ewell's divisions then bypassed Harper's Ferry, Virginia, and its ten thousand defenders and entered Maryland. By June 28, Gen. Jubal Early's division had seized York, Pennsylvania, and narrowly missed capturing the bridge over the Susquehanna River at Wrightsville, Pennsylvania, before it was burned by retreating militia. Robert Rodes's division was approaching Harrisburg, Pennsylvania, which was defended only by militia commanded by Maj. Gen. Darius N. Couch (Couch had been in command of the 2d Corps under Hooker, but had quit in disgust after Hooker's inept performance at Chancellorsville).[8]

The remainder of the Army of Northern Virginia was scattered throughout the Cumberland Valley, with its main concentration near Chambersburg, Pennsylvania. However, the majority of Stuart's cavalry was out of touch with Lee. Stuart had departed on a raid behind Union lines. When the Army of the Potomac moved north, Stuart was cut off from any communication with Lee and was forced into a more circuitous route than planned to regain contact with his chief. Thus, for a great part of the campaign, Stuart blinded Lee when it mattered most.[9] Lee did not hear any concrete information about the location of the Federals until Longstreet's spy, "Harrison," reached his employer on June 28 with the startling news that the Army of the Potomac was north of that river and closing with the scattered Confederate divisions.[10] After considering Harrison's information, Lee sent orders for his units to concentrate in the Chambersburg-Cashtown area. Sometime after sending out these orders, Lee apparently received word that was even more surprising—the Federal government had replaced Hooker with yet another officer, Maj. Gen. George G. Meade.

As mentioned above, Hooker had become dissatisfied with the government's interference in his command of the army. He did not like General Halleck personally and attempted to bypass him in the chain of command whenever possible. Lincoln, however, put a stop to this practice by ordering Hooker to keep Halleck informed of the Union army's movements. As the army crossed the Potomac and approached Frederick, Maryland, Hooker became involved in yet another squabble with his superiors. Once it was apparent that Lee's soldiers were approaching the Susquehanna River, Hooker devised a plan to cut Lee's communications with Virginia and force him to break off the Pennsylvania Campaign. He proposed abandoning Harper's Ferry and adding Maj. Gen. William H. French's garrison to the field army. French's command would unite with Maj. Gen. Henry W. Slocum's 12th Corps. This force of seventeen thousand men would then march into the Cumberland Valley to destroy the Rebel bridges across the Potomac and intercept any ammunition supply trains attempting to cross. Other units of the army would remain within supporting distance in case Lee turned back to engage Slocum's command.[11]

However, Halleck did not look kindly on this plan. He told Hooker that the Harper's Ferry garrison would remain in place because he considered the town a vital point for the Federals to occupy. Halleck also ordered General French to disregard any orders he might receive from Hooker. When Hooker's own plans had been vetoed and he learned of Halleck's stance, the general sent his resignation to Washington. Hooker complained that it was simply not possible to cover both Washington and Harper's Ferry with the troops then at his disposal.[12]

There has been much debate on whether or not Hooker was bluffing when he sent his resignation to Halleck. Perhaps he believed that the administration would not dare to change commanding generals in the midst of a campaign, and would thus bow to his demands. Perhaps he was genuinely shaken at the prospect of facing Lee in another battle. Or possibly Halleck did everything he could to goad Hooker into resigning. But whatever the reason, Lincoln and Secretary of War Edwin Stanton accepted Hooker's resignation. For a replacement, they decided on Maj. Gen. George G. Meade.[13]

Col. James A. Hardie of the War Department was dispatched from Washington on June 27 by special train to convey the orders to Hooker and Meade. While making the journey to Frederick, Hardie chatted pleasantly with Maj. Gen. Daniel E. Sickles, commander of the 3d Corps, who was en route to rejoin his corps after a furlough. Sickles was the Army of the Potomac's sole corps commander who was not a professional soldier, but Sickles was very well known by this period of the war.

Daniel Edgar Sickles, a New York City native, was born in 1819. After attending New York University, he entered law practice via Tammany Hall, the notorious, graft-ridden, Democratic machine that controlled New York politics. He later was a member of the state assembly before returning to the city as a corporation counsel. In 1853, Sickles became secretary of the American legation in London, from which position he had a hand in formulating the Ostend Manifesto that proved so embarrassing to the Franklin Pierce administration. In 1857, Sickles was elected to the House of Representatives as a member of the New York delegation.

While in this position he was suddenly thrust into national recognition when his wife became involved with Philip Barton Key, whose father was the famous Francis Scott Key of "Star-Spangled Banner" fame. Sickles, who was a notorious womanizer, found out about his wife's infidelity and took matters into his own hand. He shot and killed Key when he spied his wife's lover loitering near his house on Lafayette Square in Washington. A lengthy court case ensued. Sickles' battery of lawyers, among them Edwin Stanton, pleaded temporary insanity for the first time in American legal history. Sickles was found not guilty of murder as a result. And then, in an age when proper etiquette demanded that he divorce his wife, Sickles further surprised his contemporaries by taking her back. Not surprisingly, the notoriety he received at this period in his life derailed his political aspirations.

Upon the outbreak of the Civil War, Dan Sickles decided to fight for the Union in an attempt to refurbish his tarnished reputation. Primarily through his efforts, a brigade of five regiments was raised. After some squabbling with authorities in Washington, Sickles had his regiments, dubbed the "Excelsior Brigade," mustered into Federal service. He was commissioned a brigadier general on September 3, 1861, as thanks for his efforts to support the government. Some congressional debate, among other problems, delayed Sickles' confirmation to this rank until May 13, 1862.

Sickles rejoined his brigade later that month. His command was a part of General Hooker's division of the 3d Corps, and in this capacity Sickles participated in the engagement at Fair Oaks and the Seven Days' Battles. Political intrigues in Washington then kept Sickles out of the second Manassas and Antietam Campaigns. He reemerged as a major general of volunteers in command of Hooker's old division of the 3d Corps at the Battle of Fredericksburg in December 1862, where his command lay in reserve and was not engaged.

With Hooker's elevation to army command, Sickles received the 3d Corps for the Chancellorsville Campaign. Some of his skirmishers discovered Stonewall Jackson's flanking march and Sickles received permission from Hooker to pull his corps out of line to attack the enemy, which was supposed to be retreating toward Richmond. As Sickles' troops struggled forward through tangled woods to smash Jackson's rearguard, Jackson's main force struck the isolated 11th Corps on the Federal right, completely shattering this hapless corps. Sickles turned his command around and although he failed to return to the main line by nightfall, he authorized a night attack to clear a path back to friendly positions. While moving back to the main line, Sickles was ordered to abandon Hazel Grove, a treeless hillock in the center of the battle area. The Confederates were quick to take advantage of the terrain, and enemy artillery placed there caused many casualties to the Yankees fighting in the Chancellor House area on May 3. All in all, Sickles had done rather well in his first real test of combat leadership. Now, in late June, he was on his way back to the 3d Corps.[14]

Once Colonel Hardie reached Frederick, he set out in search of Meade. After stumbling around in the dark for some time, Hardie eventually located 5th Corps headquarters. Following some animated conversation with the guards, Hardie was permitted to go in and wake the sleeping general. Meade's first reaction at being awakened was to profess a clear conscience, an allusion to his belief that Hardie was sent to arrest him over a disagreement he had had with Hooker. Hardie then handed the startled general the War Department order assigning him to army command.[15]

Perhaps the choice of Meade took most observers by surprise, since that general was not well known, even throughout the army. Meade professed an indifference to the backbiting and politicking so prevalent in the Army of the Potomac, and thus sought no support for his own advancement. He also possessed a dedication to duty and a strong moral sense of righteousness as well as a genuine concern for the safety of his men. But Meade also had a quick temper, hence his nickname, "Old Snapping Turtle." This quality sometimes left bad impressions on those who did not know him well. Still, once it was announced that Meade had taken command, most officers thought highly of the choice.[16]

George Gordon Meade, born in 1815, was the son of a well-to-do Philadelphia businessman. He graduated from West Point in 1835, and saw brief service in the Second Seminole War before resigning his commission to become a civil engineer. In this capacity Meade participated in the survey of the Mississippi River delta, a Florida railroad, and in the Texas–Louisiana boundary dispute. He then was reappointed as a lieutenant of topographical engineers and assigned to the Philadelphia area so he could be with his wife, Margaret, whom he had married in 1840. While in Philadelphia, Meade worked on coastal lighthouses in the vicinity.

Upon the outbreak of the Mexican War, Lieutenant Meade was assigned to the staff of Gen. Zachary Taylor and was present on the battlefields of Palo Alto, Resaca de la Palma, and Monterrey before being transferred to Winfield Scott's army for the Veracruz landing. Meade was then rotated home and saw no further wartime action. Next, he was assigned to various duties along the Atlantic seaboard, primarily the construction of lighthouses in Florida, Delaware, and New Jersey. The outbreak of the Civil War found Meade, now with the rank of captain, in charge of the engineering survey of the Great Lakes, with headquarters at Detroit.

After the debacle at Bull Run, Pennsylvania Governor Andrew G. Curtin used his influence to have Meade appointed a brigadier general of volunteers to rank from August 31, 1861. The general was assigned to the command of the 2d Brigade of the Pennsylvania Reserves. He led his brigade at Beaver Dam Creek, Gaines' Mill, and Glendale, where he was severely wounded in the back and arm. He recovered quickly and led his command at Second Manassas. Meade was then elevated to the command of the Reserves and led the division at South Mountain and Antietam. When Hooker was wounded at Antietam, Meade temporarily commanded the 1st Corps. At Fredericksburg, Meade's division scored the only temporary Federal success of the day. His brigades smashed through Jackson's line near Hamilton's Crossing, only to be driven back when supporting troops failed to take advantage of the temporary breakthrough.

Soon after Fredericksburg, Maj. Gen. Ambrose E. Burnside appointed Meade to command the 5th Corps, which he led during the Chancellorsville Campaign. Although his corps was not heavily engaged, Meade was quite vocal about wanting to continue the battle after Hooker had made up his mind to retreat. Thus, by the beginning of the Gettysburg Campaign, Meade had achieved a solid combat record and was developing as a competent, reliable officer when he was suddenly thrust into the position of commanding general, Army of the Potomac.

After handing Meade the order placing him in command of the army, Colonel Hardie gave him a short, detailed letter from General Halleck outlining his duties. Halleck wrote that the army was to continue to cover Washington, and if Lee moved upon either the capital or Baltimore, the government expected Meade to intercept the Rebels and fight a pitched battle. All troops within the sphere of the army's operations were placed under Meade's control, including the Harper's Ferry garrison. Finally, in an unusual order, which echoed the importance the government placed upon the change of commanders during a critical campaign, Halleck empowered Meade "to remove from command, and to send from your army, any officer or other person you may deem proper, and to appoint to command as you may deem expedient."[17]

Meade and Hardie then rode off in search of General Hooker's headquarters, which they located just before daybreak. Hooker had already been informed that somebody important from the War Department was in camp, and had guessed Hardie's mission before he read the order relieving him of command. The two generals then entered into a lengthy discussion as Hooker briefed Meade on the location of the several corps comprising the Army of the Potomac, as well as the approximate locations of Lee's troops. Maj. Gen. Daniel Butterfield, Hooker's chief of staff, also joined the generals for this meeting.[18]

Meade later recalled that he believed Hooker did not have any concrete plans, and appeared to be extemporizing strategy according to each day's intelligence reports. The new commander of the army was different, for at 7:00 A.M. he wired a report to Halleck that offered a first glimpse of his proposed strategy:

> Frederick, Md., June 28, 1863—7 A.M.
> (Received 10 A.M.)

General H. W. Halleck,
General-in-chief:

> The order placing me in command of this army is received. As a soldier, I obey it, and to the utmost of my ability will execute it. Totally unexpected as it has been, and in ignorance of the exact condition of the troops and position of the enemy, I can only say now that it appears to me I must move toward the Susquehanna, keeping Washington and Baltimore well covered, and if the enemy is checked in his attempt to cross the Susquehanna, or if he turns toward Baltimore, to give him battle. I would say that I trust every available man that can be spared will be sent to me, as from all accounts the enemy is in strong force. So soon as I can post myself up, I will communicate more in detail.

> Geo. G. Meade
> Major-General[19]

To accomplish these objectives, Meade first had to concentrate the army. Upon assuming command, he had learned from Hooker where the several corps were located, and the widely scattered positions illustrated Hooker's uncertainty as to Lee's exact whereabouts. Army headquarters was located at Frederick, as was the Artillery Reserve, with the 5th Corps a few miles away on Ballinger's Creek. About ten miles west of Frederick, at the village of Middletown, lay the left wing of the army, commanded by Meade's close friend, Maj. Gen. John F. Reynolds. In addition to his own 1st Corps, Reynolds had control of General Sickles' 3d Corps and Maj. Gen. Oliver O. Howard's 11th Corps. Maj. Gen. Henry W. Slocum's 12th Corps had just crossed the Potomac River and was encamped near Knoxville, about fifteen miles southwest of Frederick. Maj. Gen. Winfield Scott Hancock, commanding the 2d Corps, was at Barnesville. The largest infantry corps in the army, Maj. Gen. John Sedgwick's 6th, was even farther from headquarters, bivouacked at Poolesville.

Maj. Gen. Alfred Pleasonton's Cavalry Corps was widely scattered. Brig. Gen. John Buford's 1st Division was halfway between Frederick and Knoxville. The 2d Division, Brig. Gen. David M. Gregg commanding, was guarding the northern approaches to Frederick. A third cavalry division, under the command of Maj. Gen. Julius Stahel, had just arrived at Frederick from the Washington defenses.

Finally, two brigades of the Pennsylvania Reserves had been released from Washington and were en route to join the army. Led by Brig. Gen. Samuel W. Crawford, the Reserves had just reached the mouth of the Monocacy River.[20]

Meade designed the order of march for June 28 to bring the corps closer together just in case the enemy was nearer the army than expected. By that nightfall, five of the infantry corps were in the vicinity of Frederick, with Sickles about eight miles north and Sedgwick ten miles to the southeast at Hyattstown.[21] (See map 1.)

As Meade became more familiar with his new duties during the day on June 28, he made some changes designed to improve the efficiency of the army. General Stahel was relieved from command of his cavalry division, as were his two brigade commanders. Three new brigadiers were appointed; command of the division went to Hugh Judson Kilpatrick, whose command was now designated the 3d Division of the Cavalry Corps.[22]

Meade kept the officers of Hooker's staff in their accustomed roles, but he did seek out a new chief of staff. Relations between Meade and General Butterfield were formal, if nothing else. The two appeared to work well together until the latter departed from the army immediately after Gettysburg on account of a slight wound received on July 3. Many contemporaries were wary of Butterfield, who, along with Hooker and Sickles, formed an influential trio with many powerful political connections. Meade had earlier expressed some distrust of Butterfield, and the fact that General Burnside had displaced Butterfield as 5th Corps commander with Meade surely influenced Meade to search for a replacement he could better trust.[23] Meade approached three candidates—Adj. Gen. Seth Williams; Brig. Gen. Andrew A. Humphreys, commanding one of Sickles' divisions; and chief engineer Gouverneur K. Warren. All three advised Meade that Butterfield was the best-qualified man for the post and that a change now would result in lost time as the new chief of staff would have to familiarize himself with his new duties. Thus, for better or worse, Meade retained Butterfield as his chief of staff.[24]

By daybreak on June 29, Meade had further refined his original plan. He wrote to Halleck that his line of march would incline to the right to

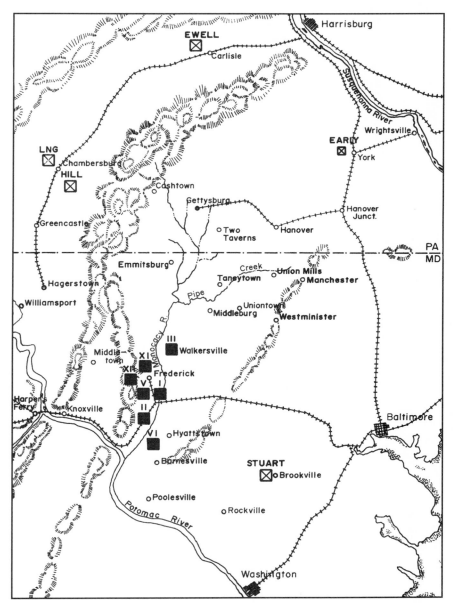

Map 1. Positions of the Armies, Night of June 28, 1863.

better cover the territory between his present position and the Susquehanna River. In other words, Meade had by this time abandoned Hooker's
idea of striking at Lee's communications and instead declared that the
Confederate army was his main objective. Meade was still not sure about
the exact location of Lee's units, but he hoped to catch his opponent before Lee could concentrate and perhaps Meade could defeat the Rebels in
detail. Meade also ordered General French to abandon Harper's Ferry,
send not more than three thousand men to escort all the movable stores
to Washington, and march to join the army with the rest of the garrison.
This last order reflected Meade's uncertainty over the eventual outcome
of the campaign and his desire to have the strongest possible force with
which to confront Lee's army, which he apparently thought was larger
than his own.[25]

The order of march for June 29 reflected Meade's change of route for
the army. Meade intended that the infantry corps would occupy a general
line from Emmitsburg, Maryland, in the west to New Windsor, Maryland, in the southeast, but a series of mishaps prevented all corps from
attaining their objectives. Hancock was three hours late in starting his
troops on the road to Taneytown, Maryland, because a clerk failed to
deliver the order on time; his 2d Corps halted for the night at Uniontown,
Maryland, near army headquarters.[26]

General Slocum complained to headquarters that the trains of another
corps blocked the road to his front. Upon closer inspection, these wagons
were found to belong to the 3d Corps. After hearing Slocum's report,
Meade dispatched a short note to Sickles, ordering him to give personal
attention to getting his trains moving. Still, Slocum encamped for the
night far short of Taneytown.[27] (See map 2.)

Part of this confusion and delay was because of the poor maps available
to the army. General Warren had to rely on a paucity of maps. To remedy
this, he sent some of his aides to scour Baltimore and Philadelphia for any
maps of central Maryland that could be found. The miserable condition
of many of the roads also contributed to some of the delays.[28]

Based upon more positive information about the location and intentions of the enemy, Meade slowed the advance for June 30. The left wing
under Reynolds encamped in the Emmitsburg area. The right wing made
a somewhat longer march that took the 5th Corps across the Pennsylvania
border to Littlestown, the 6th Corps to Manchester, Maryland, and the

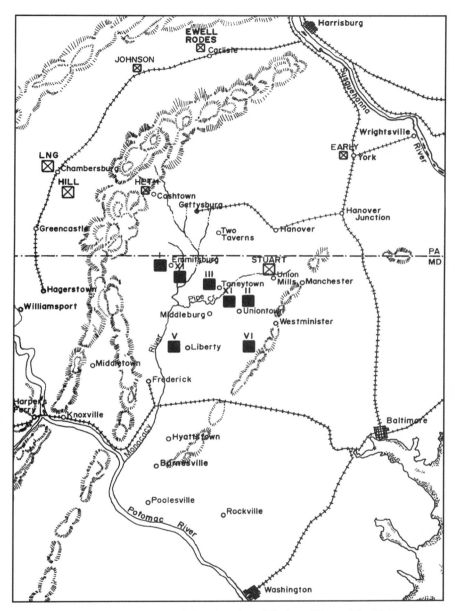

Map 2. Positions of the Armies, Night of June 29, 1863.

12th Corps to Uniontown. In the center, Meade transferred army head-quarters to Taneytown; Hancock's 2d Corps was a few miles away to the southeast.[29] (See map 3.)

Also, by June 30 Meade had received fairly accurate intelligence reports and had a good idea of the approximate enemy positions. A circular note sent to all corps commanders identified these positions—Longstreet and Hill at Chambersburg and Ewell's troops at Carlisle and York. Meade also informed his subordinates that enemy movements indicated "a disposition to advance from Chambersburg to Gettysburg."[30] The apparent concentration of the enemy divisions seemed to indicate to Meade that his rapid advance had caused Lee to hesitate and begin recalling his scattered units. Cavalry contact between elements of both armies was increasing, especially to the north and west of the axis of advance, where General Buford's division had reached Gettysburg and located enemy infantry a few miles west of the town.[31]

Since Meade believed that Lee had turned back from the Susquehanna and was concentrating his forces, he foresaw that a battle was imminent. During the day on June 30, Meade ordered Brig. Gen. Henry J. Hunt, his chief of artillery, aided by General Warren, to examine closely a possible battle line that other engineer officers had located as the army marched north. This line followed the course of Pipe Creek, from Middleburg to Manchester, Maryland, and was ideally suited for a defensive battle. Although other officers received instructions to examine other possible locations, Meade had already decided that the Pipe Creek line was the best place to defend if Lee advanced against the Army of the Potomac before Meade was ready to fight. Meade was unsure of where the impending engagement would occur, but he would do all within his power to amass every possible advantage for his men, including that of favorable terrain.[32]

Early the next morning—July 1, 1863—Meade embodied his thoughts on the Pipe Creek line in a circular letter to the corps commanders. This letter also gave the order of march for the day. The plan was provisional only, for Meade stated that "developments may cause the commanding general to assume the offensive from his present positions." This statement reflected the fact that Meade had not yet pinpointed the exact Rebel positions. Until the enemy concentration point was known in full, the Pipe Creek line would be taken up, especially if Lee attacked.[33]

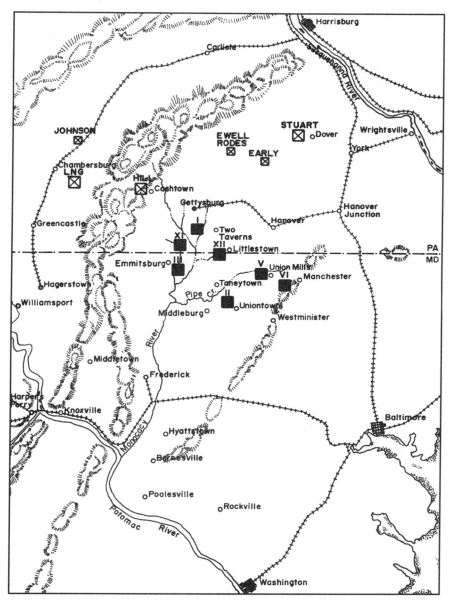

Map 3. Positions of the Armies, Night of June 30, 1863.

At noon, Meade sent Halleck a message outlining his plans:

Taneytown, July 1, 1863—12 P.M.

General Halleck:

Dispatch sent last night giving my position at Emmitsburg, Gettysburg, and Hanover.

Ewell is massing at Heidlersburg. A. P. Hill is massed behind the mountains at Cashtown. Longstreet somewhere between Chambersburg and the mountains.

The news proves my advance has answered its purpose. I shall not advance any, but prepare to receive an attack in case Lee makes one. A battlefield is being selected to the rear, on which the army can be rapidly concentrated, on Pipe Creek, between Middleburg and Manchester, covering my depot at Westminster.

If I am not attacked, and I can from reliable intelligence have reason to believe I can attack with reasonable degree of success, I will do so; but at present, having relieved the pressure on the Susquehanna, I am now looking to the protection of Washington, and fighting my army to the best advantage.

1 P.M.

The enemy are advancing in force on Gettysburg, and I expect the battle will begin today.

Geo. G. Meade[34]

The appended message to the above order referred to Meade's plan to have Reynolds fall back from Gettysburg in case of enemy pressure, allowing the rest of the army to deploy behind Pipe Creek. However, the Pipe Creek circular was obsolete by the time it was sent out, for events now forced Meade to scrap his plans.

As mentioned above, General Buford's cavalry division had reached Gettysburg on June 30; two of his brigades found the entire town "in a terrible state of excitement" owing to the Confederate advance. Buford reported that enemy infantry had approached to within half a mile of Gettysburg when the Yankee cavalrymen rode into town and compelled their hasty withdrawal. Buford pushed on through Gettysburg and bivouacked on McPherson's Ridge west of town. The general then sent a further report to Meade, writing that Confederate General Hill's corps of three divisions was massed behind Cashtown, nine miles from Gettysburg. Prisoners revealed that Rodes' division of Ewell's corps was crossing the mountain from Carlisle and approaching Gettysburg from the north. Buford also kept Reynolds informed of these movements.[35]

The Confederate movements revealed by Buford's troopers probably aided Meade in the formulation of the Pipe Creek circular that was sent out on July 1. The order of march for the day sent Reynolds and the 1st Corps to Gettysburg, with Howard's 11th Corps moving up within supporting distance. Sickles was to march to Emmitsburg to cover the roads in that area. Maj. Gen. George Sykes, who had succeeded Meade in command of the 5th Corps, moved his troops to Two Taverns, a scant five miles from Gettysburg. The 6th Corps headed for Manchester, while Hancock would halt at Taneytown, where army headquarters was located.[36]

With these dispositions, Meade could cover the entire projected line behind Pipe Creek. However, he still remained uncertain as to the exact Confederate positions. Therefore, he sent a long message to Reynolds advising him of this uncertainty and asking him to survey the Gettysburg area as a possible concentration point for the army rather than Pipe Creek.[37] (See map 4.)

As dawn broke on July 1, Buford's cavalry pickets detected Rebel infantry again moving toward Gettysburg. He deployed his two brigades along McPherson's Ridge and began firing at the advancing enemy. Buford's three thousand troopers, armed with breech-loading carbines, easily managed to fend off the first, tentative probes against his thin battle line. Alerted by the firing, General Reynolds appeared on the field and told Buford that the 1st Corps would soon relieve his tired men. The first contingents of infantry began arriving on the field about 10:45 A.M. As Reynolds supervised the deployment of the Iron Brigade, he was killed during a sudden exchange of volleys between opposing foot soldiers. But just prior to his death, Reynolds had talked with Buford, analyzed the situation, and sent a message to Howard, ordering him to bring the 11th Corps to Gettysburg. Reynolds also sent a courier to Meade to inform him of the situation.

The bearer of this dispatch, Capt. Stephen M. Weld, arrived at army headquarters about 11:20 A.M. Weld reported that Reynolds had told him, "Ride at your utmost speed to General Meade. Tell him the enemy are

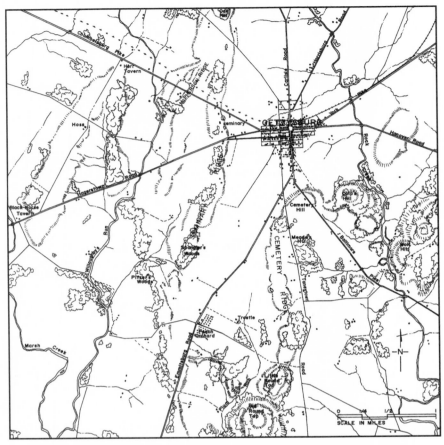

Map 4. Topographical Features of the Gettysburg Battlefield.

advancing in strong force, and that I fear they will get to the heights beyond the town before I can. I will fight them inch by inch, and if driven into the town, I will barricade the streets and hold them back as long as possible. Don't spare your horse—never mind if you kill him." General Meade at first seemed much disturbed by Reynolds's message, but after hearing it repeated, exclaimed, "Good! That is just like Reynolds; he will hold on to the bitter end."[38]

Shortly after receiving Weld's message, a courier from General Buford rode up and handed Meade the following note:

> Headquarters, First Cavalry Division,
> Gettysburg, July 1, 1863—10.10 A.M.

The enemy's forces (A. P. Hill's) are advancing on me at this point, and driving my pickets and skirmishers very rapidly. There is also a large force at Heidlersburg that is driving my pickets at that point from that direction. General Reynolds is advancing, and is within 3 miles of this point with his leading division. I am positive that the whole of A. P. Hill's force is advancing.

> Jno. Buford.
> Brigadier-General, Commanding.

General Meade,
  Commanding Army of the Potomac.[39]

On the basis of these two reports, General Meade notified the other corps commanders about the advance of the enemy upon Gettysburg. He advised Hancock that Reynolds might not have received a copy of the Pipe Creek circular. If he had not, the 1st Corps might fall back from Gettysburg through Emmitsburg rather than Taneytown, as the circular directed. If so, Meade directed Hancock to move his corps via Taneytown toward Gettysburg to cover that road should the enemy advance along that thoroughfare.[40] Meade also informed Sedgwick of the enemy advance and warned him that if it became necessary for the army to engage the enemy this day, he must hold his corps in readiness pending future orders to move in any direction. Slocum was ordered to halt his corps upon receipt of the message from headquarters and wait until he heard from Reynolds that the 1st Corps was retreating from Gettysburg. He was then to comply with his part of the Pipe Creek circular. Meade also ordered Slocum to communicate with Sykes and advise him to perform similar maneuvers with the 5th Corps should it become necessary.[41]

And then, at 1:00 P.M., Maj. William Riddle of Reynolds's staff reached headquarters with the news of his chief's death.[42] Meade immediately used the authority conferred by the order placing him in command of the army, which enabled him to appoint any officer to any command, regardless of rank or seniority. General Hancock, commanding the 2d Corps, which was bivouacked at Taneytown near army headquarters, was a close personal friend of Meade's. So, at 1:10 P.M., Meade ordered Hancock to turn command of the 2d Corps over to Brig. Gen. John Gibbon (his 2d Division commander) and proceed to Gettysburg. Once there, Hancock was to assume command of the three corps—1st, 3d, and 11th—assembled there. "If you think the ground and position there a better one to fight a battle under existing circumstances, you will so advise the general, and he will order all the troops up."[43] Thus, instead of leaving for the battlefield himself, Meade sent a trusted lieutenant to assume command and advise him of the practicability of fighting at Gettysburg instead of behind Pipe Creek.

Once Hancock departed, all Meade could do was wait for further news from the battlefield. The first dispatch arrived at 3:30 P.M. from General Howard. Sent at 2:00 P.M., the terse note must have irritated Meade very much. Howard merely reported the positions of the 1st and 11th Corps, mentioned the presence of Ewell's and Hill's corps of Lee's army, and said that he had ordered up the 3d Corps.[44]

An hour later, a courier from Buford arrived with a dispatch addressed to his superior, General Pleasonton, whose headquarters was also at Taneytown. This message was sent at 3:20 P.M. and was a call for help:

> Headquarters, First Cavalry Division,
> July 1, 1863—3.20 P.M.
>
> I am satisfied that Longstreet and Hill have made a junction. A tremendous battle has been raging since 9.30 A.M., with varying success. At the present moment the battle is raging on the road to Cashtown, and within short cannon-range of this town. The enemy's line is a semicircle on the height, from north to west. General Reynolds was killed early this morning. In my opinion, there seems to be no directing person.
>
> Jno. Buford,
> Brigadier-General of Volunteers.
>
> General Pleasonton.
> P.S.—We need help now.[45]

As a result of these two messages, Meade began to contemplate fighting the battle at Gettysburg. Shortly after receiving Buford's call for help, Meade directed Sedgwick to move the 6th Corps to Taneytown, ostensibly to act as a reserve force. Later, at 6:00 P.M., Meade sent word to Hancock, from whom he still had not heard, of Sedgwick's order, suggesting to Hancock that the battle at Gettysburg had been forced upon the army, so that, "if we get up all our people, and attack with our whole force to-morrow, we ought to defeat the force the enemy has."[46]

Meade then telegraphed Halleck, informing him of the fighting and the death of Reynolds. At the time, Meade knew that Ewell's and Hill's corps were at Gettysburg. Where Longstreet was he did not know, although Buford had postulated earlier that Longstreet was also present at Gettysburg. Meade told Halleck that he hoped to concentrate the Army of the Potomac and defeat the Rebels before Longstreet could reach the field. "At any rate, I see no other course than to hazard a general battle."[47]

Soon after Meade sent these messages, Maj. William G. Mitchell of Hancock's staff rode up to headquarters, having left Gettysburg at four o'clock. He explained the situation on the field and remarked that Hancock would hold the ground until dark to allow Meade to decide on where the battle would be fought.[48]

General Hancock had left Taneytown about 1:30 P.M. He began the thirteen-mile journey ensconced in an ambulance so he could study a map of the region as he traveled to the field without loss of time. Hancock arrived on Cemetery Hill sometime between 4 and 4:30 P.M., as the Federals were falling back toward the high ground south of Gettysburg. After Reynolds had been killed, Maj. Gen. Abner Doubleday had assumed command of the 1st Corps and repulsed the first gray assaults on McPherson's Ridge. General Howard soon reached the field and took overall control of the Northern troops arriving on the battlefield. In addition to informing Meade of the situation, Howard sent messages to Sickles at Emmitsburg and Slocum at Two Taverns, asking them to bring their corps to Gettysburg as soon as possible.

When the 11th Corps arrived on the field late in the morning of July 1, Howard posted it on the plain north of Gettysburg to guard the right flank of Doubleday's position against enemy troops reported to be advancing south from the Harrisburg area. The two Confederate divisions of Ewell's corps that entered the field from that direction attacked, and this new assault, combined with a forward movement by those units of General Hill's corps that were present, overwhelmed the Federal defenders. Howard's troops were outflanked and fell back in great confusion through the streets of Gettysburg, where hundreds became lost in the unfamiliar streets and were captured by the pursuing Rebels. This left Doubleday's corps isolated, and the remnants fell back slowly, fighting for every inch and inflicting heavy losses on Hill's two divisions.

These two corps were just rallying on Cemetery Hill south of Gettysburg when Hancock arrived. Together with General Howard, who at first demurred when Hancock told him of Meade's order placing him in command of the field (Howard ranked Hancock), Hancock managed to rally the beaten troops and began forming a defensive line. He sent the battered survivors of Brig. Gen. James S. Wadsworth's division of the 1st Corps to occupy Culp's Hill. When the 12th Corps began to arrive, Hancock sent Brig. Gen. John W. Geary's 2d Division south to the Little Round Top (Sugar Loaf Mountain) area to prevent a Confederate flanking movement from that direction. At 5:25 P.M., Hancock sent aide Capt. Israel B. Parker back to army headquarters with a written message giving Meade his thoughts on the position at Gettysburg. Meade received this note about seven o'clock:

5.25

GENERAL: When I arrived here an hour since, I found that our troops had given up the front of Gettysburg and the town. We have now taken up a position in the cemetery, and cannot well be taken. It is a position, however, easily turned. Slocum is now coming on the ground, and is taking position on the right, which will protect the right. But we have, as yet, no troops on the left, the Third Corps not having yet reported; but I suppose that it is marching up. If so, its flank march will in a degree protect our left flank. In the meantime Gibbon had better march on so as to take position on our right or left, to our rear, as may be necessary, in some commanding position. General G. will see this dispatch. The battle is quiet now. I think we will be all right until night. I have sent all the trains back. When night comes, it can be told better what had best be done. I think we can retire; if not, we can fight here, as the ground appears not unfavorable with good troops. I will communicate in a few moments with General Slocum, and transfer the command to him.

Howard says that Doubleday's command gave way.

General Warren is here.

Your obedient servant,

Winf'd S. Hancock,
Major-General, Commanding Corps.

General Butterfield, Chief of Staff.[49]

Hancock then transferred command to his senior, General Slocum, and at dark set off for Taneytown to report in person to Meade. A few miles south of Gettysburg, Hancock met General Gibbon and the 2d Corps.

Hancock halted the corps and instructed Gibbon to bivouac on the ground to guard against any possible Confederate flanking movement, then march north at first light. General Warren, Meade's chief engineer, had also arrived at Gettysburg sometime late in the afternoon. He helped rally the troops and aided Hancock with his expert advice on the strengths and weaknesses of the proposed line. He too left the field, but by a different route, to make himself better acquainted with the terrain to the rear as he rode back to report to Meade.[50]

Sometime before General Hancock departed from Gettysburg, General Sickles, having marched from Emmitsburg in response to Howard's request for help, arrived on the field with two brigades of Maj. Gen. David B. Birney's 1st Division of the 3d Corps. For Sickles, the march to Gettysburg was the culmination of three frustrating days under Meade's command. In addition to being reprimanded because his trains blocked the progress of the 12th Corps on June 29, Sickles received yet another rebuke from Meade on the thirtieth:

Headquarters Army of the Potomac
June 30, 1863.

Commanding Officer Third Corps:

The commanding general notices with regret the very slow movement of your corps yesterday. It is presumed you marched at an early hour, and up to 6 P.M. the rear of your column had not passed Middleburg, distant from your camp of the night before some 12 miles only. This, considering the good condition of the road and the favorable state of the weather, was far from meeting the expectation of the commanding general, and delayed to a very late hour the arrival of troops and trains in your rear. The 2d Corps in the same space of time made a march of nearly double your own. Situated as this army now is, the commanding general looks for rapid movements of the troops.

Very respectfully,

S. Williams,
Assistant Adjutant-General.[51]

For June 30, General Reynolds had ordered Sickles to move the 3d Corps from Taneytown to Emmitsburg, an order later reinforced by an identical message from army headquarters. However, while the troops marched toward Emmitsburg, Meade rode over to Sickles and issued him a verbal order to halt his corps where it then was, apparently because he was worried about the presence of enemy units west of Emmitsburg. Sickles would thus act as a guard force in the area. But shortly after hearing Meade's order, Sickles received a note from Reynolds detailing the position to be occupied by his troops. This last order conflicted with Meade's verbal order. Not fully comprehending the discrepancy between these instructions, Sickles halted his troops and wisely referred the matter to army headquarters. So, when the day ended, the 3d Corps remained bivouacked on the road between Emmitsburg and Taneytown.[52]

The order of march for July 1 directed the 3d Corps to take position in and around Emmitsburg while engineer officers surveyed the ground in the area for possible battle locations there. Once the corps reached this small town, Sickles sent his chief aide, Maj. Henry E. Tremain, on to Gettysburg to communicate with Reynolds and obtain information about the positions of other units of the left wing. Tremain found Reynolds before the infantry of the 1st Corps had reached McPherson's Ridge. In response to Tremain's request for information, Reynolds said, "Tell General Sickles I think he had better come up."[53]

Tremain rode back to Emmitsburg and repeated Reynolds's message to Sickles, who was unsure of what to do because the Pipe Creek circular, issued that morning, directed the 3d Corps to remain at Emmitsburg to cover a Federal withdrawal should the enemy force Reynolds back from Gettysburg. Sickles thereupon sent another aide to Gettysburg to get a fresh report from Reynolds while he waited at Emmitsburg.[54]

At 3:00 P.M., just after Tremain had returned and Sickles had dispatched another aide to Gettysburg, a courier from Reynolds hurried up to report that Reynolds had been killed and asked Sickles to move his corps to the battlefield. At almost the same instant a message from Howard reached Sickles, again requesting the presence of his troops at Gettysburg.[55]

Sickles now was faced with a crucial decision. On the one hand he had orders from army headquarters to remain at Emmitsburg, watch for the presence of the enemy, and be prepared to cover a withdrawal from Gettysburg. But now, it appeared that the 1st and 11th Corps were heavily engaged at Gettysburg and needed help. Tremain was then sent to inform Howard that the 3d Corps would march immediately for the battlefield. To conform with the order to remain at Emmitsburg, Sickles detached one brigade from each of his two divisions, together with two batteries, and placed Brig. Gen. Charles K. Graham in command, with orders to hold Emmitsburg but to fall back to Taneytown should the enemy appear in overwhelming force. Sickles sent two brigades of Birney's 1st Division on the direct road to Gettysburg. Two brigades of General Humphreys' 2d Division followed a parallel road a few miles to the west. Sickles also informed army headquarters of his decision to march to Gettysburg while leaving two brigades at Emmitsburg.[56]

Meanwhile, at Taneytown, Meade, after receiving Howard's dispatch of 2:00 P.M., became concerned lest Sickles leave Emmitsburg unprotected. At 4:45 P.M. Meade sent a message to Sickles, ordering him to remain at Emmitsburg until he heard from General Hancock, whom he mentioned had been sent to Gettysburg to take command of the troops assembled there.[57] Sickles did not receive this dispatch until his troops were well on their way to Gettysburg, so Sickles disregarded Meade's order and kept on until he reached the battlefield with Birney's two brigades sometime around six o'clock. Once he had bivouacked his men in accordance with Hancock's orders, Sickles sent the following report to Meade:

> Headquarters Third Army Corps,
> July 1, 1863—9.30 P.M.
>
> Major General Butterfield, Chief of Staff:
>
> General: Before the receipt of your dispatch (dated 4.45 P.M.), four brigades and three batteries of my corps had advanced to the support of General Howard and reached Gettysburg.
>
> I left two brigades and two batteries at Emmitsburg, assuming that the approaches through Emmitsburg toward our left and rear must not be uncovered.
>
> General Hancock is not in command—General Howard commands.
>
> My impression is, if I may be allowed to make a suggestion, that our left and rear are not sufficiently guarded. Nothing less than the earnest and frequent appeals of General Howard, and his supposed danger, could have induced me to move from the position assigned to me in general orders; but I believed the emergency justified the movement.
>
> Shall I return to my position at Emmitsburg, or shall I remain and report to Howard?
>
> If my corps is to remain in position here, I hope my brigades at Emmitsburg (and batteries) may be relieved and ordered to join me.
>
> This is a good battle-field.
>
> Very respectfully,
>
> D. E. Sickles,
> Major-General, Commanding.[58]

In this case, Sickles' discretion in advancing to Gettysburg with part of his corps was correct, given the situation at the time. He had delayed a bit because of conflicting orders from army headquarters and Reynolds, but he did eventually use correct judgment by moving to Gettysburg and leaving part of his corps at Emmitsburg to comply with the Pipe Creek circular. General Meade, after issuing the 4:45 P.M. order for Sickles to remain at Emmitsburg until he should hear from Hancock, reversed himself when more details of the action at Gettysburg became known. He had already sent a message to Halleck that reflected his change of mind to fight now at Gettysburg instead of behind Pipe Creek. Meade so notified Hancock before receiving that general's 5:25 P.M. report. At seven o'clock, Meade sent an order to General Sykes to march his corps to Gettysburg if not already ordered to do so by General Slocum. Half an hour later, Meade sent a dispatch to General Graham at Emmitsburg, informing him of the situation and ordering him to bring his troops to Gettysburg by daylight. At the same time, an orderly rode off to find General Sedgwick and present instructions for the 6th Corps to march for Gettysburg immediately. Thus, Sickles had anticipated his chief's orders to assemble the entire army at Gettysburg.[59]

However, the march of the 3d Corps to Gettysburg was far from uneventful. Sickles, with Birney's two brigades, reached the battlefield about six o'clock. The two brigades of General Humphreys' 2d Division were not so fortunate. Humphreys was ordered to march via a road parallel to the Emmitsburg Road in an effort to prevent a clogging of the main artery. His men started off with no problems. Lt. Col. Julius Hayden, inspector general on Sickles' staff, accompanied the column as guide. Sometime around 9:00 P.M., the head of the column approached the Black Horse Tavern on the Hagerstown Road. By this time, Humphreys had become convinced that the road he was on was diverging too far from the reported Federal positions south of Gettysburg. He wanted to take a road that led off to the right, but Colonel Hayden refused, maintaining that he had orders from Sickles to continue on the assigned road.

Nevertheless, Humphreys was cautious about continuing so he and a small party went ahead to reconnoiter. The general noticed the glow of a number of campfires not far ahead, indicating the presence of troops. Suspecting that his brigades were about to encounter Confederates, Humphreys signaled a halt without the use of bugles. Lt. Francis W.

Seeley, commanding Battery K, 4th United States Artillery, did not receive the order and his bugler sounded the halt. Shortly thereafter, a squad of Rebel artillerymen, thinking that the bugle call came from their battery, came up to report and were captured. Humphreys turned the column around as quietly as possible and eventually reached the Federal line on Cemetery Ridge at two o'clock in the morning of July 2, his soldiers thoroughly worn out and exhausted. This entire affair so disgusted the general that he later wrote to a friend, "You see how things were managed in the Third Corps!"[60]

In the meantime, General Meade, satisfied that all units of the army had received orders to march to Gettysburg, decided to transfer his headquarters to the field. Hancock returned to Taneytown to report in person shortly after nine o'clock, and Meade allowed him to remain there overnight to catch up on some badly needed sleep. Chief of Staff Butterfield also stayed at Taneytown to send and receive any messages that might reach headquarters the rest of the night. Any officers who remained at Taneytown would, at daybreak, pack up the headquarters wagons and move to Gettysburg to join Meade.[61]

Chapter Two

THE SECOND DAY AT GETTYSBURG

General Meade left Taneytown for Gettysburg after ten o'clock on the night of July 1. Just before the general departed, General Warren returned from the battlefield and reported what he had seen of the terrain there. His favorable views reinforced Meade's decision to concentrate the army at Gettysburg.[1] Capt. William H. Paine of the engineers then reached headquarters with a civilian guide to take the general to Gettysburg. Accompanied by Paine, the guide, and some of his staff officers, Meade set off toward Gettysburg. He was in a hurry to reach the field; Captain Paine later recalled that he remembered this ride as the fastest he made during the war. The party was delayed several times by marching troops, but in only fifty-seven minutes the general's entourage covered ten miles to reach General Gibbon's headquarters. By this time, the guide's horse had given out and most of the staff had fallen behind.[2] Meade stopped to see Gibbon for about fifteen minutes, ordering him to move the 2d Corps to Gettysburg at first light.[3]

Meade left Gibbon's camp and arrived at the gatehouse on Cemetery Hill shortly after midnight. General Howard came out of his headquarters room and invited Meade inside. Here were assembled Generals Howard, Slocum, and Sickles. From them, Meade learned about the day's fighting and that the positions the troops then occupied were good. Meade in turn informed everyone that the entire army was marching to the field. He walked outside and was shown, by the light of a full moon, the positions of the units then on the field, as well as the distant campfires of Lee's troops.[4]

At this time, units of four Union corps were on the field. Wadsworth's division of the 1st Corps occupied Culp's Hill, while the entire 11th Corps lay on Cemetery Hill. Doubleday's 3d Division of the 1st Corps was massed in reserve behind the cemetery, while John C. Robinson's 2d Division of the same corps extended from the left of the 11th Corps along Cemetery Ridge to Ziegler's Grove. From Robinson's left the ridge was vacant for about half a mile. After this gap, the crest was occupied by four brigades of Sickles' corps, two brigades from each division (Humphreys' two exhausted brigades arrived about two in the morning). To the south of these troops was massed General Geary's division of the 12th Corps, with two regiments bivouacked on Little Round Top. The other division of the corps—Brig. Gen. Alpheus S. Williams'—had been halted east of Rock Creek to counter any nocturnal enemy flanking move. Finally, Buford's cavalrymen were posted in front of the 3d Corps, occupying the general line of the Emmitsburg Road.[5]

Sometime later, just before actual sunrise, Meade, accompanied by Generals Howard and Hunt and Captain Paine, rode south along Cemetery Ridge, noting the terrain and where the troops were then positioned. Captain Paine began sketching a map of the topography and fell behind the generals. Meade rode south almost to the Round Tops, then doubled back and examined the Culp's Hill area as far east as Rock Creek. He then indicated, on the sketch map Paine had drawn, where each corps was to be posted in line. Captain Paine then made copies of this map and sent one to each corps commander, designating where each corps was to be posted. Meade also ordered General Hunt to reexamine the line after daybreak to make sure the artillery was posted properly.[6]

By the time Meade finished his reconnaissance of the battle line, he had decided to locate his headquarters at the Leister House, just behind the crest of Cemetery Ridge and adjacent to the Taneytown Road. This placed Meade near the center of the line and within easy reach of any part of it. Meade was seated on horseback in a field on the east side of the road when at six o'clock General Gibbon rode up at the head of the 2d Corps and reported for orders. General Meade issued Gibbon verbal instructions to place the troops in position on Cemetery Ridge, relieve Robinson's division, and extend the line to the south along the crest.[7]

As the 2d Corps marched onto the field, other changes were taking place in the Union line according to Meade's orders. Sometime before five o'clock, General Geary received orders to vacate his position near Little Round Top and move to Culp's Hill to rejoin the 12th Corps, which would occupy the right of the line. General Sickles was directed to relieve Geary's division and occupy Cemetery Ridge from the left of the 2d Corps to Little Round Top, which was also to be garrisoned if practicable. Once these dispositions were completed the Union battle line would be shaped something like the letter "J," with good terrain favoring a defensive battle. The remaining units of the Army of the Potomac would be available as reserves to back up any threatened part of the line.

General Sykes and two divisions of the 5th Corps reached Gettysburg about eight o'clock and were massed in reserve behind Culp's Hill. The 3d Division of the corps, two brigades of the Pennsylvania Reserves, reached the field about noon, having marched directly from the Washington defenses to join the army. The Artillery Reserve came up from Taneytown and parked beside the Taneytown Road near the center of the line. At nine o'clock, the two brigades of the 3d Corps left behind at Emmitsburg reached Cemetery Ridge and rejoined the corps. Buford's cavalry still picketed the left of the line, while other cavalry units assembled on the army's right flank. Thus, by noon, all infantry units of the army had reached the field except the big 6th Corps. Maj. Gen. John Newton, who had been detached from command of Sedgwick's 3d Division to take over the battered 1st Corps, reported to Meade early in the morning and told his chief that Sedgwick was pushing his men toward Gettysburg as fast as possible and would arrive sometime that afternoon.[8]

Once Meade established his headquarters at the Leister House, his staff, including those left behind at Taneytown, began to assemble there. Shortly after dawn, General Butterfield reached the scene. At this time General Meade was apparently worried that Lee would attempt to outflank the Union position. Hancock had reported the ease with which the position could be turned in his July 1 message to Meade. So, when his chief of staff reported for duty, Meade instructed him to become familiar with the roads in and around the battlefield and prepare contingency orders so the army could fall back in an orderly manner should Lee attempt to interpose his troops between Meade and Washington.[9]

To carry out Meade's instructions, Butterfield needed to know the location of each corps, and thus he dispatched a staff officer to each corps commander to become acquainted with the positions and roads in each area.[10] Butterfield then spent a great deal of time preparing the withdrawal order. When finished, Butterfield asked General Gibbon, who was present at headquarters several times during the day since his division was posted nearby, to read over the order and see if it was drawn up correctly. Gibbon was taken aback at this unusual request, and out of curiosity asked Butterfield what the order was. When told that it was an order directing the movement of the army corps to points in the rear, Gibbon exclaimed, "Good God, General Meade is not going to retreat, is he?" Butterfield answered that the order was merely a contingency plan, so Gibbon looked it over, compared it to a map, and pronounced it correct. Gibbon later recalled that at the time he placed little importance on this incident.[11]

Sometime between six and seven o'clock, at a time when most staff officers were absent from headquarters on various missions, General Meade walked out of the farmhouse and saw his son George, recently promoted to captain and acting as an aide-de-camp, standing nearby. The general exchanged pleasantries with his son, asking if he had written home, since he himself was too busy to write at the moment. Captain Meade later noted that his father seemed to be in excellent spirits. His tone of voice indicated that events were proceeding smoothly. General Meade then said, "George, you just ride down to General Sickles; explain to him where my headquarters are, and ask if his troops are in position yet and what he has to report." The general explained where 3d Corps headquarters was and then sent George off.[12]

Captain Meade rode down the Taneytown Road for a half mile and found 3d Corps headquarters in a grove of trees on the west side of the road. There was only one tent then pitched and only one officer visible. Meade found this man to be Capt. George E. Randolph, Sickles' artillery commander. Meade stated his message to Randolph, who replied that Sickles was in the tent resting, having been up most of the night. Randolph went into the tent and came out a few minutes later. He told young Meade that the corps was not yet in position because Sickles was in some doubt about where to place his men. George Meade was quite surprised by this statement. He later recalled that his orders from the general presupposed that an order had already been issued to Sickles and that his own mission was merely to confirm Sickles' following of prior orders. Meade then told Randolph that he would go back to headquarters and report the conversation.[13]

George rapidly galloped back to army headquarters. Upon returning, he found General Meade in the midst of a conversation with several other officers. Meade stopped the conversation to allow George to report. After hearing that Sickles' men were not yet in position, General Meade, "in his quick, sharp way when annoyed," ordered his son to ride back to Sickles and tell him that "he is to go into position on the left of the 2d Corps, that his right is to rest on General Hancock's left, and that he is to occupy the general line held by General Geary the night before and also to say to him that it is of the utmost importance that his troops should be in position as soon as possible."[14]

Captain Meade then rode back to 3d Corps headquarters. Upon his arrival he found the tent struck, several other officers present, and Sickles in the act of mounting his horse. Meade repeated his father's instructions, to which Sickles replied that his men were moving and would soon be in position. But then the general mentioned that Geary's troops had occupied no discernible position that he could find. Sickles then rode off. Captain Randolph asked Meade to ask his father to send General Hunt to help him set up suitable artillery positions. Meade returned to the Leister House and reported what Sickles had told him, and also passed along Randolph's request.[15] And so, about seven o'clock or slightly later, Sickles' corps moved into position on Cemetery Ridge, prolonging the line south of Hancock's position to the foot of Little Round Top.[16]

As the bulk of the army assembled on the battlefield, General Meade was engaged in determining the exact positions of Lee's troops. Visible enemy troop movements indicated that major units were forming opposite the Federal right flank on Culp's Hill. At 9:30 A.M., Meade ordered General Slocum, with Warren's help, to examine the ground in front of Culp's Hill to see if conditions favored an attack on the Rebels. If so, Slocum's own 12th Corps would spearhead the attack, to be supported by the 5th Corps and later by the 6th when it arrived. The two generals made a reconnaissance and decided that the ground would hinder an effective assault. The rough terrain would equally render hazardous any Confederate attack.[17]

After receiving this report, Meade canceled the proposed attack and decided to await the 6th Corps before planning any other offensive moves. He wanted to give the men presently on the field an opportunity to rest, since many units had made long marches to reach Gettysburg. Constant watch was maintained on suspected Confederate positions in an attempt to locate the enemy with a greater degree of certainty than existed on the morning of July 2. If circumstances warranted, Meade was determined to attack. Otherwise, he would wait to see what Lee might plan.[18]

The morning of the second passed quietly except for the constant scattered skirmish fire that was a regular feature of two armies in close contact. Sometime around eleven o'clock, General Sickles rode up to Meade's headquarters to report that he was not sure of the position his command was to occupy. Meade replied that he was to occupy the same position General Geary had held the previous night, connecting his right to Hancock's left and extending the line south along the ridge to Little Round Top, which Meade pointed out on the southern horizon. To Sickles' repeated solicitations for a staff officer to accompany him to survey artillery positions, Meade sent General Hunt. Before leaving headquarters, Sickles asked Meade if he was authorized to post his men as his judgment saw fit. "Certainly," Meade replied, "within the limits of the general instructions I have given to you; any ground within those limits you choose to occupy I leave to you."[19]

Sickles took Hunt out to the Emmitsburg Road and the ridge along which this artery passed. While riding out from Meade's headquarters, Hunt asked Sickles what the problem was. The 3d Corps commander replied that he wished to throw his line forward from the low ground of the southern part of Cemetery Ridge to cover the Emmitsburg Road. Hunt surmised that Sickles wanted to guard this road to ensure the safe arrival of the corps artillery train, which had been left behind at Emmitsburg when the corps marched to Gettysburg. Meade had told Hunt of this earlier in the morning. Sickles pointed out the position he wished to occupy. Hunt, on the whole, agreed that the higher ground at farmer Sherfy's large Peach Orchard commanded the lower ground where the 3d Corps was then posted. An advanced line along the Emmitsburg Road seemed to be the better position to occupy. On the other hand, Hunt also saw that Sickles' proposed line was longer than the direct line south along Cemetery Ridge and that Sickles did not have enough men to man the proposed line. Furthermore, the line would present a salient to any Confederate attack and both flanks of the corps would be unsupported unless other troops were sent to bolster this advanced line.[20]

As Hunt was talking with Sickles, some artillery fire echoed from the direction of Cemetery Hill, so Hunt rode off to investigate. When Sickles asked his permission to occupy the advanced line, Hunt remarked, "Not on my authority; I will report to General Meade for his instructions." Hunt also suggested that a reconnaissance force be sent out into the woods that fronted this line, since the artillery chief thought that the trees would screen the enemy and allow an attacking force to approach closely before being detected. Hunt then galloped off. Before heading to Cemetery Hill, Hunt surveyed the southern portion of Sickles' proposed line and noted how much farther from Cemetery Ridge it actually was than it appeared at first glance. Hunt reported to Meade what he had seen, then rode on to see what the cannonading was about.[21]

After Hunt left, Sickles ordered General Birney to send out a reconnaissance force into the woods in front of the Peach Orchard. Birney detailed Companies D, E, F, and I of the 1st United States Sharpshooters with the 3d Maine as a support, the whole force under the command of Colonel Hiram Berdan of the green-clad sharpshooters. This contingent of slightly more than three hundred officers and men formed in the Peach Orchard, moved out via the Millerstown Road into the woods on Seminary Ridge, then deployed and swept north through the woods. As the sharpshooters reached Pitzer's Woods, they encountered Rebel skirmishers and drove them back to the edge of the trees. Here, they saw more Confederates marching across an open field. The Yankees opened fire on the surprised Confederates as the 3d Maine came up and filled the gaps between the sharpshooters. After a sharp firefight lasting perhaps twenty minutes, Berdan gave the order to retreat as the enemy launched an attack with superior numbers. Berdan's force quickly retired to the Peach Orchard, while Berdan reported that there were indeed Confederates in the woods in front of the Union line.[22] (See map 5.)

The Confederate troops that Berdan's men found in Pitzer's Woods were there as the first step in General Lee's battle plan for the day. This plan had been a long time in forming and units were still moving into position when the Union sharpshooters found some of them.

After the end of the fighting on July 1, Lee was faced with personal indecision as well as some vacillation by subordinates. Wherever the blame lay, the Confederates failed to take advantage of the remaining daylight

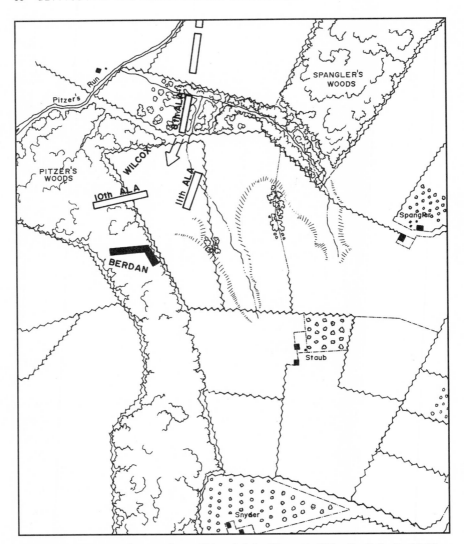

Map 5. The Berdan-Wilcox Skirmish in Pitzer's Woods, July 2, 1863.

hours after the defeated Federals retreated to Cemetery Hill and were ral-
lied there by Generals Hancock and Howard.

As the Yankees fell back to the hills south of Gettysburg, Lee was joined
by General Longstreet, whose troops were still many miles to the rear.
Longstreet surveyed the ground on which the enemy was reforming and

advised Lee that it would be better to flank the enemy out of the strong position and force Meade to attack at a place of Lee's own choosing rather than risk an assault on what appeared to be a strong natural position. For several reasons, chiefly the absence of his cavalry and the need to forage for supplies, Lee decided to stay and fight at Gettysburg while talking with Longstreet that afternoon.[23]

Once Lee made up his mind to remain on the battlefield, he spent a great part of the evening consulting with several of his subordinates as to their views on the course of action for July 2. He first rode over to General Ewell's headquarters and spoke with the commander of his 2d Corps, together with Generals Early and Rodes. These generals were averse to making an attack up the steep slopes of Cemetery and Culp's Hills, but wanted their troops to remain in position because they argued that the men would become demoralized if they were forced to yield the ground they had captured. After a long conversation, Lee acquiesced and stated that the main attack would be made on the right by Longstreet's corps.[24]

Two divisions of Longstreet's corps—those of Maj. Gen. John B. Hood and Maj. Gen. Lafayette McLaws—had reached Marsh Creek via the Chambersburg Pike shortly after midnight. These units had been on the road since early afternoon, their march delayed by the wagons of Ewell's and Hill's divisions and by Maj. Gen. Edward Johnson's division of Ewell's corps, which was guarding Ewell's trains as they moved to the battlefield. Other units of Longstreet's corps—Maj. Gen. George Pickett's division and Brig. Gen. Evander M. Law's brigade of Hood's division—were still in the rear guarding trains until relieved by cavalry, and would not reach the army until at least the afternoon of July 2.[25]

Before any attack could be launched, Lee had to plan specifically how it would commence and place his men in battle order. He and Longstreet met on Seminary Ridge before daylight on July 2. They were joined by General Hill and Maj. Gen. Henry Heth, and the whole group examined the visible Union position on Cemetery Ridge while they discussed the plan of attack. Longstreet's two divisions had broken camp at daylight and reached the field between 8 and 8:30 A.M., when both Hood and McLaws reported the presence of their men. The troops filed off the Chambersburg Pike and got under cover to await further orders.[26]

While troops were moving toward the field, Lee sent some of his staff officers to survey the enemy line and to find positions for his own troops.

Brig. Gen. William N. Pendleton had scouted the Spangler's Woods area during the late afternoon of July 1, then proceeded to Willoughby Run along Emanuel Pitzer's farm lane. He thus had found a way for troops to move along Seminary Ridge without being seen by the enemy. Early on July 2, Pendleton again reconnoitered the Confederate right flank and made a more complete tour of this "ravine road." Also that same morning, Lee ordered Col. Armistead L. Long to "examine and verify" the positions of the Confederate artillery batteries along the whole line. Long assisted Col. Reuben L. Walker of Hill's corps in posting guns along Seminary Ridge and called Walker's attention to the high ground along the Emmitsburg Road as a possible site for artillery.[27]

The most complete reconnaissance of the Confederate right was undertaken at daylight, when Lee ordered Capt. Samuel R. Johnston, one of his engineers, to make a closer examination of this area of the battlefield. Accompanied by three or four other men, Johnston rode south along Willoughby Run, turned east, and crossed the Emmitsburg Road in the vicinity of the Peach Orchard; he then followed the ridge to the Little Round Top area. Johnston claimed that he climbed this hill and looked to the north along Cemetery Ridge. Due to heavy foliage and a slight morning mist, Johnston apparently did not see Sickles' men bivouacked on the lower section of the ridge. He thus assumed that the Union army occupied only the northern, more elevated section of Cemetery Ridge. Johnston then moved south beyond Big Round Top before riding back to report to Lee.[28]

While Johnston was engaged in his scouting mission, Longstreet and Hill joined Lee at his headquarters near the seminary. The generals discussed the prospects for renewing the battle against the Federals on Cemetery Ridge. As Longstreet's two divisions reached the field, the division commanders came up to report their presence. By the time McLaws rode up to report, Lee seemed to have formed a general idea of his attack plan, but waited until Johnston returned with his report before making a final decision. After hearing his engineer's account, Lee was surprised but pleased to learn that Johnston had gotten so far without being seen by the enemy.[29]

It was Johnston's report that enabled Lee to solidify his provisional attack plan. On the basis of Johnston's report, Lee apparently believed that the Union left flank extended only partway south along Cemetery Ridge. Thus, instead of a frontal assault on the ridge, Longstreet's men would occupy the high ground along the Emmitsburg Road and launch an oblique attack on the Federal left and attempt to outflank the enemy. Richard H. Anderson's division of Hill's corps would cooperate with Longstreet, while Ewell would attack the Union right as a diversion and widen the attack if the opportunity presented itself. If all went according to plan, the Federal army would be crushed and driven from the field.[30]

While Longstreet made preparations to move his corps into position, Lee rode over to Ewell's headquarters to ascertain the state of affairs on that part of the field. After a conference with Ewell and other officers, Lee was convinced that he had made the right decision in allotting a secondary role to Ewell's troops. He then rode back to Seminary Ridge, only to find that Longstreet had barely begun to move his troops. Hence, Lee issued an outright order to his 1st Corps commander to "move with the portion of [his] command that was up, around to gain the Emmitsburg Road, on the enemy's left." This order was issued about eleven o'clock, but Lee then consented to wait until Law's brigade reached the field. Lee also ordered Captain Johnston to guide Longstreet's corps into position, taking care to avoid being seen by the Union signal station visible on Little Round Top.[31]

As Longstreet began to move his divisions, Hill's corps also maneuvered into battle array. Lee sent Hill his orders shortly after giving Longstreet his. Hill's men were to cooperate with Longstreet's assault when the opportunity was available. More specifically, Maj. Gen. William D. Pender would use his division to threaten the Union right center to prevent reinforcements from being sent to either flank when Longstreet and Ewell attacked. Anderson's division, which had been posted a few miles to the rear on the evening of July 1, was ordered to relieve some of Pender's units and be prepared to assist Longstreet when the attack up the Emmitsburg Road reached his position. As Brig. Gen. Cadmus M. Wilcox's brigade, which was Anderson's right flank unit, was moving into position between Spangler's and Pitzer's Woods, there was a short but severe clash with Federal troops in Pitzer's Woods. These Yankees were driven off and Wilcox went into line to await Longstreet's troops, who would form on his right.[32]

Once Law's brigade of Hood's division arrived, Longstreet began to move his corps into position. Captain Johnston and General McLaws rode together at the head of the column, which began to march from McLaws' bivouac area on Herr Ridge. The men marched around to the reverse side of the ridge where they would be invisible to the Union signalmen on

Little Round Top, then tramped south along Marsh Creek until they reached the Black Horse Tavern on the Hagerstown Road. At this point the column turned southeast onto a country lane. A few hundred yards south of the tavern, this road went over the crest of a small hill. As McLaws and Johnston reached the crest of the hill, they were horrified to see signal flags waving on Little Round Top. They had been detected! Longstreet soon came up to see what the delay was about and saw that another route would have to be found.[33]

There was a short delay as the troops were disentangled after the head of Hood's division became mixed up with the rear of McLaws's command. The corps then countermarched north along the west side of Herr Ridge to the area from which the march had begun, then headed east. When the head of the column reached Willoughby Run, it turned south along the run, following a narrow country lane.[34]

As the troops were marching south along this road, Longstreet rode up to McLaws and asked him how he would deploy his division:

> I replied: "That must be determined when I can see what is in front of me when I arrive in sight of the enemy." He replied: "There is nothing in your front; you will be entirely on the flank of the enemy." . . . To Gen. Longstreet's assertion, I replied: "Then I will continue my march in column of company, and after arriving on the flank as far as necessary, will face to the left, form line and advance to the attack." "That suits me," he said, and rode away.[35]

Brig. Gen. Joseph B. Kershaw's brigade emerged from the woods opposite the Peach Orchard about three o'clock that afternoon. Instead of finding an advanced Union outpost there as Longstreet had suggested, Kershaw found the enemy in superior force, amply supported by artillery. In the rear of the orchard, more troops were visible stretching toward the Round Tops. Therefore Kershaw deployed his brigade behind a stone wall at the edge of the woods and sent a courier to McLaws. The general soon arrived and surveyed the Union line. "The view presented astonished me, as the enemy was massed in my front and extended to my right and left as far as I could see."[36] While McLaws deployed his other brigades, he received several messages from Longstreet, inquiring why he did not proceed with the attack. However, after a short time Longstreet became aware of the situation and told McLaws not to attack. Hood would form on his right and would move to the attack first.[37]

Longstreet had become aware of the Yankees in and around the Peach Orchard as Hood's division moved to McLaws' right and began to deploy. While he was waiting for McLaws to attack the orchard, Longstreet received a message from Hood that the Federal line extended almost to the Round Tops and that an attack up the Emmitsburg Road would expose the flank of his command to this line. Besides, his Texas scouts had found no enemy troops near Little Round Top and said it was possible to get into the enemy rear by this route. Hood asked that the attack order be suspended and that he be allowed to move his division around the left flank of the Federal line. But Longstreet refused Hood's repeated solicitations, replying that Lee's order was to attack up the Emmitsburg Road. Finally, after some more delay as the troops formed the line of battle, Col. Edward Porter Alexander's artillery opened a massed fire on the Union positions sometime between 3:30 and 4:00 P.M. Shortly after four, Hood's first two brigades surged forward and Longstreet's assault was finally under way.[38]

Once Berdan reported Confederates in the woods in front of the Peach Orchard, General Sickles decided to take action to prevent enemy occupation of the ridges to his front. Earlier, about the time that Sickles went in person to Meade's headquarters, General Pleasonton ordered Buford's two brigades of cavalry to the rear to refit and guard supply trains. But Pleasonton failed to provide replacement units. Meade did not find out about Pleasonton's oversight until early afternoon when he ordered his cavalry chief to send horsemen to replace Buford. The regiment detailed from Gregg's division did not reach the Union left before the fighting began.[39]

The withdrawal of the cavalry, together with Berdan's report, influenced Sickles' next decision. Late in the morning he had moved some of his troops forward a few hundred yards to what General Hunt termed the "Plum Run Line." When Berdan's report reached him, Sickles decided he could wait no longer for orders from headquarters and so ordered his corps forward to the Peach Orchard area.[40] Shortly after two o'clock, General Birney received orders to change his front to meet an expected attack from the south. He moved the left flank of his division forward to Houck's Ridge while the right of his line marched forward to occupy the Peach Orchard. General Humphreys advanced his brigades from Plum Run toward the Emmitsburg Road, halting the leading brigade just behind the crest of the ridge to shelter the men from artillery fire. As Humphreys' lines advanced across the fields toward their initial position, their formation caught the attention of Hancock's soldiers, in line farther to the north. Hancock himself was in company with General Gibbon and some other officers, and Humphreys' splendid lines caught their eyes also, as well as their astonishment and speculation at whether or not the 2d Corps might have missed an order to advance. When deployed, Sickles' line roughly resembled a "V," with the apex of the "V" at the Peach Orchard.[41]

While Sickles was moving his corps into position, Meade summoned all his infantry corps commanders to army headquarters for consultation and future planning. This summons went out at three o'clock, just as the lead elements of the 6th Corps were sighted on the Baltimore Pike.[42] As this message was dispatched, Meade also sent a telegram to General Halleck, informing him of the situation at the time:

> Headquarters near Gettysburg, Pa.,
> July 2, 1863–3 P.M. (Received July 3, 10.20 A.M.)

Maj. Gen. H. W. Halleck,
General-in-Chief:

I have just concentrated my army at this place to-day. The Sixth Corps is just coming in, very much worn out, having been marching since 9 P.M. last night. The army is fatigued. I have to-day, up to this hour, awaited the attack of the enemy, I having a strong position for defensive. I am not determined, as yet, on attacking him till his position is more developed. He has been moving on both my flanks, apparently, but it is difficult to tell exactly his movements. I have delayed attacking, to allow the Sixth Corps and parts of other corps to reach this place and to rest the men. Expecting a battle, I ordered all my trains to the rear. If not attacked, and I can get any positive information of the position of the enemy which will justify me in so doing, I shall attack. If I find it hazardous to do so, or am satisfied the enemy is endeavoring to move to my rear and interpose between me and Washington, I shall fall back to my supplies at Westminster. I will endeavor to advise you as often as possible. In the engagement yesterday the enemy concentrated more rapidly than we could, and toward evening, owing to the superiority of numbers, compelled the Eleventh and First Corps to fall back from the town to the heights this side, on which I am now posted. I feel fully the responsibility resting upon me, but will endeavor to act with caution.

> Geo. G. Meade,
> Major-General.[43]

Sickles did not appear at headquarters as the other generals assembled there, so a second peremptory order was sent to him. While this took place, some cannonading was heard from the direction of the 3d Corps line. Almost simultaneously, one of Warren's aides rode up to report that affairs on Sickles' front were "not all straight." This report led Meade to mount his horse and ride out to the front to see about Sickles' command. As he did, he ordered General Sykes to bring the 5th Corps over to the left as rapidly as possible. Just then Sickles rode up to headquarters, but Meade told him not to dismount and to return to his men and that he would follow.[44]

General Meade, accompanied by several members of his staff, together with Warren and some of his aides, then rode out to Sickles' position. As the entourage passed the line of Cemetery Ridge, Warren exclaimed that here was the proper line for the 3d Corps to occupy. Meade expressed great surprise that there were no troops in position on the ridge. He then met Sickles in the rear of the Peach Orchard and had the 3d Corps commander point out his line. After Sickles briefed him on the subject, Meade fairly exploded with incredulity and demanded to know why his orders had not been obeyed and why the troops were out on this advanced line. Sickles replied that he thought he was acting within the general instructions he had received earlier. Meade then turned in his saddle and pointed to Cemetery Ridge, telling Sickles that the line he should have occupied was back there. He said: "General Sickles this is neutral ground, our guns command it, as well as the enemy's, the very reason you cannot hold applies to them."

At this point, Sickles expressed regret at occupying a position that did not meet with Meade's approval and said, "Shall I bring the troops to the line indicated?" Meade said he might as well but the enemy would not permit the withdrawal without taking advantage of it. As Sickles rode away to issue withdrawal orders, Confederate artillery opened fire all along the line, so Meade quickly countermanded his order and told Sickles to stay put and that he would order up reinforcements, including the 5th Corps and a division of Hancock's command. He also told Sickles to send to the Artillery Reserve for more guns and then galloped back to headquarters to coordinate the movements of the reinforcements.[45] (See map 6.)

While Meade was riding out to the Peach Orchard, he directed General Warren to go to the left of the line and investigate the situation.[46] Warren made his way to the summit of Little Round Top, where a Signal Corps detachment was then stationed. The general discovered that there were no combat troops on the hill. He also saw at once that Little Round Top was the key to the entire Federal line at Gettysburg. Enemy cannon placed on the crest could command the entire length of Cemetery Ridge to the north. Capt. James S. Hall, the senior officer on the hill, told Warren that he thought he had noticed, just before the general's arrival, enemy troops moving in the woods on the east side of the Emmitsburg Road. He had just communicated this observation to Generals Meade and Sickles. Warren then sent one of his aides down the western slope of the hill and up above the Devil's Den to Capt. James E. Smith, commanding the 4th New York Independent Battery, asking him to lob a shell over the woods in question.

> He did so, and as the shot went whistling through the air the sound of it reached the enemies' troops and caused every one to look in the direction of it. The motion revealed to me the glistening of gun barrels and bayonets of the enemy's line of battle already formed and far outflanking the position of any of our troops, so that the line of his advance from his right to Little Round Top was unopposed. I have been particular in telling this, as the discovery was intensely thrilling to my feelings and almost appalling.[47]

Warren sent a hasty message to Meade about the lack of troops on Little Round Top and asked for at least a division to defend the hill. Meade quickly ordered General Humphreys to pull his division out of line and secure the hill. However, a few minutes after Humphreys started moving the two brigades directly under his command, the 5th Corps was reported to be coming up, so Meade sent Humphreys back into line along the Emmitsburg Road.[48]

Warren dispatched his aides to seek troops to defend Little Round Top. Lt. Chauncey B. Reese went to Meade and was in turn sent to bring the 5th Corps to the left of the line.[49] Lt. Ranald S. Mackenzie went to Sickles to ask for some of his troops, but Sickles refused, telling the lieutenant that he needed all his men to defend the advanced position.[50] But while returning to Little Round Top, Mackenzie chanced upon General Sykes and Gen. James Barnes on the road in rear of the Wheatfield. Sykes had come onto the field in advance of the 5th Corps to find positions for the troops when they arrived. When he heard of the necessity for troops to defend Little Round Top, Sykes sent an aide for one of Barnes' brigades. Mackenzie then rode back to Warren to report his actions.[51]

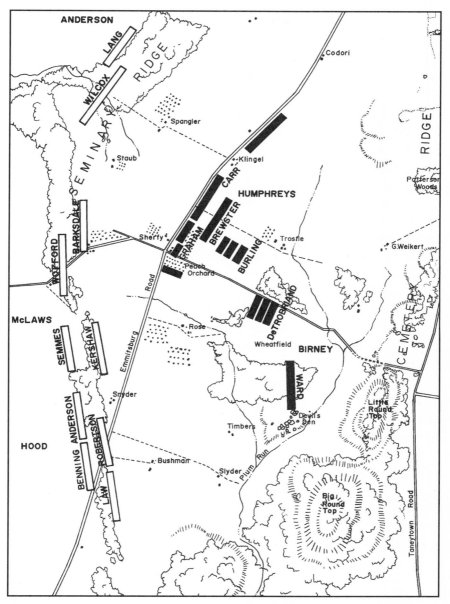

Map 6. Positions of Troops on Sickles' Third Corps Line at 4:00 P.M., July 2, 1863.

Col. Strong Vincent intercepted Sykes' aide and on his own responsibility took his brigade to Little Round Top. But because of Vincent's approach route, Warren failed to notice the brigade as it went into position on a spur at the southern end of the hill. Vincent's four regiments were hardly in position when they were attacked by parts of Generals Law's and Jerome B. Robertson's brigades of Hood's division, shortly after five o'clock. While this engagement was going on, Warren was not idle. Noticing the movement of troops toward the Wheatfield, he mounted and galloped down the north slope of Little Round Top to find the commander of the units. By a stroke of luck, Warren found that these troops belonged to his old brigade, now led by Brig. Gen. Stephen H. Weed, who had ridden on ahead to find General Sickles to see where his men were needed. After some arguing with the brigade adjutant, Warren detached the 140th New York and sent it up the hill, guided by Lt. Washington A. Roebling of his staff. This regiment appeared on the crest just as some of Robertson's Texans were flanking Vincent's position. The arrival of the New Yorkers repulsed the Confederates and saved the line. Meanwhile, General Sykes found Weed, who had marched his troops from the Little Round Top area at the behest of Capt. Alexander Moore of Sickles' staff, and ordered Weed to move the brigade back to the high ground. Warren also ordered an artillery battery to the summit. Then, thinking the hill was safe, Warren went off to report to General Meade.[52]

The Union troops had the good fortune of reaching Little Round Top just ahead of the enemy, but this close call was typical of the problems that Sickles' forward move created for Meade. Since the Confederate cannonade preceding the infantry assault opened about the time Meade was conversing with Sickles near the Peach Orchard, Meade did not have enough time to plan an orderly movement of reinforcements to Sickles. As a result, troops were necessarily rushed into the battle piecemeal, leading to confusion as units from different corps fought on the same line, often at the same time. By the time the fighting sputtered to a halt after dark, Meade had sent forward the entire 5th Corps, two depleted divisions of the 1st Corps, three brigades of the 12th Corps, and five full brigades plus detached regiments from Hancock's 2d Corps. In addition, many of the brigades of the 6th Corps were sent directly to the left as soon as they reached the field. The use of troops from other parts of the line to plug gaps in Sickles' position dangerously weakened the right flank. Only Brig. Gen. George S.

Greene's brigade of the 12th Corps and the timely arrival of darkness stopped an otherwise effective attack by troops of Ewell's corps on Culp's Hill. Many of the units that fought on Sickles' front were rendered ineffective for the remainder of the battle owing to a high percentage of casualties, which reduced many regiments to mere skeletons. Chief among these decimated units was the 3d Corps, which lost over forty-two hundred men of about eleven thousand engaged. The list of wounded included Dan Sickles, whose right leg was crushed by a stray cannonball as he was preparing to move his headquarters back from the Trostle Farm as the line began to break at the Peach Orchard.[53]

Chapter Three

After being wounded, Sickles' leg was amputated on the battlefield. He
was taken to Washington so he could recover some of his strength
before making the longer journey home to New York. While in the capital,
Sickles told his version of the Battle of Gettysburg to everyone who
would listen, President Lincoln included. During this recuperation period,
Sickles may have begun his plan to have Meade removed from command,
but it is difficult to state precisely when he first decided on this course of
action. The extant references to Sickles' stay in Washington during July
1863 do not mention exactly what Sickles told Lincoln or any of his other
visitors about Meade. One of Sickles' staff officers, Lt. Col. James F.
Rusling, wrote that Sickles "certainly got his side of Gettysburg well into
the President's mind."[1]

Events during the autumn of 1863 widened any gulf that might have
existed between Generals Meade and Sickles. Meade submitted his official
report of the Gettysburg Campaign to Halleck in early October. The general was quite restrained when writing about Sickles' forward move:

> About 3 P.M., I rode out to the extreme left, to await the arrival of the Fifth
> Corps and to post it, when I found that Major-General Sickles, commanding
> the Third Corps, not fully apprehending the instructions in regard to the
> position to be occupied, had advanced, or rather was in the act of advancing
> his corps some half a mile or three-quarters of a mile in front of the line of
> the Second Corps, on the prolongation of which it was designed his corps
> should rest.[2]

The insinuation that he had not understood his orders would surely have rankled a character such as Dan Sickles. To make matters worse, a rumor that Meade would have court-martialed him except for his wound might have reached Sickles' ear.[3] Also, by October 1863, Sickles was eager to resume command of the 3d Corps. He journeyed to Fairfax Station, Virginia, to ask Meade for permission to return to active duty. The two generals met on October 18, and although relations were cordial on the surface, Sickles became further enraged when Meade refused to allow him to resume command because of his wound, citing Confederate General Ewell's long convalescence due to a similar wound.[4]

Finally, General Halleck, in his report of the Gettysburg Campaign, which was based on Meade's, was even more critical of Sickles. The general in chief wrote: "General Sickles, misinterpreting his orders, instead of placing the Third Corps on the prolongation of the Second, had moved it nearly three-quarters of a mile in advance—an error which nearly proved fatal in the battle."[5]

These developments during the autumn of 1863, together with Sickles' forced inactivity in Washington, made him the perfect ally of the Radical Republican–dominated Committee on the Conduct of the War. The Joint Congressional Committee on the Conduct of the War—to use its full name—was composed of three senators and four representatives. Radical Republican Senator Benjamin F. Wade (Ohio) and Senator Zachariah Chandler (Michigan) dominated the committee. The committee had been established to oversee both the military and civil conduct of the war and to advise the president of its findings. Because of its proximity to Washington and its repeated defeats, the Army of the Potomac had become a favorite subject of investigation by late 1863.[6]

The activities of the committee reflected the views of Senators Wade and Chandler, two violent Radicals who opposed Lincoln's conciliatory attitude toward the South. Further, both senators mistrusted West Point, an institution they regarded as flirting with treason because of its stance toward slavery and the South in general. Late in February 1864, the committee began to call witnesses to testify about the Army of the Potomac's operations since Meade had taken command. As events proceeded, it became clear that the committee had five main points to prove with the officers they called upon to testify:

1. Hooker was defeated at Chancellorsville because of a conspiracy of unfriendly corps commanders, not through his own incompetent generalship.
2. Halleck did not cooperate fully with Hooker, but did so with Meade.
3. Meade did not have any campaign plan at Gettysburg—he merely followed what Hooker and Butterfield had previously mapped out.
4. Meade planned to retreat from Gettysburg but was prevented from doing so when the army became engaged in battle on July 2.
5. Meade failed to pursue Lee's beaten army after the battle and smash the enemy.

The object of all of this was to have Meade, a West Pointer, removed from command and replaced by Hooker, another West Pointer, who, although defeated at Chancellorsville, was more in line with the Radicals and thus was a suitable candidate for army command.[7]

Daniel E. Sickles was the first officer to testify before the committee. He began his statements about Meade's handling of the army by dwelling at length on Meade's July 1 circular order for the army to concentrate behind Pipe Creek. Sickles understood this to be a retreat order, but when he received a dispatch from General Howard, advising him of the fighting at Gettysburg and asking for his aid, Sickles regarded the fighting as more important. Therefore, he left a part of his corps at Emmitsburg and marched with the remainder to the sound of the guns. This part of the 3d Corps arrived at Gettysburg shortly after Howard's men had been forced back through the town to the high ground south of Gettysburg. Sickles made it a point to mention that the arrival of his command "seemed to reassure General Howard in the security of his position." Meade subsequently approved of Sickles' march to Gettysburg and ordered the entire army to concentrate there.[8]

General Sickles then talked at length about July 2. He stated:

> At a very early hour on Thursday morning, I received a notification that General Meade's headquarters had been established at Gettysburg, and I was directed by him to relieve a division of the Twelfth Corps (General Geary's division, I think), which was massed a little to my left, and which had taken position there during the night. I did so, reporting, however, to General Meade that that division was not in position, but was merely massed in my

vicinity; the tenor of his order seemed to indicate a supposition on his part that the division was in position.[9]

The general went on to state that since he had not received any orders about his position (presumably after reporting that Geary's division did not have any position), and because he observed "from the enemy's movements on our left, which I thought to be conclusive indications of a design on their part to attack there," he went in person to headquarters and reported this observation. Sickles asked for orders, he said, but Meade did not issue him any. Then Sickles made a statement that fit in nicely with the committee's plans. When he left headquarters, Sickles related, "I was satisfied, from the information which I received, that it was intended to retreat from Gettysburg."[10]

When enemy activity drove in his pickets, Sickles determined to wait for orders no longer, but proceeded to move his corps to the Peach Orchard line and make dispositions to receive the attack. Sickles pointed out that the line he occupied, which was disapproved of by General Halleck in his report, was not taken through misinterpretation of orders. "It was either a good line or a bad one, and whichever it was, I took it on my own responsibility." Sickles told the committee that he took this advanced line because it enabled him to occupy commanding ground and thus deprive the enemy of it.[11]

Sickles then mentioned that as the enemy advanced to the attack, he succeeded in getting into position "on Round Top and along the commanding ridge to which I have referred" and these positions were firmly held by the 3d Corps. As the battle opened, General Meade arrived at the front and remarked that Sickles' line was too much extended. Sickles agreed but stated that if he was supported he could hold the line. He also offered to withdraw, but Meade told him to remain where he was and said reinforcements would be sent. The 5th Corps arrived after almost an hour's delay, while Hancock furnished troops from the 2d Corps to protect the right of the 3d Corps line. The position was held at heavy cost to both sides until Sickles was wounded and carried from the field.[12]

The committee members then questioned Sickles about the dilatory pursuit of Lee's army, a subject he knew very little about since he was not present. But Sickles answered several questions put to him about the pursuit, evaluating the morale of both armies, Lee's ammunition shortage, and

Meade's failure to use the additional soldiers available at Harper's Ferry, Baltimore, and Washington. The general also commented on the division of opinion among the corps commanders at the several councils of war held during the campaign, and on the near-disastrous implications of removing Hooker from command on the eve of a major battle. After all, Sickles stated that the rank and file had "entire confidence" in Hooker, so his removal must have been due to personal relations between Hooker and Halleck. Finally, Sickles made a few adverse comments on the October Bristoe Station Campaign, during which Meade had retreated from a foe supposedly badly beaten at Gettysburg.[13]

Maj. Gen. Abner Doubleday was the second witness called before the committee. At the time, Doubleday was an "unemployed" general, having left the army after Meade replaced him as commander of the 1st Corps with John Newton, whose commission date made him junior to Doubleday. This incident certainly did not endear Meade to Doubleday, a fact that may well have colored Doubleday's testimony before the committee.[14] Doubleday said he did not know of any retreat order on July 1, but when asked by Senator Wade why Meade relieved him from command, Doubleday replied:

> General Meade is in the habit of violating the organic law of the army to place his personal friends in power. There has always been a great deal of favoritism in the Army of the Potomac. No man who is an anti-slavery man or an anti-McClellan man can expect decent treatment in that army as at present constituted.[15]

The third witness was Brig. Gen. Albion P. Howe, an erstwhile division commander in the 6th Corps. Howe told the committee that Meade had considered withdrawing from Gettysburg on the night of July 2. This information came from a conversation that Howe had with General Sedgwick, his corps commander. Howe also stated that the position at Gettysburg provided the victory. "There was no great generalship displayed; there was no manoeuvring [*sic*], no combination." He detailed the slow pursuit of Lee, then mentioned the retrograde movement of the Bristoe Station Campaign and how Meade seemed beset by indecision.[16]

After hearing the testimony from these three generals, Senators Wade and Chandler felt they had heard enough. On March 3, these two politicians appeared before President Lincoln and Secretary of War Stanton.

"In behalf of the army and of the country," they demanded that Meade be relieved from command because of his incompetence. Wade and Chandler advocated Hooker's reinstatement, but left it up to Lincoln and Stanton to appoint whomever they felt to be more competent than Meade.[17]

General Meade arrived in Washington on March 4, his visit connected with the impending reorganization of the Army of the Potomac. The general was "greatly surprised to find the whole town talking of certain grave charges of Generals Sickles and Doubleday." Meade was summoned to appear before the committee the next day. Meade wrote that when he made his appearance, he found only Senator Wade present to question him. Wade told Meade that there were no charges against him, and said further that the committee was compiling a history of the war and was engaged in gathering the evidence necessary to enable it to give an account of the Battle of Gettysburg.[18]

Apparently Meade took Wade's comments at face value, for he proceeded to give an extremely detailed account of the army's operations from Gettysburg through the Mine Run Campaign of November 1863. The general began by informing Senator Wade that when he was appointed to army command, he determined to advance until he was sure that Lee would be forced to give up his march into Pennsylvania and then seek a battle. Meade said he never deviated from this policy, but said he would also modify the object of seeking battle by endeavoring to secure as many advantages for his soldiers as possible. By nightfall on June 30, Meade was satisfied that Lee was concentrating his army, so on July 1 he advised his corps commanders that he favored giving battle behind the Pipe Creek Line. His morning circular gave instructions about the positions to be occupied behind this waterway.[19]

The circular had already been sent when Meade received word that the 1st Corps had met the enemy at Gettysburg and that General Reynolds had been killed. Meade immediately sent Hancock to Gettysburg with orders to take command of all forces on the field. Even more importantly, Meade instructed Hancock to survey the ground and report if conditions favored a battle there rather than along Pipe Creek. After receiving Hancock's favorable assessment, Meade ordered all units to concentrate at Gettysburg.[20]

Once at Gettysburg, Meade at first wanted to attack, but unfavorable terrain reports dissuaded him. Hence, he decided to await the late arrival of the 6th Corps before repositioning his troops. When Sedgwick's brigades began to arrive, Meade ordered the 5th Corps to move into reserve behind the army's left flank, while the 6th would bolster the right. Meade stated that sometime between 3 and 3:30 P.M., he rode over to the left to see about the posting of the 5th Corps and inspect the position of Sickles' command. Instead of finding Sickles' men on Cemetery Ridge as expected, Meade discovered that the 3d Corps occupied a position very much in advance of the ridge, leaving a gap between its right wing and Hancock's left, while Sickles' left flank rested in front of Little Round Top. While Meade was talking with Sickles about withdrawing the 3d Corps to Cemetery Ridge, Confederate artillery opened fire, making any change in position impossible.[21]

Meade then remarked that he rode over to the left in person because he was in some doubt about the position of the 3d Corps. He said that previous instructions had been sent to Sickles, ordering him to form on Hancock's left and prolong the line south to Little Round Top, which was to be occupied if practicable. Later in the morning, when Meade sent an officer to see if Sickles was in position, the reply was that there was no position there. The officer then went back with the same instructions issued previously. A short time afterward, Sickles came in person to army headquarters and again received the same orders from Meade himself. Sickles remarked that there was some favorable ground for artillery near his position and asked for a staff officer to accompany him to survey this terrain. He also inquired whether or not he was authorized to post his corps as he saw fit. Meade replied, "Certainly, within the limits of the general instructions I have given to you; any ground within those limits you choose to occupy I leave to you." Meade then detailed General Hunt to go with Sickles to his position. It was because of all these messages to Sickles that General Meade decided to inspect the 3d Corps line in person.[22]

Meade told Senator Wade that he made these remarks *in extenso* because the public did not fully comprehend the advanced position and also because he did not expound upon it in his official report. The general made it clear that he did not intend to censure General Sickles in any way. As far as Meade was concerned, "I am of the opinion that General Sickles did what he thought was for the best; but I differed from him in judgment. And I maintain that subsequent events proved that my judgment was correct, and his judgment was wrong."[23]

General Meade went on to describe the fighting of July 3, then elaborated about operations after the battle. The pursuit of Lee was slowed by rainy weather and the necessity of bringing up supplies. The character of the easily defended passes through South Mountain also hampered pursuit. On July 12, the army was finally in position before Lee's entrenchments at Williamsport, Maryland. Rather than attack blindly and risk defeat, Meade called a council of corps commanders and asked for opinions. Meade himself wanted to attack, but only two officers agreed with him, so he postponed the attack for a day while the enemy positions were developed more fully. However, Lee slipped across the Potomac River before the attack could begin. After examining the abandoned earthworks, Meade believed the attack would have failed disastrously because of the strength of the Confederate line. Pursuit was then continued across the Potomac into Virginia, but Lee refused to stand and fight. Eventually the two armies reached the same area from which the campaign had begun.[24]

After giving his testimony to Senator Wade, Meade made a call on Secretary Stanton. The Secretary frankly told him that there was pressure from a certain party, including Sickles, to have General Hooker placed in command, and that this group was behind the present activities of the committee. Stanton assured Meade that they would not succeed in their quest to have him removed as a preliminary to getting Hooker reappointed. The Secretary of War's reassurances notwithstanding, Meade was still concerned about the damage his reputation would suffer.[25]

Meade returned to Brandy Station and the army after finishing his business in Washington. But having been alerted to the danger from the committee, the general kept his ears opened. During the following week in March, Generals Pleasonton and Birney gave some damaging testimony dealing with the council of war held on the evening of July 2 and the dilatory pursuit of Lee's army. The newspaper attacks on his reputation also increased during this period, but Meade remained quiet, determined to await the final report of the committee. If it failed to do him justice, Meade was prepared to publish a booklet presenting his side of the matter.[26]

President Lincoln invited Generals Grant and Meade to dine with him on March 12. Since he was going to Washington, Meade took the opportunity to request the committee to allow him to add more evidence to his testimony. This request was granted. Meade thus appeared before the committee on March 11, bringing along copies of his orders of June 30 and July 1 to illustrate that there was no intention to withdraw the army once contact was made with the enemy. Meade included a copy of his instructions to Hancock when he sent that officer to Gettysburg to report on conditions there. Copies of orders to the 5th and 6th Corps to move to Gettysburg as rapidly as possible were also introduced as evidence. Meade told Senator Wade that the idea he had planned to retreat from Gettysburg on the morning of July 2 would appear "entirely incomprehensible" when compared to the exertions made on the night of July 1 to concentrate the army at Gettysburg. Meade concluded his testimony by stating that the conference of corps commanders on the evening of July 2 agreed with his own view to remain on the field and await further attacks by the enemy before assuming the offensive.[27]

Having given this additional testimony, Meade began to believe that the tide was turning in his favor. He had again talked with Stanton while in Washington, and the Secretary told him that Senator Wade had been to see him and stated that Meade's testimony was perfectly satisfactory in explaining away the charges against the general. Meade had also ascertained that committee members Benjamin F. Harding, Daniel W. Gooch, and Moses F. Odell were friendly to his cause, while Chandler and M. S. Wilkinson were his enemies.[28]

However, by coincidence or not, the day after Meade's second appearance before the committee, an article on the Battle of Gettysburg appeared in the *New York Herald*.[29] The author, writing under the pseudonym "Historicus," identified himself as an eyewitness of the battle, writing that the essential history of the battle needed to be made public. His only motive for writing was to "vindicate history, do honor to the fallen, and justice to the survivors when unfairly impeached." After summing up the first day's battle, Historicus told of the opportune arrival of the 3d Corps, implying that Sickles' presence on the battlefield brought an end to the fighting (when in fact Sickles reached the battlefield long after the shooting had stopped).

Historicus then repeated the same story that Sickles told the committee; that on July 2, Sickles did not receive any orders about where to place his men and that Meade was planning a retreat when Longstreet's attack prevented it. He went on to say that when Confederate columns were detected moving toward Little Round Top, Sickles was first to act on his own. Moreover, Ward's brigade and Smith's battery took position on that vital hill while the rest of the corps advanced some three hundred yards to support Ward. Historicus said that Sickles' great aim was to "prevent the enemy from getting between his flank and the Round Top alluded to." He added that the 5th Corps came up after nearly an hour's delay, which almost proved fatal. The story said that one of Sickles' staff officers finally managed to convince General Crawford to move his division without orders from General Sykes. Crawford arrived on Little Round Top "just in time to prevent its falling into the enemy's hands." Historicus further denigrated the performance of the 5th Corps by stating that the Union line was first broken when Barnes' division "suddenly gave way" and despite the remonstrances of General Birney, Barnes would not advance and hold his position in line. Aides quickly brought up Gen. Samuel K. Zook's brigade of the 2d Corps, which advanced into action over the 5th Corps troops, who were told to lie down so Zook's men could charge forward. After describing the battle of July 3 as being against the Union left flank, Historicus closed his lengthy epistle with a blistering condemnation of Meade's failure to pursue the battered Army of Northern Virginia and attack while the Potomac River was swollen in flood and could not be crossed.

Until this time, Meade had been largely unmoved by the slander against his reputation, but the article by Historicus stung him into action. In a March 15 letter to the War Department, Meade enclosed a copy of the article and complained that whoever wrote it had access to official documents and papers not yet made public, let alone issued to the army. The general came straight to the point as to whom he believed authored the Historicus account: "I cannot resist the belief that this letter was either written or dictated by Maj. Gen. D. E. Sickles." Meade wrote further that he gave Sickles the benefit of the doubt by writing in his official report that Sickles advanced his command through a misapprehension of orders, not from a deliberate wish to violate orders. The general also asked the department to ascertain whether Sickles and Historicus were one and the same. If so, Meade said he must request a court of inquiry to investigate fully the subject and make the truth known.[30]

General Halleck responded to Meade's letter a week later. Halleck also believed that Sickles was behind the Historicus article. He advised Meade to ignore the whole matter because Sickles would like nothing better than to engage in a newspaper dialogue, given his ability to color the New York

press. Halleck told Meade that any attacks on his reputation would probably backfire. Meade replied that he would abide by Halleck's wishes, saying that he hardly expected Sickles to admit to writing the article, but did
expect him at least to have the "manliness" to say that even if he did not
write the story, that its contents were true in his judgment. Meade con-
fessed that he was not as philosophical as Halleck, for he considered it bad
policy to allow such maliciousness to pass unnoticed.[31]

Meade's hands were tied, but several 5th Corps officers took offense at
the slanders of Historicus toward their commands. Col. William S. Tilton,
commanding one of Barnes' brigades, sent a letter to the general, calling
attention to the Historicus article. Colonel Tilton said it was "sickening" to
give so much praise to Sickles at the expense of others, for "had Sickles'
orders to some of Sykes' Brigade Commanders been obeyed, the rebels
would surely have had both Round Tops early in the fight." Tilton stated
that his brigade, which held the division's right flank, did not fall back until
he discovered Confederates moving toward the rear of his position. After
falling back to the woods north of the Wheatfield, Tilton added that his
chief annoyance in keeping his men in line was from squads of 2d and 3d
Corps soldiers breaking through his files in their haste to get to the rear.
He also wrote that "I had men injured too by being jumped upon by flee-
ing 3d Corps men as we lay behind a stone wall after our change of front."[32]

Very soon after the Historicus article, three replies appeared in the
Herald. The March 16 edition included the first of these. Signed "Another
Eye-Witness," this reply attacked several of Historicus' statements. The
author first responded to the inference that the arrival of the 3d Corps on
July 1 put an end to the fighting at Gettysburg when in reality the battle
was over by three o'clock. The eyewitness objected to Historicus' omission
of General Hancock's name anywhere in his article, comparing the omission of Hancock's name to "the play of Hamlet with the part of the Prince
of Denmark omitted." After all, Hancock wielded overall command until
General Slocum arrived later in the afternoon. The author then went on to
describe how Sickles detached his corps and gave battle with both flanks
unprotected and in advance of the army. The 2d and 5th Corps prevented
the enemy from penetrating through these gaps on both flanks of the 3d
Corps. "Another Eye-Witness" closed his letter by stating that the ground
Sickles occupied was no place for his corps, "nor is there a just defense for
the movements of General Sickles."[33]

Two days later, the *Herald* printed a rebuke by "A Staff Officer of the 5th Corps."[34] Claiming to be another Gettysburg eyewitness, the officer listed seven points of contention he had with Historicus. He claimed that the 5th Corps was never placed under the orders of General Sickles nor was it posted on the left of the 3d Corps by Sickles. Moreover, General Sykes never relieved Ward and Smith on Little Round Top for the very good reason that these units were never on that vital hill. Barnes' two brigades were posted in line before any musketry fire began, so the allegation that the hour's conflict involved the 3d Corps alone was a false statement.[35] Further, he stated that Crawford's division advanced into line by direct order from General Sykes, not through any orders from Sickles. He noted that the danger of losing Little Round Top did not result from any failure to relieve Ward's brigade, but from an order of Sickles' taking Weed's brigade from that hill. Sykes ordered Weed back just in time to prevent the Confederates from seizing the hill. The staff officer closed by stating that "when a dispassionate writer seats himself to bolster up one officer at the expense of others, neither 'hearsay evidence' nor 'slight errors' should have a place in his narrative. Unadulterated truth should stamp its every assertion."

The *New York Herald* of March 21 contained a thundering reply to Historicus by General Barnes, who took offense at the statements concerning the sudden withdrawal of his two brigades during the action on July 2.[36] Barnes' denial of these allegations was straightforward and to the point:

> All this is pure invention. No such occurrence as is here related took place. There is not a particle of truth in it. No order was given to me by General Birney. None was received by me through any one from General Sickles. I did not see or hear from General Zook. I did not meet him in any way. I did not know he was there, and the article above referred to is the first intimation that I have had that any one pretended that any such event took place. There was no order to advance—no refusal; no orders to lie down given to the command by me or by any one else to my knowledge; no passing over my command . . . nothing of the kind occurred that ever came to my knowledge, and I think I should have heard of such a thing before this late day if it, or anything like it, had taken place; the whole story is untrue in every particular, and my astonishment at now hearing of such a thing for the first time may possibly be imagined.

Barnes then detailed the movements of his division on July 2. It is ironic that in advancing to the position assigned by General Sykes, Barnes' men passed over a line of 3d Corps troops lying down in reserve.[37] He quoted from the official reports of Colonel Tilton and Col. Jacob B. Sweitzer to reinforce the fact that he did not order a retreat until the enemy passed through a gap on his right and threatened the rear of his position. Barnes ended his reply by stating that he did not intend to blame anyone for the dispositions that led to the gap on his right, but only wanted to show that the movements of his division were not as disorderly as Historicus said they were. It was his belief that Historicus, who said he was an eyewitness, may have been overly anxious in the midst of danger, preventing him from "distinguishing between an orderly and a disorderly movement." As far as Barnes was concerned, Historicus' narrative was "filled with errors, detracting from the merits of some and exalting the moderate claims of others to a ridiculous excess."

Historicus was not long in replying to his critics. In a second article published by the *Herald*, he said that his outline of the battle was not only correct but nearly every detail and incident mentioned was correct.[38] In dealing with "Another Eye-Witness," Historicus stated that it was not his intention to disparage the soldiers of the 2d Corps by failing to mention General Hancock. It was no fault of his that General Sickles figured so prominently in the fighting on July 2. He replied to the charge that Sickles had advanced his command far beyond his supports by writing that if Sickles had indeed committed such an error, he would have been cashiered from the army. Since he had not, he must not have erred. Sickles made a "simple" maneuver required by the enemy movements. He merely changed front to the left by wheeling forward his center and right to confront the flank attack. "No military critic would call this an advance." Sickles did not abandon support because he had none; the 5th Corps was not yet up from reserve on the right.

Refuting the "Staff Officer of the 5th Corps," Historicus replied that Sykes was indeed ordered to report to General Sickles and that Sickles requested he take position on his left and relieve the troops on Round Top Mountain. He also replied that it was true that Smith and Ward were not on Round Top; they were on adjacent Little Round Top instead. Historicus finally said that much of what the 5th Corps officer found fault with in his narrative was a "mere quibble and unworthy of the gravity of the subject."

In answer to General Barnes, Historicus quoted a letter he had received from General Birney, who stated that Birney himself had ordered Barnes' men to lie down so that Zook's brigade could charge. He revealed that Birney found out from Sykes that he heard "the same thing" about Barnes' troops from Colonel Sweitzer after the council of war on the night of July 2.[39]

Historicus closed his reply with some more slanderous remarks directed at General Meade, beginning with the statement that the testimony of several officers before the Committee on the Conduct of the War "is known to be so ruinous to the Commander of the Army of the Potomac that it will be a singular indifference to public opinion on the part of the government if he is allowed to remain longer in that important post." He then said that many in the army shed tears when Meade's vacillation allowed Lee to escape across the Potomac. And now Meade wished to break up the 1st and 3d Corps and dismiss some of the army's most heroic officers.

While the controversy raged in the pages of the *Herald*, Meade was assailed from yet another direction. Sickles was very anxious to get General Butterfield to testify before the committee. In fact, Sickles had addressed a private note to Senator Chandler, stating that Butterfield had come to Washington from his assignment in the 20th Corps without Halleck's permission, and should be subpoenaed so he could add his statements about Meade's generalship.[40]

Chandler called Butterfield before the committee on March 25. Butterfield portrayed Meade as appearing dazed and confused when he was appointed to army command; in fact, Butterfield continued, Meade was so bewildered that he asked Butterfield for help in formulating plans. Meade asked the New Yorker to remain as chief of staff, and he so took pity on the new commander that he revealed Hooker's campaign plans. Meade eagerly seized these plans, making only a few minor changes that did not affect the outcome. Therefore, although Butterfield did not say it in so many words, Gettysburg was Hooker's victory, not Meade's.[41]

Butterfield went on to state that it was he who suggested sending Hancock to Gettysburg on July 1. According to Butterfield, Meade himself went up to the field that night, leaving his chief of staff to send a vital message to Sedgwick. This message stated that Meade planned to make a vigorous attack on July 2. Furthermore, since the 6th Corps would not arrive on the field before the matter would be settled, Sedgwick was to take position in the rear to cover a retreat should it become necessary. Or, in the event of success, he could push his men forward to aid in the pursuit of the enemy. Butterfield noted that the Regular Engineer Battalion would be detailed and placed under Sedgwick's command so that any earthworks necessary could be constructed.[42]

Butterfield said he himself arrived on the battlefield shortly after daylight on July 2, that Meade was glad to see him, told him of the march of the 6th Corps toward the field, then asked him to do a task that was Butterfield's most damning accusation of his former commander. "General Meade then directed me to prepare an order to withdraw the army from that position." Butterfield replied that this order would require a great deal of preparation, including his personal knowledge of the roads in the vicinity and the deployment of the troops. Meade said he could not wait for Butterfield to inspect the lines and made a rough sketch of the area for him. The chief of staff then spent a considerable amount of time preparing this order. It met with Meade's approval, but to make sure "no misunderstanding should arise from the manner in which it was worded or expressed," Butterfield showed the order to three other officers—John Gibbon, Seth Williams, and Rufus Ingalls—who all said it was prepared correctly. Meade sent for his corps commanders while General Williams' clerks began to copy the order for distribution. But as Sickles rode up, the battle opened in front of the 3d Corps, and there was no council held to discuss the impending retreat.[43]

Here was the most critical testimony regarding Meade's generalship at Gettysburg. Although Butterfield did admit that the retreat order may only have been prepared for an emergency, his sketch of his own activities on July 2 made it clear that he regarded the opening of the battle as a stroke of luck because it prevented the army from withdrawing. Butterfield went on to discuss the council of war on the evening of July 2, during which Meade said Gettysburg was no place to fight a battle, but the army would remain there. He then told about the conference on July 4, then ended his statements by dwelling on the failure to pursue Lee's army.[44]

Once Meade heard of Butterfield's statements about the withdrawal order, he appeared a third time before the committee and added some testimony to refute Butterfield. He told Chairman Wade that Butterfield must have misapprehended the order to retreat. When Butterfield arrived early on July 2, Meade did admit that he directed his chief of staff to familiarize himself with the topography and to study the roads in all directions. Meade stressed that this order to Butterfield was based on the possibility that a retreat might be necessary because of Lee's movements. The general then went on to ask some rhetorical questions, such as if he had indeed directed Butterfield to prepare a retreat order, why was it not issued? There were no obstacles to prevent a withdrawal at the time this supposed retreat order was prepared. Meade included as evidence copies of his ten o'clock order to Slocum to examine the ground in his front preparatory to an attack, as well as his three o'clock telegram to Halleck as proof of his determination to remain at Gettysburg. Meade concluded that Butterfield, through an "excess of zeal and desire to do more than he was called upon to do," probably did compile a retreat order. If he did, Meade said that he did not know about it, nor did he ever sanction such an order.[45]

In spite of all the adverse criticism of Meade's generalship, there were several officers who gave favorable testimony in the face of loaded questions from some of the committee members. General Warren defended Meade by stating that to his knowledge there were no plans to retreat from Gettysburg made at the council of war on the evening of July 2. As far as Sickles' position was concerned, Warren only mentioned that there was some doubt about the line his corps was to occupy, and when he went with General Meade to examine the position on the left, they found his troops out of position; in fact, "his troops could hardly be said to be in position."[46] General Hancock stated that he knew of no order to retreat, and in reference to Sickles, did know of the order to the 3d Corps to prolong the line south to Round Top.[47]

John Gibbon's testimony was solidly in favor of Meade. Gibbon also understood Sickles' position was to be on the left of the 2d Corps, and was surprised when the 3d Corps marched out to the advanced position on the afternoon of July 2. When asked whether or not the advanced line was a good position, Gibbon replied vigorously that it was not, pointing out the isolation of the 3d Corps in respect to the rest of the army, the lack of support on either flank, and the invitation to attack presented by this position. Gibbon also recalled that the opinion of the meeting on July 2 was unanimous to stay and fight. The general then volunteered some information for which the committee did not specifically ask. He said he was of the opinion that Meade wanted to stay and fight at Gettysburg because of the several messages received during the morning, urging him to bring the 2d Corps into position as soon as possible. Later, while present at army headquarters, Gibbon was asked by Butterfield to read over the draft of an order that he had just prepared and compare it with a map. When Gibbon found out that the order pertained to a withdrawal, he exclaimed, "Great God! General Meade does not intend to leave this position?" Butterfield replied that the order was only prepared so if it became necessary to pull back, then the plan was there.[48]

Chief of Artillery Henry Hunt also provided some support for Meade. Hunt said he was sure no retreat had ever been planned. If so, he would certainly have been one of the first to know because the artillery trains blocked the roads to the rear and would have to be moved before the army could withdraw. He described Sickles' advanced position and his own reconnaissance on the morning of July 2, pointing out both its good and bad features.[49]

General Sedgwick then testified. He also stated that he did not hear of any retreat order until the subject appeared during the committee hearings. He thought it odd that such an idea could be advanced in the face of the exertions of the 6th Corps to reach the battlefield.[50]

Finally, Meade's adjutant general, Seth Williams, provided some key points to defend Meade. Since Williams was responsible for copying and distributing all orders given to him by the chief of staff, he would certainly have known about any retreat orders. When asked about such an order, Williams replied:

> In regard to the order of the 2d of July, to the best of my recollection and belief, the chief of staff either handed me or my clerk an order looking to a contingency which possibly might happen of the army being compelled to assume a new position. To the best of my belief such an order was prepared, and I presume it may have been signed by me, and possibly the copies may have been prepared for the corps and other commanders. Orders of such a character are usually made out in manifold in order to save time. The particular order in question, however, was never distributed.

He further elaborated on this order when Mr. Gooch questioned him about it:

> To the best of my belief the chief of staff handed me or my clerk the manuscript of the order, with the understanding that no copies were to be sent out until I received further instructions from him, and I infer this from the fact that no copies of the order were sent out. The order was prepared a short time before the engagement on that day commenced. I only know such an order was never in fact issued.

Williams observed that all Meade's actions led to the irresistible conclusion that he intended to stay and fight at Gettysburg.[51]

The final report of the committee was published at war's end.[52] As was to be expected, the report was biased against Meade. The major criticisms of his generalship were the several wasted opportunities to attack Lee—immediately after Pickett's Charge, the dilatory pursuit and failure at Williamsport, and the failures during the Bristoe Station and Mine Run Campaigns. Senator Wade wrote that because of Butterfield's help, Meade followed Hooker's plans. He also wrote that Pleasonton was the general who decided the battle would be at Gettysburg by sending Buford there. There was not much comment about Sickles in the report, but the insinuation was there that his forward movement prevented a disastrous flanking attack by the enemy. Finally, the report went into great detail to examine the proposed retreat from Gettysburg. Copious quotations were inserted to investigate the results of the conference at three o'clock in the afternoon of July 2 as well as the evening meeting at army headquarters. The report concluded that the opening of the engagement on July 2 broke up the meeting called to consider retreat, and the council that evening voted to stay and fight. When it was all over, Meade remained in command of the Army of the Potomac, but the publicity attendant to the committee hearings had damaged his reputation.[53]

Chapter Four

POSTWAR DEVELOPMENT
OF THE CONTROVERSY, 1869–1930

With the opening of the 1864 campaign, the Meade-Sickles feud lapsed until after the war. In 1869, John Watts De Peyster, a former 3d Corps officer, published an article entitled, "The Third Corps at Gettysburg, July 2, 1863. General Sickles Vindicated."[1] De Peyster proposed to answer the question of whether Sickles was right or wrong in moving out to the advanced position he occupied on July 2. The author chiefly relied on the Committee on the Conduct of the War testimony, but he did use other material as well, such as General Lee's official report and Edward A. Pollard's history of the war. De Peyster wrote that Sickles was wrong if the position his corps occupied was advanced and separated from the rest of the army and if he did not have a sufficient cause for moving forward. He was right if he was better able to check a dangerous enemy movement.

To no one's surprise, De Peyster concluded, after examining all the evidence, that Sickles was justified in occupying the Peach Orchard line because his advance forced Longstreet into a frontal assault rather than flanking the Army of the Potomac.

> Sickles had learned a great lesson at Chancellorsville, on Saturday, 2d May. He had seen what fatal results had followed his not being permitted to attack Jackson, when making the flank movement which effectually disposed of our right wing. . . . With Sickles' intelligence, experience and consequent cool judgment, he could not repeat the same fatal error, or stand still and see it repeated on a more momentous field.[2]

In citing the opinion of various officers, De Peyster committed the sin of leaving out portions of committee testimony detrimental to Sickles,[3] and omitting the names of officers with whom he said he had conversations after the war.[4] The author also made too much of the appearance of Confederate skirmishers in the vicinity of the Peach Orchard as early as eight o'clock in the morning of July 2, leaving the reader to believe that the enemy flank movement started very early in the morning when in fact it did not begin until almost noon. He also "proved" that the 3d Corps did not take up the advanced line until the Confederates were advancing to the attack. De Peyster did point out that the 3d Corps absorbed the shock of Longstreet's assault and disrupted it so much that the gray-clad attackers failed to reach Cemetery Ridge with sufficient force to capture and hold the ridge. Here De Peyster may have had a valid point, but the question of what the result might have been had Sickles remained in position on Cemetery Ridge is one that cannot be answered.

In November 1869, an episode occurred that was later to prove the catalyst for the escalation of the controversy in 1886. During a speech made before the Reunion Society of Vermont Officers, Col. William W. Grout made the following statement in reference to the Battle of Gettysburg:

> Sickles had the day before sent word to Meade that he had gone to the relief of Howard at Gettysburg and suggested the propriety of concentrating at that point. Thus the responsibility of that selection was largely upon him, and with true manliness, himself took the only weak place in what must be conceded was a naturally strong line for a defensive battle; and it should be remembered that we were then on the defensive. Under these circumstances Sickles, perhaps made a little anxious by the adverse judgment of Meade, and because too, of the exposure of his position, thought to improve it by occupying a ridge in his front and moved out for that purpose. But the practiced eye of Lee it seems had caught this same ridge as threatening round-top hill on our left, which in turn threatened the whole federal position; and had ordered Longstreet to take possession of it, which he was then in the act of doing. Thus, in manoeuvering for the crest of this ridge, Sickles, with his corps and the whole left wing of the army, became unexpectedly engaged, to the great chagrin of Meade, who was still intent upon falling back to his favorite position near Taneytown. Some have spoken of this step on the part of Sickles as unfortunate. In my judgment history will record it otherwise. It is not my purpose, however, on this occasion to defend it; my only object is to show how that step precipitated the engagement, and prevented the possible retreat of the army to Pipe Creek.[5]

Col. George G. Benedict, a member of the audience, and at the time the editor of the *Burlington Free Press*, took up the issue of Meade's proposed retreat from Gettysburg via some editorials in his newspaper. Benedict claimed to have never had any prejudice against either Meade or Sickles, but thought Grout's claims were so unjustified, as well as a distortion of history, that he sided with General Meade's supporters. Benedict sent copies of his writings to Meade, who wrote a long letter in reply, a document Benedict kept secret until 1886.[6]

After this brief flurry, the controversy submerged for over a decade, primarily because of Sickles' involvement in politics in a variety of posts. General Meade died in 1872, and it remained for historians to write about the controversy until it heated up again in the 1880s. In June 1882, Sickles visited Gettysburg as part of a reunion called by John B. Bachelder,[7] and the general's version of the battle found its way into the newspapers.[8]

Sickles mentioned that he sent out a reconnaissance early on July 2, and "soon became convinced that the enemy intended attacking in force." Sickles said he rode over to Meade's headquarters and found that the commanding general did not expect an attack. In fact, he said, the 3d Corps commander concluded that Meade's intention was to retreat from Gettysburg. Indeed, General Butterfield informed Sickles that orders were even then being prepared for a withdrawal to Pipe Creek. Sickles then spoke of General Hunt's survey of the advanced line. According to Sickles, Hunt told him that although their views on the position were in agreement, he could not order Sickles to take position there, but he would report to Meade his survey of the terrain. Sickles continued that Hunt rode away to headquarters, but before the order to advance could arrive, the danger of attack became so imminent that Sickles was forced to march out to the high ground to his front.

Soon after taking position, Sickles said he was called to headquarters for a conference of corps commanders. Before he arrived at headquarters, the enemy opened fire on the 3d Corps. As he rode up to the conference, General Meade told him not to dismount and to go back to his command. Meade soon joined Sickles and inspected the position, expressing apprehension that the line was too extended. Sickles did offer to withdraw, he said, but Meade told him to stay in position and that he would send up reinforcements. While Hancock responded promptly with some of his best troops, Sykes took much longer to bring the 5th Corps into battle.

One of the reinforcing brigades was sent to Little Round Top in response to General Warren's urgent appeal for troops to defend that vital hill. As a conclusion to his remarks, Sickles stated that present-day military critics were wrong in saying that the 3d Corps should have taken position in the low ground of southern Cemetery Ridge, since this position would have given the enemy the commanding ground to the front and would have left Little Round Top "entirely uncovered."

The year 1886 saw a rapid escalation of the controversy. During a speech before the 3d Army Corps Union in the Boston Music Hall on April 8, Sickles launched into a defense of his July 2 actions at Gettysburg in response to criticism of the 3d Corps during the twenty-three years since the battle.[9] During the course of this oration, as well as in an evening speech at the Revere House, Sickles constantly indicated the importance of Little Round Top as the key to the Union position. He used Meade's committee testimony to substantiate this view, and stated that the best way to defend the hill was by going out in front of it, as he did. Sickles also quoted from Lee's official report to show the importance of the line his men occupied on July 2.

But even though he took this position on his own responsibility, Sickles told the admiring audience that he was not to blame. The enemy had been massing in his front since the early morning of July 2. Although he sent word of this to army headquarters several times, "I, the corps commander on our extreme left flank, had received no instructions as to any dispositions for battle." He cited from Meade's committee testimony to illustrate that he had not received any orders, and, in the Revere House speech, challenged contradiction. Earlier, in the Music Hall oration, Sickles may have suggested why he did not receive any orders when he said:

> Now, I know it is said . . . that General Sickles was imprudent in engaging General Longstreet in battle when he had but one corps at his disposal. That is true. I acknowledge the truth of that criticism. It may have been imprudent to advance and hold Longstreet at whatever sacrifice, but was it not a sacrifice to save the key of the position? What were we there for? To fight. Were we there to count the cost in blood and men when the key of the position at Gettysburg was within the enemy's grasp? Comrades, what little I know of war, I learned under good soldiers. What little I know of conduct on the field of battle, I learned from Hooker and Kearney [*sic*]. What would Hooker or Kearney [*sic*] have done finding himself in an assailable, untenable position, without orders from headquarters as to his dispositions for battle, when he

saw the masses of the enemy marching to seize a point vital to the integrity of the Union position? Would those men have hesitated? Would they have sent couriers to headquarters asking instructions what to do? Well, I learned war from them, and I didn't send any either. I simply advanced out on to the battlefield and seized Longstreet by the throat and held him there.[10]

General Sickles' next statement was a speech at Gettysburg on July 2. This oration was supposed to be delivered outdoors in the Wheatfield before another reunion of the 3d Corps, but due to inclement weather the meeting was held indoors in a rink. The air in this building became so oppressive that Sickles never finished his speech.[11] The speech was later published in its entirety in the *National Tribune*. Several other papers featured excerpts.[12]

Sickles began the speech by giving credit to Hooker for forcing Lee to suspend his invasion and concentrate his army. As for the position at Gettysburg, General Howard received the credit. The 3d Corps marched to Gettysburg on July 1 and Meade never acknowledged Sickles' foresight. In fact, Sickles never received any orders all the time he was present on the battlefield. Sickles, by using Meade's 3:00 P.M. telegram to Halleck and Hunt's committee testimony, showed that prior to the enemy attack on July 2, Meade had not even formed a plan of battle, and was taken completely by surprise when Longstreet sent his troops forward against the Union left.

This attack came as a surprise to everyone except Sickles. He did not like the low ground on which the 3d Corps was posted and feared that his left flank could easily be turned. Sickles cited Hancock's report to Meade, which mentioned how easily the position might be flanked. Thus, Sickles took precautions to guard against such a move. Of course, there was no help from army headquarters. To the contrary, Sickles declared, Meade withdrew Buford's cavalry and did not replace it; Sickles was forced to use infantry as scouts. The result was Colonel Berdan's reconnaissance, which uncovered the enemy plan to move around his left flank. Still, no orders were received although couriers were sent to headquarters to report the situation. Sickles quoted from letters he received from Capt. Alexander Moore, Capt. John B. Fasset, Henry Tremain, and Alfred Pleasonton as proof of his statements. Finally, Sickles continued, when it appeared that the enemy was about to attack, he advanced his corps to occupy the high ground in his front and thus foiled Hood's movement by threatening Hood's own flank and forcing him into a frontal assault.

According to Sickles, just as he was deploying his corps, he received a message to report to headquarters for a conference of corps commanders. At this point in the speech, Sickles brought up the rhetorical question of why this conference was convened. He then proceeded to quote from Butterfield's committee testimony about the chief of staff's preparation of a retreat order, alleging that this order would be issued at the conference. Sickles again quoted from the three o'clock telegram to Halleck to reinforce his belief that the withdrawal was indeed planned.

Sickles then returned to a discussion of the fighting on July 2. He stated that, all throughout the battle, he did not receive any orders from General Meade, except that which ordered him to occupy General Geary's position, which was impossible to obey since Geary did not have any position. Since he did not receive any orders, Sickles claimed "I am, therefore, alone responsible for the lines on which the battle of July 2 was fought." He went on to remark that Meade slighted the 3d Corps in his official report, but then showed that Meade omitted much of the actions of the 12th Corps as well.

Finally, Sickles concluded by stating that he had not spoken out to quell the prejudices against the 3d Corps, but now it was time to right the wrongs that, by his previous silence, time had endorsed as true. He then enumerated twenty-six points as the most conspicuous errors that needed correcting. Sickles backed these up with references to official reports and committee testimony. Among the major points the general stressed was the notion that the forward movement exchanged weak ground for strong. Furthermore, the Peach Orchard line effectively covered Little Round Top, which would have been lost to the enemy had the corps remained on Cemetery Ridge. In fact, Sickles declared that the orchard salient was the best part of the line since it threatened the flank of the Confederates who were endeavoring to turn the Union left. Thus, Sickles claimed, his line forced the enemy into a frontal attack. Sickles reiterated that he never received any orders. If it were not for his vigilance and discovery of the elaborate Southern preparations that were under way since daylight, the later enemy assault would have been a complete surprise to the Union commander.

This much-publicized speech by General Sickles brought forth a storm of criticism by Meade supporters. Maj. James C. Biddle, one of the general's aides, responded with an article in the July 14 issue of the Philadelphia *Weekly Press.*[13] Biddle accused Sickles of misleading the 3d Corps veterans by telling them that their conduct in the fighting on July 2 was the chief criticism against the forward movement because the corps was driven back.

> The real and serious accusation is against General Sickles, . . . to the effect that on July 2, 1863, he, through ignorance, or from a worse motive, disobeyed the orders of General Meade, his commander, and by that disobedience imperiled the safety of the army, which was saved from serious disaster by the energy of General Meade in sending and bringing reinforcements from other portions of his line.

Biddle wrote that there were several opportunities for Sickles to receive orders. After Meade's inspection of the field early on July 2, orders were sent to all corps commanders. Under these orders, Sickles' command was to go into position on the left of the 2d Corps and extend the line south to Little Round Top, which was to be occupied if practicable. When these orders were repeated later that morning, Sickles was also ordered to occupy General Geary's position. Finally, when Sickles came in person to headquarters, Meade, in addition to repeating his earlier orders to Sickles, pointed out Little Round Top when reaffirming the order. Biddle then recalled what he remembered of the conversation between the two generals when Meade rode out to the Peach Orchard just as the battle opened.

Former Confederate Maj. Gen. Lafayette McLaws also responded to Sickles' speech.[14] McLaws wrote primarily to defend his former soldiers against Sickles' claim that Crawford's division drove McLaws' men back to end the action on that part of the line. After dealing with this charge, McLaws went on to discuss Sickles' thesis that his move led to the Union victory at Gettysburg. He admitted that if Sickles meant by victory the fact that his position had disorganized and exhausted Longstreet's two divisions by the time they broke the 3d Corps line, then Sickles was right.

On the other hand, McLaws wrote that a discussion of what might have happened as a result of Sickles' forward move must also be included. McLaws argued that if Sickles had taken position where Meade had intended him to, Little Round Top would have been made impregnable, and the Confederate attack that did come close to seizing that hill might well have been cancelled. Chief among these "what if" theses was that if Stuart had done a better job, Pickett's division would have been on hand when Longstreet launched his attack; this extra division might have provided the manpower necessary to break the Federal line. Also, if Ewell had cooperated with a more general assault on the Union right, reinforcements could not have been drawn from that part of the line to aid Sickles. In effect, Sickles' move almost led to a disaster on the Union left. "It would, therefore, appear that the arrangements of the troops made by General Meade, which contemplated the occupation of Round Top, were the best possible to meet all emergencies."

In conclusion, McLaws cited his own experience to comment on Sickles' statement that the enemy concentration against the Federal left began at daybreak. McLaws did admit that Longstreet's assault probably was a surprise to General Meade, but then Burnside's assault on Marye's Heights at Fredericksburg was also a surprise to General Lee, as was Hooker's flanking move at Chancellorsville. The opposing general rarely knows where the enemy will strike and thus almost any attack is somewhat of a surprise, McLaws argued.

Before closing with a commentary on political generals who were always seeking fame, McLaws penned the following:

> General Meade was in command of the army, and upon him rested the responsibility as to the manner and mode of driving back the invaders— whether to do this he chose to stand on the defensive in his stronghold or assume the offensive was for him alone to say. It was not personal fame he was looking after, but safety to his people and the success of his cause. He was in the occupation of a line which on his left could have been made impregnable, and his right was, so General Sickles says, also impregnable. That the commander on his left should leave the position which could be made impregnable and offer battle in front of that position, thereby imperilling the position, and this without the knowledge or consent of the Commander-in-chief, thus taking it upon himself to force the defensive plan into an offensive movement, will have to be characterized by those whose interests he was serving. The assault, as it was, was unsuccessful. But if it had been made on the same troops occupying an impregnable position, the attacking party would have been defeated with far greater loss to themselves and much less loss to the defenders than the records show.

An anonymous reply to Sickles' speech appeared in the Saint Paul *Pioneer Press* on August 15. The author, who identified himself as "Chief of Staff for Gen. Humphreys, commanding the Second Division of the Third (Sickles) Army Corps," revealed that it was common knowledge "before noon" at division headquarters that the essence of Meade's orders to Sickles was "to continue Hancock's left and cover Round Top." But, Sickles advanced his corps to await Longstreet's attack instead of remaining in position. This staff officer ended his letter by stating that "the true story of Gettysburg may safely be left to the impartial historian of the now near future without a shadow of fear that a leaf will be touched in the wreath so honestly won and modestly worn by George G. Meade."[15]

The most important reply to Sickles appeared in the Philadelphia *Weekly Press* of August 11.[16] Col. George G. Benedict now made public General Meade's 1870 letter. Benedict had respected the wishes of the long-dead general not to publish this letter, but Sickles' speech so outraged Benedict that he felt the truth would be better served with its publication.

General Meade, after thanking Benedict for his favorable editorials, had written the Vermonter that the defense against the charges of Sickles and Butterfield could be found in his testimony before the Committee on the Conduct of the War. Over the years, Meade had "avoided any controversy with either of these officers—though both have allowed no opportunity to pass unimproved which permitted them to circulate their ex parte statements, and . . . to distort history for their purposes." The instruction to Butterfield to prepare a retreat plan was a contingency measure formulated in case Lee did what Meade feared most—attempt to get between the army and Washington.

Meade then revealed an important piece of information. He wrote that when he prepared his official report, he honestly did believe that Sickles did not know where he was to place his command in position and thus the forward move was due to a misapprehension of orders. But since the war Meade told Benedict that he learned some new facts from General Geary, who told him that after he had received the order to move his division to Culp's Hill, he was ordered to await relief by the 3d Corps before vacating his bivouac area. Geary waited "some time" for his relief. When none appeared, he sent a staff officer to Sickles to explain where his position was and the importance of the Round Tops. Sickles replied that he would attend to it "in due time." Geary remained "till his patience was exhausted," then marched off to rejoin the 12th Corps. As far as Meade was concerned, here was evidence that Sickles knew of Geary's position and yet failed to carry out his orders to replace Geary in line. When Sickles came to headquarters later in the morning and told him that he did not know where to place his command, Meade replied, "Why, you were to relieve the

Twelfth Corps." The commanding general then pointed to the Round Tops, visible on the southern horizon, telling Sickles his left flank was to anchor on that point and that his right was to connect with Hancock's left.

Sickles' reply to Benedict's article was not long in coming. The August 14 *New York Times* contained a three-column-length answer.[17] Sickles told the reporter sent to get his reaction that Meade's 1870 letter "must have been written without deliberation, without revision, and without comparison with the official records. It contradicts his own official report . . . and his testimony before the Committee on the Conduct of the War." After speaking of inaccuracies in Meade's official report about the actions of the 12th Corps at Gettysburg, Sickles spoke of his July 1 march to the battlefield and how he wrote to Meade that Gettysburg was a good place to fight a battle, but the position was weak on the left, as it proved to be on July 2. Sickles then said that every officer who was instrumental in selecting Gettysburg as the place to fight—Doubleday, Robinson, Wadsworth, Buford, Reynolds, and Howard—suffered disgrace at the hands of General Meade. Somehow, Sickles forgot Hancock's name on this list.

In reference to the July 2 battle, Sickles asserted that it was Meade who authorized the withdrawal of Buford's cavalry division, in spite of his own and Hancock's warnings that the left flank was vulnerable. Sickles again mentioned Meade's 3:00 P.M. telegram as evidence that there was no battle plan at the time Longstreet's artillery opened fire. He told the reporter that General Pleasonton mentioned that Meade ordered him to gather what cavalry and artillery he could and take position in the rear of the army to cover the intended retreat.

Sickles again insisted that he was without orders all during the battle. He said that he had "become weary of so many visits to headquarters during the day," begging for orders and warning of enemy movements toward the left. In answer to the statement that the 3d Corps was ordered to relieve Geary, Sickles said that "the Twelfth Corps was never at any time until the very close of the battle on the 2nd of July, in position on the left." Sickles also said that his corps could never have held the assigned ground on Cemetery Ridge because he did not have enough men to establish a sufficient line of battle. Moreover, the lower half of Cemetery Ridge was dominated by the Peach Orchard line. As far as Sickles was concerned, "he was in position according to his humble judgment." He said the advanced position of the 3d Corps was held at the end of the day's combat by Crawford's division on the left at the Wheatfield, and on the right by Humphreys' division, which, although initially driven back, advanced at nightfall and held a position close to the Emmitsburg Road.

Sickles concluded the interview by again remarking that Meade's letter contained several obvious errors. He then quoted from Meade's official report, but an examination of the *Official Records* reveals that this "quote" is nowhere to be found. Sickles was adamant that the only specific order he received from Meade on July 2 was to relieve Geary's division, which Sickles said he could not locate—because Geary sent no guides to show him the position. Sickles also asked why Meade was unwilling to bestow praise when it was due, citing the forced march of the 3d Corps to Gettysburg on July 1 as a case in point.

The year 1886 closed with Gen. Henry Hunt's "The Second Day at Gettysburg" article in the December issue of *The Century Magazine*.[18] In gathering information for his study of the Gettysburg Campaign, Hunt had written to Sickles and to Meade's son for information.[19] When he contracted with the Century Company to write a series of three articles on Gettysburg, Hunt said, in a private letter, that he would avoid the Meade-Sickles controversy and simply present the facts, leaving the reader to draw his own conclusions.[20] But after finishing the study, Hunt was inclined to write Colonel Meade that his (Hunt's) opinion of General Meade was higher than it had ever been as a result of his work on these articles.[21]

Hunt's bias showed in his second day article. The general wrote that Meade decided to concentrate the army at Gettysburg even before receiving Hancock's report. By doing so, Meade exposed the army to great risk because if the Confederates had attacked before the Army of the Potomac had assembled on the field, the result would have been disastrous. As for the retreat order mentioned by General Butterfield, Hunt said it was a precautionary measure only, as General Meade stated in his committee testimony, and "his acts and dispatches during the day were in accordance with his statement." Hunt bolstered this defense of Meade by mentioning his own role as artillery commander at Gettysburg. As he had testified before the Committee on the Conduct of the War, he said that if a withdrawal was indeed planned, he would have been one of the first to know because the artillery trains would have to be moved on the roads prior to a general withdrawal.

Hunt also recounted his survey of the Peach Orchard line with Sickles and how he was favorably impressed with this line, since it would be a good position for the enemy to hold as well. On the other hand, the "direct line through the woods, and including the Round Tops, could be occupied, intrenched, and made impregnable to a front attack." But this line was purely defensive, and Hunt considered the Peach Orchard the better tactical position to occupy, provided there were enough troops to man this line. And until the 6th Corps arrived on the battlefield, Meade did not have enough troops to do so and at the same time keep an adequate reserve force to meet any emergency. Hunt also mentioned that Gettysburg was not a good strategic position for the Union army since the ground there was limited to the tactical defensive. But Meade was wise enough not to take risks and fought the battle to the best of his ability.

After 1886, the controversy submerged again for a few years. Some evidence damaging to Sickles appeared in 1890 in the "Gettysburg" chapter of Philippe Regis de Trobriand's *Four Years with the Army of the Potomac.*[22] De Trobriand was one of Sickles' brigade commanders at Gettysburg and on the whole had been favorably inclined toward his former chief.[23] In his memoir of his military service, de Trobriand commented adversely on Sickles' advance to the Peach Orchard:

> A crossroad to the right led us to the position occupied by the Third Corps, on the rocky slope of a hill, where it was much to be desired that the Confederates should come to attack us. Except the railroad with shelving banks, which did not exist here, our line recalled the one which the enemy occupied at Fredericksburg. It was not, then, without regret that about two o'clock in the afternoon we received the order to advance.[24]

Colonel de Trobriand thought that the forward move to oppose Longstreet "showed more ardor to advance to meet the fight than a nice appreciation of the best means to sustain it." He praised Meade for not attempting to hold the advanced line but instead remain on the defensive in the original position intended for Sickles and the 3d Corps.

Sickles reentered the fray via the popular magazine *North American Review.* The March 1891 issue of this magazine contained the article "Further Recollections of Gettysburg," a series of four papers by Generals Sickles, Butterfield, Gregg, and Newton.[25] In his portion of this article, Sickles chose his words carefully. Hooker received credit for choosing

Gettysburg as the battlefield, his "revenge for Chancellorsville." Sickles called the line along Cemetery Ridge "perhaps the more desirable tactical position for me to occupy, unless overruled by superior considerations." He enumerated these to be the swampy, low profile of the terrain and an insufficient number of troops. The former corps commander recounted the skirmishes that revealed the Rebel movement toward the Union left, his repeated warnings to Meade, and General Hunt's favorable view of the Peach Orchard line. Sickles again cited Meade's 3:00 P.M. telegram as proof that the army lacked a battle plan. In a new twist of history, Sickles revealed that it was he who dispatched Weed's brigade to Little Round Top upon receiving Warren's urgent appeal for troops. When he was carried wounded to the rear late in the day, Sickles knew that the Federals had won the victory.

The June 1891 *North American Review* contained a stinging rebuke by John Gibbon.[26] Gibbon's main purpose in writing this article was to inform the public of some details of military orders. He did not argue for or against the forward move undertaken by Sickles. Rather, he initially stated that the 3d Corps was "placed in a position to which it was not ordered by General Meade." Meade ordered Sickles to occupy a line on the left of the 2d Corps, and although Sickles was adamant about not receiving any orders to that effect, "neither did he receive any orders to go where he did go."

Gibbon reached the central point of his argument by writing:

> In cases of this kind there is and can be but one rule in armies. If a soldier is ordered to go to a certain point on a field of battle, he goes there if he can. If he does not get orders to go there, he does not go, with the one single exception that overwhelming necessity requires him to make the move, when he is so situated that he cannot solicit or receive the orders of his commanding officer.[27]

In this case, Gibbon remarked, Sickles was in close proximity to Meade and had no orders to move out to the Emmitsburg Road. Gibbon concluded that most of the remarks directed against Meade were based on hindsight and it was generally "idle" to sit and speculate upon what might have happened under different circumstances.

The June 28 issue of the *New York Sun* contained an anti-Sickles article authored by Carswell McClellan, who at Gettysburg had been a member of General Humphreys' staff.[28] McClellan (unrelated to the former commanding general) at this time was engaged in writing a history of the 5th Corps and this article was purportedly an excerpt from it.[29] After detailing the march of the 3d Corps to Gettysburg on July 1, McClellan spoke of the possible animosity between Sickles and Meade as a result of Hooker being relieved from command of the Army of the Potomac. McClellan claimed that Sickles, due only to his great patriotism, consented to remain in command of the corps after his friends warned him that Meade was hostile to him. McClellan also pointed out that Sickles' trains blocked the march of other units of the army; Meade had to tell the general to get them moving. This incident might also have strained relations between the two generals.

After detailing the July 1 controversy about Sickles' march to Gettysburg, Colonel McClellan delved into a discussion of the position of the 3d Corps early on July 2. He recounted Captain Meade's visit to 3d Corps headquarters to ascertain the position of the corps and the problem he encountered there.[30] McClellan then used the official reports of Generals Geary, Birney, and Humphreys to show that shortly after 7:00 A.M. the 3d Corps was in the position desired by General Meade. McClellan then summed up the controversy:

> Had disaster overtaken the Federal army while Gen. Sickles occupied the position assigned him and had made judicious dispositions for its defence, history could well listen to whatever argument he might adduce to clear himself of blame. Failing that, it is unnecessary to follow the controversy attempted against Gen. Meade further in detail. Whatever may have been the opinion of Gen. Sickles, Gen. George G. Meade, and not Gen. Daniel E. Sickles, was in command of the Army of the Potomac on July 2, 1863, and until the latter can demonstrate the right of a subordinate to move from an assigned position in the face of an enemy into one which compels the commander of an army to alter his dispositions, and dangerously to weaken his line at other points, in order to ward off disaster courted thereby, attempted arraignment of his superior can only recoil upon himself.

The author then went on to describe the actions of the 5th Corps on July 2 and how its timely arrival enabled General Warren to save Little Round Top. Sickles contributed nothing to the victory "save the emergency that gave needless and fearful opportunity for showing the wonderful endurance of his command and the magnificent courage of its supports."

Sickles replied to McClellan's attack via the *New York Times*.[31] The former 3d Corps commander commented that he had done more fighting for his reputation since the end of the war than he did fighting the enemy during the conflict. Personally, he had nothing against General Meade, who was a "careful, conservative, and conscientious officer." It was only Meade's friends who constantly attacked him. Sickles preferred to let the records speak for themselves. He told the reporter, "I have yet to find in the records an order from Gen. Meade that I did not obey." Sickles said that his forward move to confront the Confederate flanking march was within his discretion as a corps commander. He cited the statements of Howard, Doubleday, Warren, Hunt, and Philip H. Sheridan on the Union side, and Lee, Kershaw, and John C. Haskell on the Confederate side to back up his claim of the importance of his move. Sickles closed his remarks by condemning Meade's lack of attention to his left flank.

After the 1891 skirmish, the controversy began to die out as many of the principal characters in the drama passed away. However, those yet alive published their reminiscences. Helen D. Longstreet published a memorial volume to her late husband in 1904.[32] General Sickles wrote the introduction to Mrs. Longstreet's volume, which in effect was a defense of Longstreet's conduct at Gettysburg. Sickles wrote that had the Confederates attacked early in the morning, all the Federal troops that opposed him later in the day would also have been on hand that morning. On the other hand, if Longstreet had delayed his attack just one hour, "I would have been on Cemetery Ridge, in compliance with General Meade's orders, and Longstreet could have marched, unresisted, from Seminary Ridge to the foot of Round Top, and might, perhaps, have unlimbered his guns on the summit."[33]

Sickles gave Longstreet credit for holding the Union army on the battlefield because his attack stopped the planned retreat. A reconnaissance party from the 3d Corps discovered Longstreet's flank march and prevented complete surprise, enabling Sickles to change front to meet the anticipated assault on his position. This action delayed Longstreet long enough for Meade to bring up reinforcements to save the Federal position. Sickles interpreted Lee's order to attack up the Emmitsburg Road as impossible to obey until his advance occupied that position.[34]

In 1905, Sickles' chief aide at Gettysburg, Maj. Henry E. Tremain, published his recollections of the battle.[35] The major revelation as far as the controversy was concerned, was that Tremain went to army headquarters five times during the day. The first trip was to report the arrival of General Graham with the two brigades from Emmitsburg and to report that the corps trains had not yet arrived. Later that morning, Tremain was sent to Meade to report that there were no other troops on the left of the 3d Corps. He then accompanied General Sickles to headquarters at 11:00 A.M. Upon returning to the corps, Tremain guided Sickles and Hunt on the survey of the Peach Orchard line. In the afternoon, Tremain rode to army headquarters to report suspected enemy movements to Meade, who exclaimed, "Generals are always expecting attacks on their own fronts." Finally, he went with Sickles when the general was summoned peremptorily to attend the corps commanders' conference. Tremain also mentioned that the skirmish that uncovered the enemy flank march deflected the march to a more southerly course and delayed it long enough for Sickles to occupy the high ground to his front.[36]

Colonel George Meade, who had served as an aide to his father at Gettysburg, had his *The Life and Letters of George Gordon Meade* published posthumously in 1913.[37] In the section on Gettysburg, Meade recounted his two visits to 3d Corps headquarters on the morning of July 2 and how his initial mission presupposed that orders had already been issued to Sickles and he was merely to ascertain their obedience. He also detailed Sickles' eleven o'clock visit to army headquarters and Meade's further instructions at that time. After relating the movements of both armies through the early afternoon, Meade described Sickles' advance to the Peach Orchard line, referring to it as direct disobedience of orders.[38] Meade also included his father's Civil War letters, many of which pertained to Gettysburg, as well as the 1864 committee hearing testimony. In 1930, the Gettysburg chapters of *Life and Letters* were published separately as *With Meade at Gettysburg*.[39]

The final published recollection of a participant in the origins of the controversy was that by John Gibbon. Although Gibbon's memoir was published in 1928, most of the Gettysburg-related material had been published in the Philadelphia *Weekly Press* in 1887.[40] Gibbon recalled that Meade awakened him while riding to Gettysburg on the evening of July 1 and gave him verbal instructions to move the 2d Corps to the field at first light. "There seemed to be no doubt in his mind then that the site of the battle was already determined upon." Gibbon also described Butterfield's request that he examine the supposed retreat order and see if it was drawn up correctly. Gibbon included correspondence between himself and General Meade during the committee hearings in 1864 and with other officers regarding the council of war on the evening of July 2.[41]

After Gibbon's book in 1928 and Meade's in 1930, all recollections by participants in the controversy had been made public. A summary of General Meade's position reveals that he gave Sickles the benefit of the doubt by writing in his official report that his 3d Corps commander misapprehended his orders and did not willfully disobey his orders by advancing to the Peach Orchard. However, when General Geary told him that Sickles never bothered to ascertain the position of his 12th Corps division before he had to march off to Culp's Hill, Meade changed his mind and decided that Sickles had indeed known where his original position was to be. Even so, Meade never entered into any public condemnation of Sickles' conduct at Gettysburg; he preferred to let his committee testimony speak for him. After Meade's death in 1872, some of his staff officers, notably his son George, Major Biddle, and friends Warren and Gibbon, upheld Meade when the late general was assailed by Sickles and his supporters.

Yet Sickles never missed an opportunity to publicize his own rationale behind the forward move to the Peach Orchard line. An analysis of what he said in defense of this advance reveals that he concocted four major points around which he spun the vindication of his actions at Gettysburg. First, Sickles declared on numerous occasions that he had never received any orders concerning the position of his corps. At times, when he did admit to an order, Sickles declared that it was so indefinite that he was forced to act on his own discretion as to the best position to occupy. Second, since the Peach Orchard ridge commanded the lower ground on which his corps was first posted, Sickles proclaimed that it was necessary to occupy the higher ground to his front to prevent enemy seizure of it. According to Sickles, such an event would have left his position along Cemetery Ridge untenable because of the low ground there and the fact that the 3d Corps was not strong enough to occupy the assigned position.

Third, Sickles stated that his skirmishers uncovered Confederate plans to flank the Union army out of its strong position at Gettysburg. Therefore, he moved his corps to the higher ground to forestall enemy occupation of that vital real estate. The result was Longstreet's frontal assault on the 3d Corps, which prevented the flank move and gave Meade time to bring up reinforcements to occupy Little Round Top, the key to the position.

Finally, Sickles painted a picture of Meade as a weak, indecisive general. He claimed that Meade did not have any definite plans on July 2, and was actually planning a retreat from Gettysburg when the battle opened on Sickles' front; it was this fighting that prevented the withdrawal from taking place. Before analyzing these four points, we should survey how Civil War historians have interpreted Sickles' actions at Gettysburg.

Chapter Five

THE CONTROVERSY WITHIN THE CONTEXT
OF GETTYSBURG HISTORIOGRAPHY

Having examined the Meade-Sickles controversy as it developed in the postwar years through the efforts of the participants, we now survey the controversy as historians of the Gettysburg Campaign interpreted it. Included in this survey are all major Gettysburg books and those Civil War histories that treat the battle in some depth.

The several books that appeared in the 1860s showed a wide variety of interpretation of the feud. Many of these early authors were extremely sketchy about myriad details of the battle because of the lack of published material available to them. The first two books about Gettysburg, by local authorities Michael Jacobs and Samuel M. Schmucker, suffered from this dearth of sources. Jacobs did not even mention Sickles' forward move, while Schmucker gave no reason for Sickles' advance.[1] Many succeeding authors followed these two interpretations at first. General Civil War histories by Thomas P. Kettell, John S. C. Abbott, and James Moore failed to mention the controversy or the forward move, and while works by Elliott G. Storke and L. P. Brockett, and Joel T. Headley did say something about Sickles, they failed to include any reasons for his action.[2]

Some of the late-1860s authors also began to attempt an explanation of the 3d Corps movement to the Peach Orchard line. British Capt. Charles C. Chesney, writing in 1865, was of the opinion that Sickles' move was a mistake. He attributed the advance to Sickles' misplaced desire to better the orders of his commanding general.[3] Another British observer, Henry C. Fletcher, paraphrased General Meade's official report, in which Meade said Sickles misapprehended his orders, as the reason for the move.[4] American writer W. A. Crafts also used Meade's report in his work on the war.[5]

The first detailed work about Gettysburg appeared in 1866 as a chapter in newspaper correspondent William Swinton's *Campaigns of the Army of the Potomac*. Swinton was able to use unpublished reports from both armies and was fortunate enough to consult officers who had participated in the battle. He included Meade's original instructions to Sickles (to connect with Hancock and extend the line south to the Round Tops), which Sickles disregarded because he wanted to occupy the higher ground in his front to forestall enemy occupation of this area. Lee's order to Longstreet to attack up the Emmitsburg Road was based on Sickles' position in the Peach Orchard.[6] Swinton also published a book entitled *The Twelve Decisive Battles of the War*, in which he used Meade's committee testimony to explain Sickles' actions at Gettysburg. However laudable Sickles' motives for taking the advanced position, Swinton maintained they were wrong because of the salient angle at the Peach Orchard and because his line was unsupported on both flanks.[7]

New York Tribune editor Horace Greeley also published a lengthy work about the Civil War. In reference to Sickles at Gettysburg, Greeley believed that the 3d Corps commander moved his troops forward because he was eager to fight and was acting within the discretion allowed a corps commander. Even so, Greeley condemned the move and his book was favorable to Meade, on the whole.[8]

Finally, the 1860s produced Benson J. Lossing's *Pictorial History of the Civil War*. He wrote the following in reference to Sickles at Gettysburg:

> General Birney sent out a regiment of sharpshooters, under Colonel Berdan, who advanced into a wood a mile beyond the Emmettsburg [*sic*] road, reconnoitering the Confederates. Berdan reported that the foe was moving in three columns, under cover of the woods, with the evident intention of turning the National left. It was this correct report which caused Sickles to advance his corps.[9]

By the end of the 1860s, all interpretations of Sickles' forward move that would be used by future historians had been set forth. The reasons given for Sickles' move can be summarized as follows:

1. Sickles misapprehended his orders, which may have been vague to begin with (Fletcher, Crafts).
2. Sickles deliberately disobeyed orders (Chesney).
3. Sickles was eager to fight (Greeley).
4. Sickles was entranced by the high ground to his front, and was dissatisfied with his original position (Swinton).
5. Berdan's reconnaissance found Confederates moving south under cover of woods across Sickles' front (Lossing).

Future authors would use these reasons, in varying combinations. In most cases, it is almost impossible to discover where historians of the 1860s, and indeed, those through the turn of the century, got their information, owing to a lack of footnotes. Thus, unless a competent writer such as William Swinton stated where he obtained his material, it is virtually useless to try to determine where the content of these early histories originated.

The most-repeated interpretations as to why Sickles moved his corps forward have been that the high ground at the Peach Orchard was a better position than the one on Cemetery Ridge, that Berdan's reconnaissance revealed enemy troops moving south to turn the Union left, and an explanation combining these two reasons. Before surveying these interpretations, we should mention those authors who advanced the other ideas listed above.

Willard Glazier, in his *Battles for the Union*, continued the thesis that Sickles advanced his corps because he was eager to fight.[10] Asa Mahan wrote that Sickles advanced without orders,[11] while William R. Balch maintained that Sickles received vague orders from General Meade. This, coupled with the increasing skirmish fire on his front, induced Sickles to move forward.[12] Finally, several historians failed to mention any reasons for the forward move, or failed to include any discussion of Sickles' actions at all. These men included John B. Bachelder, Theodore A. Dodge, John Formby, James K. Hosmer, Vernon Blythe, Walter Geer, and John B. McMaster.[13]

Of these authors, the most important by far was John B. Bachelder, an artist whose avocation—and obsession—became the battle of Gettysburg. He held important positions on the Gettysburg Battlefield Memorial Association and until his death in 1894 was widely regarded as *the* leading authority on the battle. However, Bachelder never mentioned the Meade-

Sickles controversy, either in his many published booklets and articles or in his massive unpublished history of the battle. Bachelder steered clear of any controversy and generally tried to present simply the facts of the battle without any interpretation.[14]

The interpretation that Sickles was lured forward by the higher ground at the Peach Orchard was continued by many authors. John W. Draper, author of a three-volume work on the Civil War, wrote the following:

> Meade, in the posting of his troops, had intended to occupy the ridge continuously from Cemetery Hill to the Round Tops, but Sickles, finding a depression at the point designated for him, advanced three fourths of a mile to the higher ground in front. He posted his troops along the Emmettsburg [sic] Road, but was construed to refuse his left toward the Round Tops. . . . About 3 P.M., Meade, visiting this part of the line, saw the peril in which Sickles was placed, and was in the act of discussing with him the propriety of withdrawing when the enemy, quick to detect a weak point, opened upon him.[15]

John L. Wilson also wrote that Sickles wanted the higher ground to his front.[16]

In the 1880s, three authors continued this same interpretation. Abner Doubleday, in his 1882 work on Chancellorsville and Gettysburg, listed the following reasons for Sickles' change of position:

> *First*, because the ground was low, and *second*, on account of the commanding position of the Emmetsburg [sic] road, which ran along a cross ridge oblique to the front of the line assigned him, and which afforded the enemy an excellent position for their artillery; *third*, because the ground between the valley he was expected to occupy, and the Emmetsburg road constituted a minor ridge, very much broken and full of rocks and trees, which afforded an excellent cover for an enemy operating in his immediate front.

Doubleday also mentioned General Hunt's reconnaissance of the advanced line, and suggested that Sickles took up this position through Hunt's views, which carried the implied sanction of General Meade. However, Doubleday did not include in his text the entire analysis of the terrain by Hunt, who also voiced some objections to Sickles' proposed line.[17]

Chambersburg resident Jacob Hoke published a lengthy book about the Gettysburg Campaign and generally followed the high ground interpretation about Sickles. He included a discussion of Meade's original orders to Sickles, Geary's 1870 letter to Meade, and Sickles' 11:00 A.M. visit to army headquarters to seek more definite instructions about his position. According to Hoke,

> General Sickles, for some unaccountable reason, concluded that there was no position upon Round Top, and taking advantage of the discretion given him concerning his occupying that place,—or, rather construing it liberally, so as to include his whole position,—moved forward to a slight ridge about three quarters of a mile in advance of the prolongation of Hancock's lines. . . . His reason for doing so was, that the ground between the left of Hancock and Round Top was considerably lower than that along the Emmittsburg [sic] road, and his position, in case he occupied that ground, would be untenable if the enemy was permitted to occupy the higher ground in front.

Finally, Hoke included an appendix about Sickles' alleged disobedience of orders on July 2. He included James C. Biddle's *Weekly Press* article, Sickles' July 2, 1886, Gettysburg speech, Lafayette McLaws's response in the *Weekly Press*, and Meade's 1870 letter to Colonel Benedict. Hoke concluded that Sickles did indeed receive an order, but one qualified in terms that allowed him wide discretion in choosing a line of battle for his corps.[18]

After the appearance of Hoke's book, Rossiter Johnson, British historian Cecil Battine, Henry S. Burrage, and William R. Livermore continued this interpretation.[19] More recently, James S. Montgomery, James W. Bellah, and Shelby Foote also have contributed to the high-ground thesis.[20]

Many historians have also advanced the thesis that Sickles moved forward after Colonel Berdan's reconnaissance discovered Confederate troops moving south under cover of the woods on Seminary Ridge. Implicit in the writings of these authors is the idea that Sickles moved out to the Peach Orchard because he wanted to forestall Rebel occupation of this high ground. As mentioned previously, Benson Lossing was the first to propose this interpretation. Samuel P. Bates was the next writer to do so. In his *The Battle of Gettysburg*, Bates recounted Meade's early morning order to Sickles and his repetition of the order when Sickles visited army headquarters later in the morning. At eleven o'clock, because of the increased volume of skirmish fire on the 3d Corps front, Sickles directed General Birney to send out a reconnaissance force, and

> [t]his reconnoissance [sic] showed that the enemy was moving in three columns under cover of the woods to the left. At length General Sickles, finding his outposts gradually driven back, determined to wait no longer for

more explicit orders, and moved out his whole corps upon the advanced ground.

Bates found it "inexplicable" that General Meade did not issue specific orders to Sickles and see about the posting of the 3d Corps in person.[21]

Willis C. Humphrey was the next writer to take up the theme of Berdan's reconnaissance as the major reason for Sickles' advance. In a general history of the Civil War published in 1886, Humphrey wrote the following about Berdan:

> He found the enemy approaching in force. A severe action took place in which his command lost nearly one half of its numbers. The advance of the enemy was greatly delayed by the desperate resistance of this handful of men. General Berdan and his brave men deserve great credit for this check given the enemy, which saved, for the time, Little Round Top to the Federals.[22]

Three years later, Boston newspaperman Charles C. Coffin published his *Marching to Victory,* which included an extensive treatment of the Gettysburg Campaign. Coffin's words echoed Humphrey's, but Coffin was one of the few early writers of this period to use occasional footnotes to denote where he got his information. In this case, Coffin cited a speech Berdan delivered on the Gettysburg battlefield in 1886 as his evidence for the importance of the skirmish in Pitzer's Woods on July 2.[23]

A second historian of the Army of the Potomac, James H. Stine, also took the Berdan discovery of Confederates as the reason for Sickles' forward move:

> This heavy force of sharpshooters drove the enemy's pickets in, and revealed the fact that three columns of their forces were marching to our left. Berdan was immediately attacked by a heavy force under Longstreet, and driven back in the Peach Orchard, with a loss of about 60 killed and wounded. Berdan did very valuable service that day with his sharpshooters. [24]

The official New York State version of Gettysburg was published in 1900 when the New York Monuments Commission presented its final report on the Pennsylvania battlefield. William F. Fox wrote the lengthy battle summary for the commission, which was chaired by Daniel E. Sickles. Fox disparaged Meade's generalship in several areas. He wrote that it was Butterfield who suggested to his commander that Hancock go to Gettysburg on July 1. When Buford was withdrawn on July 2, Meade authorized Pleasonton to do so. Fox cited the unusual character of the three o'clock council of war that afternoon, and although he did not directly denigrate the gathering, he suggested that it was a bad precedent.[25]

In examining Sickles' actions at Gettysburg, Fox relied heavily on the poor-ground argument. Sickles wished to avoid a repetition of Chancellorsville and thus moved forward. The general could not easily abandon the Emmitsburg Road line without losing control of that road and communication with Emmitsburg, where General Meade had ordered Humphreys to scout in case that ground was favorable for giving battle. Sickles' movement was not an advance; Birney's men simply wheeled to the left and the remainder of the line was a refused position "incidental" to the rest of the line. And Sickles did not bring on the battle as some of his critics had claimed. Lee had already decided to attack. In summation, Fox argued that the real question was "which line was better to adopt under the existing circumstances," not a debate over the merits of each of the two positions held by the 3d Corps. Had Buford been allowed to remain and had more troops been sent to cover the Round Tops, Sickles would not have been constrained to change his position.[26]

Three other major historians have also used this interpretation for Sickles' advance. Francis Marshal Pierce's book, which is pro-Meade in argument, incorporated this theory, as did that of West Pointer Gustav J. Fiebeger.[27] Finally, Glenn Tucker took this approach in his *High Tide at Gettysburg*. Tucker wrote that Meade's orders to Sickles were ambiguous. He cited Captain Meade's visits to 3d Corps headquarters and Sickles' eleven o'clock talk with Meade as examples. When Berdan's sharpshooters drove back enemy skirmishers, they "unveiled three long enemy infantry lines, waiting, 300 yards away." Sickles advanced at three o'clock after receiving Berdan's report of this skirmish.[28]

Several authors combined the high-ground thesis and the story of Berdan's discovery of Rebel troops as their interpretation of Sickles' forward move. The first English translation of the Count of Paris's detailed work on Gettysburg appeared in 1883. His writing was the first extremely detailed history of the battle, encompassing a balanced, impartial approach, unlike most of his American counterparts.[29]

In reference to the Meade-Sickles controversy, the Count provided a detailed text that was the best attempt yet to unravel the problems inherent in the feud. He wrote of Geary receiving orders to move to Culp's Hill at 4:00 A.M. and of his men marching off an hour later. Sometime between six and seven o'clock, Captain Meade arrived at 3d Corps headquarters with positive orders about Sickles' position, but Geary had already vacated his bivouac, so Sickles was unsure of where to deploy his men. When Captain Meade returned a second time, he nevertheless found Sickles about to deploy his corps to the best of his ability. Thus, by nine o'clock, Birney's division was deployed, although Humphreys was left in massed formation on Hancock's left because Sickles discovered that the line entrusted to him was too long for his corps to occupy with sufficient force. The length of Sickles' line was one of Meade's mistakes, since he did not check the terrain in person.[30]

The Count said that Sickles became more and more dissatisfied with his position, and soon moved part of Humphreys' division forward to the edge of Plum Run, slightly in advance of his first position. Sickles finally rode over to army headquarters at eleven o'clock, when Meade repeated his earlier orders to Sickles. The Count reasoned that by late morning Sickles had guessed the enemy's intentions to attack the Union left because of the increased skirmish fire on his front. The signal station on Little Round Top also had detected the southward advance of the Confederates. The skirmish between Berdan's sharpshooters and Wilcox's brigade clinched Sickles' thought that he had fathomed the Rebel strategy, so he moved his corps forward to the higher ground in his front.[31]

The Count disapproved of Sickles' move because of the salient at the Peach Orchard, the extreme length of the new line, the nearness of woods to this line, and the detached position of the 3d Corps. Also, the Count thought that Sickles ignored the military value of Little Round Top. On the other hand, the Count criticized General Meade for ignoring his left flank and not attending to Sickles in person. However, he did believe that Meade did not intend to retreat from Gettysburg, and that the contingency plan that he ordered Butterfield to draft was a wise precaution.[32]

Two books published in the 1890s discussed the controversy in some detail. The first of these, Samuel Adams Drake's *The Battle of Gettysburg, 1863*, was very anti-Sickles in tone but also contained evidence of errors in research. Drake wrote that Sickles moved forward because he was dissatisfied with his position and uneasy at seeing no enemy in front of his command. When Berdan's men reported enemy infantry moving south across his front, Sickles became even more worried; since his orders were either "vague or unsatisfactory," he moved his corps out to the Peach Orchard. In essence, Drake contended that Sickles had disobeyed Meade's orders.[33] John M. Vanderslice's guide to the battle and the military park also contained a discussion of Sickles' actions. Vanderslice wrote about Berdan's skirmish with Wilcox's brigade and then stated that Sickles, convinced that a strong enemy force was in his front, moved the corps "to what he thought was a better position."[34]

Robert K. Beecham's *Gettysburg*, published in 1911, also incorporated several reasons to explain Sickles' forward move. The author was generally favorable to Sickles and the book as a whole was adversely critical of Meade's generalship. Beecham wrote that Sickles was impressed by the commanding position of the Peach Orchard ridge and saw that the valley in front of the ridge offered Lee the chance to move between the Army of the Potomac and Washington, which is why Meade said that Gettysburg was no place to fight a battle. Further, in reference to the controversy, Beecham stated that Meade was not sure which position was the stronger and thus gave Sickles discretionary orders so as not to assume full responsibility for his decision. Beecham wrote the following about Meade's orders:

> Meade himself was fearful of that very movement; otherwise being the commanding general, he would have said to Sickles in plain English, so there could have been no misunderstanding, "Form your corps on Hancock's left, and continue his line southward along the ridge to Little Round Top," and surely Sickles would have followed such instructions; but Meade simply did not care to assume the whole responsibility, so he gave a kind of ambiguous order that Sickles construed according to his ideas of the necessity of the case.

Once Sickles occupied the advanced position, he became uneasy over it and sent out the sharpshooters, who discovered the enemy flank march.[35]

The next author to combine several reasons to explain Sickles' conduct at Gettysburg was Jesse Bowman Young, in his *Battle of Gettysburg*, published in 1913 for the fiftieth anniversary of the battle. Young, a 3d Corps veteran, declared that he would not enter into the controversy but would only present the facts. Accordingly, Young began his exposition by mentioning Meade's order to Sickles to extend Hancock's line south along Cemetery Ridge and relieve Geary, but then wrote that Geary's division marched off before Sickles could relieve him. As it was, the 3d Corps line

was much too long to occupy in depth, and no officer from army headquarters appeared to direct the corps into line, although Sickles did make
more than one request for such an officer to indicate a clearer line.[36]

Young wrote that Sickles' apprehension about enemy occupation of the
high ground in his front was increased by the skirmish fire and the shots
fired at the two brigades that came up the road from Emmitsburg. After
Berdan's sharpshooters found Southern troops moving south under cover
of the woods to his front, Sickles made one more appeal to headquarters.
As a result, Meade sent Henry Hunt to Sickles. Hunt was noncommittal
about Sickles' request to move his corps forward, so Sickles took it upon
himself to do this after Hunt departed, and Meade did not learn of the
change in position until 3:00 P.M. As a conclusion to his narrative, Young
used the writings of ex-Confederate Armistead L. Long to criticize Sickles'
move, the work of British historian Cecil Battine to suggest that Sickles'
position acted like a breakwater to stem the force of Longstreet's attack, the
Count of Paris's book to disapprove of the forward line because of terrain
problems in reinforcing it, Doubleday's work to show both sides of the
controversy, and William F. Fox's narrative to represent yet another favorable view of Sickles. Young himself viewed Sickles' position as preventing a
Confederate attack on Cemetery Ridge.[37]

Two amateur historians writing in the 1950s also discussed the controversy in some detail. Bruce Catton, in his *Glory Road*, wrote that Meade's
order did not seem clear to Sickles, who was worried about the higher
ground at the Peach Orchard. When Berdan's sharpshooters found Confederates in the woods to his front, Sickles apparently determined to
prevent a repetition of Chancellorsville and so moved forward. Without
waiting to consult headquarters, Sickles took it upon himself to answer
the perceived threat; by acting rashly, Sickles made the wrong decision.[38]
Retired Gen. Edward J. Stackpole wrote that Meade's orders to Sickles
"were oral and not nearly as explicit as they should have been." Even
though the orders were repeated when the 2d Corps arrived on the field,
adequate staff work was lacking so the orders were not carried out. Sickles
did not think highly of his position and when Berdan's men reported large
enemy forces that were growing steadily by the minute, Sickles moved
forward.[39]

Edwin Coddington's *Gettysburg Campaign*, considered by many scholars
to be the single finest work on the campaign, includes a lengthy commen-

tary on the Meade-Sickles controversy. Coddington detailed Meade's pre-dawn survey of the proposed battle line, Captain Meade's visits to Sickles, Sickles' eleven o'clock trip to army headquarters, and General Hunt's tour and views on the Peach Orchard line. He also examined Meade's order to Butterfield to prepare a contingency retreat plan. Coddington was the first modern Gettysburg historian to search out unused sources of information that shed some new light on interpretations of the battle.

In analyzing the Meade-Sickles feud, Coddington's approach was pro-Meade on the whole. He illustrated how Sickles contrived his testimony before the Committee on the Conduct of the War to cover up his pre-meditated course of action in advancing to the Peach Orchard line. Even though Halleck and Meade, in their official reports, gave Sickles the bene-fit of the doubt by writing that the 3d Corps commander had misinter-preted his orders, Sickles would have none of it. Coddington believed Sickles would rather have been guilty of insubordination than of plain stupidity. He acted as if he had an independent command, and no matter how good the position at the Peach Orchard might have been, Sickles sim-ply disobeyed orders. Coddington reasoned that Sickles' orders were clear enough to be easily understood. As far as Sickles' thesis that his orders were either vague or that they were never received, Coddington pointed out the lack of evidence available to justify the forward move. There were no signs of an early Confederate advance on Sickles' front, and Berdan's skir-mish with Wilcox in Pitzer's Woods uncovered inconclusive evidence of enemy movements. Coddington compared Sickles' action at Gettysburg with his experience at Chancellorsville, and criticized the line as too long and too far in advance to enable rapid and judicious reinforcement of it.[40]

In the years since the publication of Coddington's fine book, one addi-tional study that treats the controversy in some detail has appeared, Harry Pfanz's *Gettysburg—The Second Day*. Pfanz's treatise is primarily a detailed tactical study of the fighting on the southern end of the battlefield on July 2. While preparing this excellent study, the author decided to avoid both the Meade-Sickles and Lee-Longstreet controversies, except where necessary in the narrative.[41]

Pfanz examined the position of the 3d Corps in some detail, recounting Captain Meade's visits to corps headquarters as well as Sickles' later ride to army headquarters. He cited General Birney's report that his division took position that morning, followed by a lengthy analysis of the corps battle line as it was finally constituted. He examined the 3d Corps picket line, Buford's withdrawal, and the Pitzer's Woods skirmish. Later, Pfanz shifted to the Confederate side to examine Lee's attack plan, based upon flawed reconnaissance of the Union left flank. In a general conclusion to the Meade-Sickles feud, Pfanz believed that if indeed Sickles truthfully did send word of the Berdan-Wilcox skirmish to headquarters (Meade's supporters claimed ignorance of this), then Meade's staff poorly served their chief by not keeping him informed of all messages received from his troops. Meade should have paid more attention to his left flank, especially after he decided not to launch an attack with his right.[42]

Three recent general histories of the Civil War offer contrasting views about the Meade-Sickles controversy. Herman Hattaway, in his *Shades of Blue and Gray* (1997), wrote that Sickles "had gone somewhat forward, without explicit permission." Russell F. Weigley's *A Great Civil War* included a twenty-page chapter on Gettysburg. Weigley wrote that Sickles did not receive the permission he requested from Meade to move forward to the Peach Orchard ridge, and when his men detected Rebels moving across his front, Sickles, "the impetuous politician-commander," moved the 3d Corps forward. After mentioning the postwar controversy, Weigley conceded that Sickles did indeed err in moving forward, but pointed out that the higher ground at the orchard "went a long way toward compensating for the weakness of a salient." More important, reasoned Weigley, Sickles' advance provided Meade with a cushion of ground that could be yielded to Longstreet's attack without jeopardizing the main Federal line. Finally, Gettysburg occupied more than fifty pages in David Eicher's new volume on the war. Eicher surveyed Sickles' actions on July 2, presenting the factual story of how Sickles wanted to move forward, and when Berdan's men found Confederates, he acted unilaterally and advanced the 3d Corps to the Peach Orchard. In concise prose, Eicher said of the controversy that developed after the battle: "the army commander was clearly right and Sickles clearly wrong. The events provided some of the more entertaining sessions for the ill-starred but powerful Senate Committee on the Conduct of the War and added yet another series of foolish events into the story of Gettysburg."[43]

Before closing this examination of the historiography of the controversy, we should focus some attention on the biographies of Meade and Sickles and their authors' approach to the controversy. The fact that most biographers tend to be overly partial to their subjects, however, is evident in the biographies of these two generals.

General Meade has been the subject of three major book-length biographies. The first of these, by relative Richard M. Bache, was published in 1897. Bache included an extended discussion to show that by midmorning on July 2, Sickles' corps occupied the general line that Meade had intended. He cited Captain Meade's visits to corps headquarters, Sickles' eleven o'clock visit to army headquarters, and General Hunt's survey of the proposed line. But this is as far as Bache went in his treatment of the controversy. He failed to analyze Sickles' move or any possible reasons for it.[44] A second biography by Isaac R. Pennypacker failed to improve very much on Bache's work. Pennypacker also wrote of Captain Meade, Sickles' visit to Meade's headquarters, and Hunt's reconnaissance. As for Sickles' advance to the Peach Orchard, Pennypacker believed it to be the result of an "insubordinate disregard of Meade's direct orders."[45]

Finally, there is a 1960 biography by amateur historian Freeman Cleaves. The author wrote that Meade issued orders to Sickles shortly after arriving on the field. Cleaves then reviewed Meade's moonlight reconnaissance of the battle line, his planned attack by the right wing, Captain Meade's actions, Sickles' 11:00 A.M. visit to headquarters, and Hunt's views on the proposed line. In reference to Sickles' advance, Cleaves mentioned the Berdan-Wilcox skirmish in Pitzer's Woods, but referred to this action as being against Longstreet's corps, which was delayed for forty minutes. Sickles moved out because of this skirmish, and Cleaves thought there was an analogy between this advance and Sickles' movements at Chancellorsville. Cleaves also admitted that, through hindsight, Meade should have personally inspected his left flank earlier than he did after three o'clock on July 2.[46]

Dan Sickles has been the subject of only two major biographies. The first, by Edgcumb Pinchon, appeared in 1945. Pinchon's approach was laudatory to Sickles, giving him credit for anticipating Longstreet's flank march and, by implication, saving the Army of the Potomac from disaster. He wrote that Geary's command had occupied no discernible position and that Sickles did not have enough men to fill the line from Hancock's left to Little Round Top. Pinchon drew upon the Chancellorsville analogy to explain the 3d Corps advance to the Peach Orchard after Berdan's men found Confederates moving south across Sickles' front.[47]

Sickles' other biographer was W. A. Swanberg, whose *Sickles the In-credible* appeared in 1965. He followed the oft-repeated story of Captain Meade's visits to Sickles, the general's morning ride to see General Meade, Hunt's reconnaissance of the proposed line, and Berdan's fight in Pitzer's Woods, giving the latter as the reason for Sickles' forward movement. Swanberg thought that Sickles believed he was acting in the best interests of the army by moving to the high ground, and that his advance was the result of "careful deliberation" rather than rash impulse. Swanberg was the single biographer of either general, with the exception of some brief remarks by Cleaves, to detail Sickles' postbattle incriminations against General Meade before the Committee on the Conduct of the War, as well as the general's lifelong defense of his role at Gettysburg.[48]

Maj. Gen. George G. Meade was placed in command of the Army of the Potomac on June 28, 1863, much against his wishes. The general was an embattled figure for the remainder of the war, but he remained in command of the army until the conflict's end, despite personal attacks from all sides.

Maj. Gen. Daniel E. Sickles, the political general from New York City who spent a career defending his actions at Gettysburg.

Maj. Gen. Daniel Butterfield, the New Yorker who sided with Sickles and tried to destroy Meade's reputation before the Committee on the Conduct of the War.

Brig. Gen. Gouvernour K. Warren was the Army of the Potomac's chief engineer and quickly recognized Sickles's blunder at failing to occupy Little Round Top.

LEFT: Maj. Gen. Winfield Scott Hancock, nicknamed "The Superb." Meade sent his trusted friend to assess the situation at Gettysburg on July 1.

Maj. Gen. Henry W. Halleck, the Union army's commanding general in 1863, conspired to help remove Hooker from command and then stood by Meade when that general was assailed by Sickles and friends.

RIGHT: Capt. George Meade, 6th Pennsylvania Cavalry, was General Meade's son and aide-de-camp during the Gettysburg campaign.

Chapter Six

CONFEDERATE MOVEMENTS ON THE RIGHT FLANK
AT GETTYSBURG, JULY 2, 1863

One of the major points around which General Sickles had based his defense of the forward move at Gettysburg was his statement that Confederate forces began to move toward the Union left flank at daybreak on July 2. In his testimony before the Committee on the Conduct of the War, Sickles made the following statement:

> Not having received any orders in reference to my position, and observing, from the enemy's movements on our left, what I thought to be conclusive indications of a design on their part to attack there, and that seeming to me to be our most assailable point, I went in person to headquarters and reported the facts and circumstances which led me to believe an attack would be made there, and asked for orders.

The general also indicated to the committee that Meade did not believe an attack would take place on his left. Sickles said that when he asked for the commanding general to go back with him to examine the ground, Meade declined, sending instead the army's chief of artillery, Henry J. Hunt. After the reconnaissance along the Emmitsburg Road, Hunt said he would report the facts to Meade. Sickles stated that after Hunt left, the enemy demonstrations became more and more pronounced. When his outposts were being driven back upon their supports, he decided to occupy the advanced line to forestall Confederate occupation of that terrain.[1]

Sickles elaborated further upon this thesis that early-morning Confederate moves forced him to occupy the advanced line. If Sickles did author the two "Historicus" letters in the *New York Herald*, then he included the same statements in these articles that he had made before the committee. In the first article, published in the March 12, 1864, edition of the *Herald*, Historicus remarked that the enemy was massing large bodies of troops on the Union left flank, intimating that this process occurred all morning. The second article essentially repeated the same words.[2]

Sickles next mentioned this line of reasoning in a speech at Gettysburg on July 2, 1882. During the course of this speech, Sickles remarked, "Early the next morning [July 2], we were astir, and I sent out a reconnaissance along the front of the line that I afterwards occupied, and soon became convinced that the enemy intended attacking in force." Sickles then stated that he rode to headquarters "quite early in the morning" to express his concerns to General Meade, who said he did not share in his view that the enemy would attack the left flank.[3]

When the controversy came to a head in 1886, Sickles verbalized on three separate occasions his view that the enemy planned to attack early in the morning and that he was aware of these preparations. In a speech before the 3d Army Corps reunion in Boston on April 8, Sickles remarked that his skirmishers reported the enemy was massing a large body of troops on his front, "with a line of direction to my extreme left, and with the evident purpose of occupying Round Top, the key of our position." He further stated that these facts were communicated to army headquarters, and yet no orders were issued. Reports throughout the afternoon confirmed these earlier messages.[4]

In one of his most controversial speeches, delivered at Gettysburg on July 2, Sickles again repeated that Confederate forces were moving against him since daybreak. In his eighteenth point of contention against Meade's supporters, Sickles remarked that the Confederate attack was "carefully nurtured and concealed by the enemy from daylight until their columns were unmasked by their fire in the afternoon."[5]

In his rebuttal to Colonel Benedict's article in the Philadelphia *Weekly Press*, Sickles stated that Lee was in the saddle "from early dawn . . . carefully reconnoitring [*sic*] our left and making eleborate preparations for the assault made at a later hour."[6] Finally, in his part of the "Further Recollections of Gettysburg" article in the *North American Review*, Sickles again said he was aware of enemy attack preparations against his corps from early morning on July 2.[7]

However, the actual Confederate movements in the Seminary Ridge area on July 2 were vastly different from what General Sickles imagined them to be. At the close of the action on July 1, Pender's division of A. P. Hill's 3d Corps was in position on Seminary Ridge. The division's left flank rested near the Hagerstown Road while the remainder of the command stretched south along the ridge as far as Spangler's Woods.[8] Anderson's division of the same corps bivouacked a few miles west of Gettysburg near Marsh Creek. Wilcox's brigade of this division was detached and stationed at Trostle's Mill, about one-third of the distance between the Chambersburg Pike and the Hagerstown Road, to act as a flank guard.[9] Hill's 3d division, led by Maj. Gen. Henry Heth, remained near the Chambersburg Pike in the approximate area from which it had begun the battle.[10] Finally, two divisions of Longstreet's 1st Corps, those of Maj. Gen. John B. Hood and Lafayette McLaws, arrived at Marsh Creek sometime around midnight and bivouacked along the creek.[11]

Shortly after daybreak on July 2, Col. William L. J. Lowrance, commanding Pender's right flank brigade, was ordered to hold his position "at all hazards" until relieved. The permanent brigade commander, Brig. Gen. Alfred M. Scales, had been wounded in the desperate fighting on July 1, and his five North Carolina regiments had sustained very severe losses while driving Doubleday's troops off Seminary Ridge. When Lowrance took command of the brigade, he found it in a "depressed, dilapidated, and almost unorganized condition." With the brigade so reduced in numbers, Lowrance was extremely worried about the vulnerability of his position, so he

> threw out a strong line of skirmishers, extending fully one-half mile to the right inclining to the rear, which was placed under command of Lieutenant [A. J.] Brown, of the Thirty-eighth North Carolina troops, who most gallantly held the line against several strong skirmish lines thrown against him until 1 P.M., at which time the brigade was relieved by General Anderson's division.[12]

Colonel Lowrance's report places his skirmish line as the right of the Army of Northern Virginia early on July 2. He reported the pressure brought against his line until relieved by Anderson's troops. This report seems to refute Sickles' argument that the unusual activity and depth of the enemy skirmish line indicated an early movement toward the Union left flank. However, such pressure on the North Carolinians, ordered to hold the line "at all hazards," may have led them to be unusually active and thus create an illusion of great strength to the Yankee pickets opposing them. Perhaps this is what prompted the dispatch of the Union reconnaissance force into the woods beyond the Emmitsburg Road.

The official reports of the Union skirmishers along the front of the 3d Corps are vague and do not furnish exact details of what transpired during the morning of July 2. There was considerable skirmish activity along the 2d Corps front during most of the day, especially in and around the Bliss Farm buildings, between units of Pender's division (and later Anderson's division) and troops from Gibbon's and Gen. Alexander Hays's divisions of Hancock's command.[13]

Farther south, the activities of the 3d Corps pickets are more ambiguous. Col. Hiram Berdan, commanding the two sharpshooter regiments, reported that he sent out a detail of one hundred men at 7:30 A.M. to cover the front of the corps. Various infantry regiments aided the sharpshooters during the day. Maj. John A. Danks, commanding the 63d Pennsylvania, reported that his regiment was placed on picket duty along the Emmitsburg Road early in the morning, and that enemy pickets opened fire on his outposts sometime before noon. The 4th Maine was detailed for similar duty until relieved at eleven o'clock. Lt. Col. Charles F. Sawyer reported: "On the morning of the 2d, some picket firing took place, which was not responded to." The 1st Massachusetts, which replaced the 4th Maine, reported there was "considerable skirmishing along the line during the day."[14]

In addition to the infantry pickets, Brig. Gen. John Buford's 1st Cavalry Division was on the 3d Corps front until sent to the rear late in the morning. Buford mentioned in his report that his men were engaged with Confederate sharpshooters until relieved by infantry pickets. Col. Thomas C. Devin, commanding one of the Union cavalry brigades, wrote that while Union sharpshooters were engaged in reconnoitering the rear of the enemy's right, they became engaged with a division of the enemy advancing to feel out his position. Devin dismounted two squadrons and deployed them in support of the sharpshooters, then unlimbered one section of Lt. John H. Calef's horse artillery battery as an additional support, but the enemy did not press his advance.[15]

Two postwar regimental histories of cavalry units in Buford's division shed little additional light on the cavalry's role on July 2. Sixth New York troopers recalled that they picketed the Peach Orchard area, watching the enemy and directing the different commands arriving on the field to their proper places. The enemy did not push their line forward and the regiment departed for Westminster at eleven o'clock.[16]

Newal Cheney's history of the 9th New York Cavalry contains detailed information about the morning of July 2, but his tale cannot be verified by any other existing source. Cheney recorded that on July 2, Capt. B. J. Coffin's Company E patrolled the roads in front of the division and discovered Longstreet approaching. A detachment of six or eight troopers led by Sgt. W. T. Bradshaw rode out the Millerstown Road to Pitzer's Schoolhouse. Here, the cavalrymen spotted a large force of Southern infantry moving rapidly into line in the open fields to the north. The Yankees withdrew after exchanging a few shots with approaching Rebel skirmishers. As the Unionists retired, they brought along one of Longstreet's black servants who had escaped and was endeavoring to reach safety. At almost the same instant, Berdan's sharpshooters were seen deploying west of the Emmitsburg Road. Captain Coffin met General Sickles and informed him of the situation, then told Buford as well. Buford unlimbered a battery in support and had all nearby fences leveled for ease of movement. All then remained quiet until noon, when the cavalry withdrew. Although a detailed story, Captain Coffin's activities cannot be verified, and it is highly unlikely that he spied Longstreet's troops moving into position.[17]

Together with the Union picket line battle reports, there is other evidence that sheds some light on the activity of the Confederate pickets. Between nine and ten o'clock, the two 3d Corps brigades left behind at Emmitsburg (Burling and de Trobriand, plus two batteries) reached the field. Of the twelve official reports on file by officers in these units, only three mention any skirmish firing as they reached the battlefield.[18] The many postwar accounts written by members of these two brigades are divided on the mention of enemy skirmishers. Most accounts agree that the skirmishers who fired on the column were from Longstreet's corps, and that any delay on the march from Emmitsburg would have enabled Longstreet to cut them off from the rest of the army.[19]

Some of the more reliable accounts are more detailed in their views. Colonel de Trobriand wrote that the Emmitsburg Road was free except for a few long-range shots fired at the column as it approached the Peach Orchard, where the troops turned off the road toward Cemetery Ridge.

Likewise, the author of the 2d New Hampshire regimental history mentioned that only an "occasional shot" was heard. Captain Winslow, commanding Battery D, 1st New York, recalled that the column was fired upon just before turning off the Emmitsburg Road at the Peach Orchard.[20]

Finally, after General Sickles had gone to Meade's headquarters at approximately eleven o'clock and had obtained the services of General Hunt to see about artillery positions, Sickles took Hunt on a tour of the proposed line along the Emmitsburg Road. Evidently the party was not bothered by any Confederate skirmish fire, as no account of Hunt's tour of the proposed line mentioned any skirmish fire.[21]

Having examined the positions of the Confederate forces on Seminary Ridge on the morning of July 2, and the activities of the opposing picket lines, it is now time to analyze one of the least understood and most controversial phases of the battle of Gettysburg—the Berdan-Wilcox skirmish in Pitzer's Woods. Colonel Berdan's reconnaissance into the wooded area in front of Sickles' advanced position was, according to Sickles, the skirmish that disclosed Longstreet's flank march toward the Union left flank and prompted the advance of the 3d Corps to the Peach Orchard line.

The details of the facts surrounding Berdan's reconnaissance are controversial to the extreme. There is even no agreement upon who suggested the expedition—Hunt, Berdan, and Birney each took credit for it.[22]

The official reports of Colonel Berdan and Lt. Col. Caspar Trepp of the 1st United States Sharpshooters and of Col. Moses B. Lakeman of the 3d Maine form the basis of the Union version of the skirmish.[23] After receiving an order from General Birney to proceed with the reconnaissance, Berdan took four companies (D, E, F, I) of the 1st Sharpshooters, with the 3d Maine as a support. This force totaled just over three hundred officers and men. Berdan led his command down the Emmitsburg Road to a point opposite the extreme left of the 3d Corps line, then moved west into the woods on Warfield Ridge. The sharpshooters deployed in skirmish formation, then began moving north through the woods. The 3d Maine followed within supporting distance.

Upon encountering Confederate skirmishers, the green-clad Federals drove them back three hundred yards, to discover what Berdan described as "three columns in motion in rear of the woods, changing direction, as it were, by the right flank." The 3d Maine double-quicked up to the firing line, and the Yankees held the surprised Rebels in check until Berdan decided he had accomplished the object of the expedition and ordered a withdrawal. Losses were nineteen for the sharpshooters and forty-eight for the 3d Maine, which was in a more exposed position because the sharpshooters had taken advantage of the natural cover by the time Colonel Lakeman's men arrived in line.

Conversely, the official report of Brig. Gen. Cadmus M. Wilcox, who commanded a brigade of five Alabama regiments in Anderson's division, furnishes the chief source for the Confederate version of the skirmish.[24] Wilcox wrote that he and Anderson rode south at the head of the brigade to find a suitable position for the Alabamians, who were to be the right flank of the division. Anderson determined that Wilcox's men would occupy a position on the right of Col. David Lang's Florida Brigade, which was then moving into Spangler's Woods. The Alabamians would take position in an open field between Spangler's and Pitzer's Woods.

Unsure of whether or not there were any Union troops in the latter woodlot, Wilcox ordered Col. William H. Forney, commanding the 10th Alabama, to occupy the woods. As Forney's men entered Pitzer's Woods, the 11th Alabama followed across the intervening field in support. General Wilcox then reported what happened:

> The regiments, being preceded by skirmishers, were ordered to advance, the Eleventh to its position in line in rear of a fence, and the Tenth to keep on a line with the Eleventh, to protect it from the enemy's fire should he be found in the woods, the remaining regiments being held in rear till it should be ascertained if the enemy were in the woods.
>
> The Eleventh advanced more easily than the Tenth, being in the open field. Having moved forward about 300 yards, this regiment received a heavy volley of musketry on its right flank and rear from the enemy concealed behind ledges of rock and trees in the woods on its right. The Tenth Alabama moved forward promptly, and soon encountered a strong line of skirmishers. These were driven back upon their supports, two regiments of infantry—the Third Maine and First New York (U.S.) Sharpshooters. A spirited musketry fight ensued between the Tenth Alabama and these two Federal regiments. Having continued for some fifteen or twenty minutes, Colonel Forney gave the command to charge, and led his regiment in person. This broke the enemy's line, and they fled precipitately from the woods, leaving 20 or 25 dead and twice that number wounded and prisoners.[25]

The report above appeared in the *Official Records*. General Wilcox also wrote an earlier report that General Lee disapproved of because of the strong language with which Wilcox criticized Anderson's handling of his division at Gettysburg. Wilcox described the Pitzer's Woods skirmish as follows in his initial report:

> In front of my brigade were several houses, in and about the enclosures of which small parties of the enemy were seen; the head of the division (my brigade) arriving at this time, they marched down the wooded slope and halted, and one regiment 10th Ala. Col. Forney ordered to scour the woods on which the right of the brigade was to rest, a second regiment the 11th Ala. Col. Sanders ordered to keep in the open field in a line with the 10th Ala.
>
> These regiments had advanced but little over a hundred yds when a few musketry shots were heard and the fire quickening and increasing in volume indicated something more than an ordinary picket fight; the firing continued for ten minutes or more when cheers were heard from the regiment in the woods, and soon the firing had ceased. The firing was so heavy that the division commander sent a staff officer to ascertain if any support was required.
>
> Two regiments of the enemy occupied this wood as an advanced post, the 1st N.Y. or Berdan Sharp shooters, and the 3rd Maine; after a few shots the 10th Ala. charged them and they broke to the rear, leaving 20 or 30 killed, and more than twice that number wounded and prisoners. My loss was 56 killed and wounded.[26]

Wilcox's report is supplemented by a July 17 letter from Pvt. Fleming W. Thompson of the 11th Alabama. Thompson wrote the following about the fight in Pitzer's Woods:

> On the morning of the 2d our division was ordered to the front & our brigade to the front of the division, formed a line of battle and moved on, when we had gone about 2 hundred yards in line of battle our regt. was ordered to the front of the brigade and part of the regt deployed as skirmishers. We then marched up into an open field when the Yanks opened on our skirmishers, drove them back & opened a pretty hot fire on our regt. from a thick wood that they had placed several regts. of men in, in order to ambush us. As we came in, the fire was so hot that the Col. ordered us to fall back to the fence which was some hundred yards in our rear, & when we got back there, we formed with the rest of the brigade & advanced on them and made them move in doublequick from there [sic] stronghold. In this little skirmish we lost but few men wounded & none killed. Our Major was shot here through the leg & some ten or fifteen men from the regt. wounded. The brigade lost 30 killed and a good many wounded, but I tell you we made the ground look blue with Yanks.[27]

Col. Hilary A. Herbert, commanding the 8th Alabama at Gettysburg, also wrote about the fighting in Pitzer's Woods as part of a regimental history he wrote during the winter of 1863–1864, then revised it early this century upon the solicitations of the director of the Alabama Department of Archives and History. Herbert wrote the following about the Pitzer's Woods fight:

> On the morning of the 2nd of July, about 7 A.M., the brigade was moving by the right flank below the crest of a ridge that was to our left between us and the enemy—this to avoid being seen as we were taking our position in the intended line of battle. The 10th Alabama was in front, the 11th next, and the 8th next. The 10th was sharply attacked by Berden's [sic] battalion of sharpshooters, and the 2nd [sic] Maine regiment from behind a rock fence. When the attack was made on the 10th, the 11th was moving diagonally across a field to take its intended position on the left of the 10th. While it was thus moving in line into its right flank, which was pointing towards the stone wall, there came a volley from behind the rock wall. This sudden attack upon its flank caused the 11th to fall back. At this time the 8th was behind the 11th and was moving by the right flank to a point still further on the left where we were to take position. When the firing began we halted, forming line parallel to the rock fence. The 10th Alabama in the meantime had stood its ground on the right and was gallantly driving the enemy back. As soon as unmasked by the 11th the 8th advanced upon the enemy and drove them from the wall.[28]

In addition to this history, Herbert wrote three postwar letters that give some added details to the skirmish. Herbert recalled that the brigade was moving by the right flank, leisurely, in columns of four, when Berdan's men opened fire on the 10th Alabama. The sudden volley caught the 11th Regiment in the midst of an open field, across which it was moving to take position on the 10th's left. According to Herbert, the volley caused the startled Alabamians to fall back "in some disorder." Herbert let the retiring 11th pass over his regiment, which was third in line, and then ordered a charge against the Union force posted behind a stone wall on the edge of the woods, capturing the wall while "under a heavy fire." The 8th and 10th advanced in line and drove the Yankees from Pitzer's Woods. Colonel Herbert mentioned that only these three regiments of the brigade were engaged. The fighting ended before the remaining two regiments could deploy in support of their comrades.[29] A postwar letter by General Wilcox also mentioned that the fighting was over in "twenty or more minutes."[30]

George Clark, a member of the 11th Alabama, published his Civil War reminiscences in 1914. The old veteran recalled that his regiment was crossing a wheat field, and when about halfway across, was fired upon from the woods, "which produced some confusion and a retreat back to the fence so as to escape the fire from the rear." The 10th Alabama soon came up on the right and drove away the enemy force.[31]

There are two major differences of opinion between the Union and Confederate accounts of the skirmish. One problem is reconciling the discrepancies in the time when the skirmish took place. This is one of the most difficult facets of the event to discern. Colonel Herbert, in his letter to J. C. Kelton, mentioned that he talked with Colonel Forney and both agreed that it took place between nine and ten o'clock in the morning. However, in his regimental history, Herbert wrote that the fighting occurred at seven o'clock. General Wilcox, in his first official report, thought the encounter was over by nine o'clock. Lee's chief of artillery, Brig. Gen. William N. Pendleton, reported that a sharp skirmish took place sometime around noon.[32]

Federal accounts of the Berdan-Wilcox skirmish generally agree that it took place around noon. General Birney reported that he sent out the reconnaissance force at noon. General Humphreys recalled that he spoke with Capt. Joseph C. Briscoe of Birney's staff about noon, and since Briscoe accompanied Berdan's troops, Humphreys' testimony would indicate a postnoon operation. An 11:55 A.M. message from the Little Round Top signal station reported the following: "The rebels are in force, and our skirmishers give way. One mile west of Round Top signal station, the woods are full of them." Coddington believed this message referred to the Berdan-Wilcox encounter. Finally, Robert K. Beecham, in his *Gettysburg*, wrote that Birney reported the affair as lasting from 11:45 A.M. to 12:55 P.M. but provided no reference for this information. Given the time of Sickles' eleven o'clock visit to army headquarters, it would appear that the Yankees were more accurate than their counterparts in recalling the time of the fight.[33]

The second major problem with the skirmish is the placement of the Confederate skirmish line when Berdan's men encountered Wilcox's troops. In his report of the affair, Berdan wrote that when his sharpshooters began sweeping north through the woods, they "soon came upon the enemy and drove them sufficiently" before discovering the three columns of troops behind the gray-clad skirmishers. Colonel Trepp reported that his men met the enemy soon after crossing the Emmitsburg Road and drove them three hundred yards before they made a stand.[34]

Federal postwar accounts also mention the enemy skirmish line quite often. L. Y. Allen of Company F recalled that after the sharpshooters had progressed about a third of a mile, he was astonished to see a line of Rebel skirmishers in the open, swinging around the right and heading in the opposite direction. A member of the 3d Maine recalled that Berdan's men drove in the enemy skirmishers and pickets and were hotly engaged. The official history of the sharpshooters contains a tale that a young lad inhabiting a nearby house had already seen a large force of the enemy concealed in the woods, and scoffed when he saw the handful of Berdan's men moving to attack the more numerous foe.[35]

Yet, if the reports of Wilcox's men are accurate, the Alabamians had just arrived at Pitzer's Woods and were barely moving into position when Berdan's men suddenly opened fire on them. Wilcox himself reported that the two regiments chosen to scout the battle line were preceded by skirmishers, a logical precaution when deploying into line over unknown terrain. Colonel Herbert recalled that the 10th Alabama was suddenly fired upon as it entered Pitzer's Woods, and that the 11th Alabama's right flank received the brunt of the sudden volley that broke the advancing line and sent the men scampering for cover. In 1889, Wilcox wrote that the 10th had moved into the woods "but a short distance when a few shots were heard, followed quickly by a brisk fire." Taken together, the Southern reports indicate that the 10th Alabama had not advanced far when its skirmishers were driven back and Berdan's main body soon appeared and engaged the Rebels. If so, the story of the lad who warned the advancing sharpshooters of the imminent danger appears to be another Gettysburg myth.[36]

In contrast to the useful postwar Confederate accounts, the several accounts by Union participants are unreliable, and at times a bit melodramatic. In 1892, Charles A. Stevens published the official history of Berdan's Sharpshooters. On the whole, his description of the skirmish in Pitzer's Woods followed the official reports, being further supplemented by personal reminiscences of survivors. However, in judging the results of the skirmish, Stevens made it much more important than it actually was:

> The heroic deeds of Leonidas and his 300 Spartans, betrayed and slaughtered by the Persian hosts, has for ages been recounted in verse and story. But no greater display of heroism, no more self-sacrificing spirit of patriotism can be cited in the annals of war, than was the courageous attack of Berdan's 300 on the marching columns of 30,000 foes. And surely, it may be fairly said to be a turning point in the Rebellion.[37]

The attack on thirty thousand was a reference to the belief that Berdan's men had discovered Longstreet's flank march and delayed it long enough for Sickles to move forward and deny the Peach Orchard ridge to the enemy. Stevens included statements by Longstreet and Sickles about the importance of the skirmish to show that this delay saved the Army of the Potomac from certain destruction.[38]

Before surveying the movements of Longstreet's corps on July 2, a further analysis of Civil War histories sheds some light on the growth of the myth that Berdan's men stopped Longstreet for forty minutes and thus enabled Sickles to blunt the Confederate attack and save Little Round Top. Of forty-one histories written before 1920 discussing Gettysburg in some detail, only twelve include any account of the Pitzer's Woods skirmish. Until the 1880s, only two historians—Benson J. Lossing and Samuel P. Bates—wrote of the skirmish.[39] All of these early historians, in discussing the Meade-Sickles controversy, were unanimous in writing that Sickles advanced because of the lure of high ground to his front. No mention was made of the Berdan-Wilcox skirmish as the specific catalyst for the advance of the 3d Corps.

During the 1880s, some historians began to mention that the skirmish caused the forward move, not the lure of high ground alone. In general, every historian who mentioned Pitzer's Woods stated that this skirmish is what caused Sickles to move his corps forward off Cemetery Ridge. Those not mentioning the skirmish were of the opinion that Sickles was lured by the higher terrain in his front, in part aided by hazy or discretionary orders from General Meade.

There are several reasons for this change in historiography during the 1880s. By this decade, much of the bitter enmity still dividing North and South was fast disappearing, especially after the official end of Reconstruction in 1877. As the twenty-fifth anniversary of the battle approached, historians and veterans alike began to take a more active interest in the battle. The 1880s witnessed the majority of the monuments erected on the battlefield by Union veterans. This decade also saw the beginning of the great Gettysburg reunions, which received much publicity throughout the country.

This renewed interest in the battle also reopened old wounds. It was during the mid-1880s that the Meade-Sickles controversy, dormant since the war, erupted into open conflict. It appears from the available evidence that Col. Hiram Berdan had a great deal to do with the wider publicity that the Pitzer's Woods skirmish now received. Berdan had been absent from the United States since 1868, returning in 1886 to prosecute the government for an alleged infringement on his patent for a rifle. The former colonel of the sharpshooters became involved in the plans to erect a monument to his former comrades in Pitzer's Woods. He made several speeches at reunions, expounding upon the vital role of his command at Gettysburg.[40]

The best study of Berdan is that by Roy M. Marcot, *Hiram Berdan, Civil War Chief of Sharpshooters, Military Commander and Firearms Inventor.* Older studies are those by Richard A. Sauers, "Colonel Hiram Berdan and the 1st United States Sharpshooters," and Wiley Sword, *Sharpshooter: Hiram Berdan, His Famous Sharpshooters and Their Sharps Rifles.*[41] While some of Berdan's speeches were melodramatic to the point of absurdity, a summation of four orations results in a story as follows: Berdan noticed by 9:00 A.M. on July 2 that the enemy was making some sort of movement under cover of the woods in front of the Peach Orchard, but his skirmish line was not strong enough to discover what was afoot. About eleven o'clock, the colonel approached General Sickles about sending out a reconnaissance in force, which the general immediately approved. Berdan took his detachment to the extreme left of the line to ascertain whether any Confederates had penetrated that far south, then swung north through the woods in front of the Peach Orchard. Berdan recalled how he was some three hundred yards ahead of his men, mounted so he could see over the undergrowth and thus prevent any surprise. He came upon Wilcox's brigade, leading Longstreet's column of twenty-five thousand, marching south through the trees. Rather than withdraw and risk losing the Round Tops, Berdan gave the command, "Follow me, advance firing," although outnumbered "doubtless 20 to 1." Berdan claimed that his sudden attack on Wilcox delayed Longstreet's march from sixty to ninety minutes and thus saved the day for General Meade.[42]

General Longstreet added to the postwar historiographic confusion by agreeing with his old battle opponent that the forward move of the 3d Corps won Gettysburg by preventing a Confederate flank march. At the 1888 reunion, Longstreet was quoted as having the following conversation with Berdan:

> The old Union man, in discussing the battle this morning, asked Longstreet if he remembered the firing on his front before his troops made a forward move. "Remember it?" The Southerner pricked up his ears and,

showing more animation than he had at any other time since his arrival on the field, said that the firing in question saved Sickles and the day. It caused him a loss of 40 minutes, and could he have saved five of those minutes he believed that the battle would have gone against Meade on the second day.[43]

In 1902, Longstreet sent a letter to Sickles, apologizing for not being able to meet him at Gettysburg for the unveiling of the Slocum statue. The ex-Confederate general also wrote the following: "I believe that it is now conceded that the advanced position at the Peach Orchard, taken by your corps and under your orders, saved the battlefield to the Union cause."[44]

Sickles' theory of the early Confederate move toward the Union left flank was aided to a degree by the Lee-Longstreet controversy on the Confederate side. Longstreet was used as a scapegoat for the defeat at Gettysburg by several officers, most notably Jubal Early and William N. Pendleton. Until recently, very few historians publicly sided with Longstreet to defend his actions at Gettysburg on July 2.[45] Along with other reasons, the anti-Longstreet bias in the South drove Longstreet to side with Sickles about the forward move at Gettysburg. The lack of support for Longstreet has obscured the movements of his command prior to the opening of the fighting on July 2. A closer examination will reveal that the actual movement of Longstreet's corps was far from what Sickles thought it was.

Two divisions of Longstreet's 1st Corps, those of McLaws and Hood, arrived within four miles of Gettysburg late on the evening of July 1. The troops moved out of bivouac shortly after sunrise on July 2, McLaws's division leading. While McLaws rode ahead to report to Lee, the division's four brigades, led by Brig. Gen. Joseph B. Kershaw's South Carolinians, filed off the Chambersburg Pike, marched south along Herr Ridge, and halted with the head of the column near the Hoss House. Kershaw later recalled that while at this location he could see Federal troops moving up the Emmitsburg Road toward Gettysburg.[46]

McLaws found Lee in company with Longstreet on Seminary Ridge. Lee talked with McLaws and pointed out on a map where he wished McLaws to place his troops. Although McLaws wanted to reconnoiter the terrain in person, Longstreet ordered him back to his division. Lee mentioned to a perplexed McLaws that his engineer, Capt. Samuel R. Johnston, had already set off to scout the area.[47]

Captain Johnston, accompanied by three or four men, had started out to reconnoiter the terrain south of Pender's division about four o'clock that morning, or just shortly before sunrise. The party apparently moved south along Seminary Ridge to the approximate area where McLaws formed for battle later in the day. In Johnston's words,

> [I followed] along that ridge in the direction of Round Top, across the Emmettsburg [sic] road and got up on the slope of Round Top where I had a commanding view, then rose south along the base of Round Top, to beyond the ground that was occupied by Gen'l. Hood and where there was, later on, a cavalry fight, when I thought that I had gone far enough, I turned back, of course moving with great caution.

Nearing the Emmitsburg Road, Johnston observed a group of Federal cavalrymen moving up the road toward Gettysburg. He let them get out of sight and then took a direct route back to General Lee. Johnston made his report, noting that Lee was surprised that he had gotten so far in his reconnaissance, and that "he showed clearly that I had given him valuable information."[48]

It was apparently this information that influenced Lee to decide to have Longstreet's corps attack up the Emmitsburg Road and turn the Federal left flank. Hill's 3d Corps would aid this effort. Ewell would attack the Federal right should an opportunity present itself. Lee ordered Longstreet to move at eleven o'clock, but then consented to wait until almost noon, when Law's brigade of Hood's division reached the field after a forced march from Chambersburg. Based upon Johnston's report, Lee must have believed that the Union left did not extend all the way south along Cemetery Ridge. Thus, an oblique attack following the line of the Emmitsburg Road from the Peach Orchard ridge would outflank the visible Federal troops and perhaps catch them in a trap between Ewell and Longstreet.[49]

At any rate, Longstreet's corps, with McLaws's division leading, finally began moving sometime around noon. Captain Johnston was assigned to act as a guide, and at first McLaws and Johnston rode in advance of the infantry column, led by Kershaw's brigade. Kershaw left the Hoss House area, countermarched behind Herr Ridge, then moved south along Marsh Creek, reaching the Hagerstown Road at the Black Horse Tavern. The column continued south along another country lane. Only a few hundred yards south of the tavern, this road surmounts a small hill. As McLaws and Johnston reached the crest of this hill, they were horrified to see flags waving from the Union signal station on Little Round Top. Longstreet rode up and saw the same sight, whereupon, after a short consultation, he ordered a countermarch to find another route out of sight of the signalmen.

Col. Edward Porter Alexander, commanding one of Longstreet's artillery battalions, found the infantry halted here as he rode back for "something." That morning, Longstreet had placed Alexander in charge of the entire 1st Corps artillery, and ordered him to ride south to examine the terrain, then bring up the guns. Accompanied by a courier or two, Alexander took about an hour to reconnoiter. The colonel then took his own battalion and moved the six batteries south to a position near the Pitzer Schoolhouse, where he halted to await the infantry. Riding back for some purpose, Alexander discovered McLaws' troops at the foot of the small hill, in sight of the signal station. Earlier, the cannon had approached this same spot, but the colonel moved the column of batteries to the left, around the hill through some fields, before again picking up the lane. Alexander told the officers at the head of the infantry column about his route, but Longstreet, McLaws, and Kershaw all seem to have been absent. As a result, Alexander's suggestions fell on deaf ears.[50]

During the short halt at the hill, Hood's division had closed up on the rear of McLaws's troops and some units had become entangled, causing some momentary confusion. The troops got straightened out, and McLaws's division apparently retained the lead in this countermarch. McLaws led his men back to the area near the starting point of the march, then moved them directly east along a country lane to Willoughby Run. The column then followed the run south to the Pitzer School, where it turned east onto the Millerstown Road. As the head of Kershaw's brigade emerged from the woods in front of the Peach Orchard about three o'clock, McLaws was surprised to see numerous batteries supported by infantry in and around the orchard, since Longstreet had told him that when he reached the orchard, his men would be on the enemy's flank. McLaws quickly deployed his four brigades under cover of the woods, while Hood's division, once Longstreet learned the truth of the situation, moved behind McLaws and took up position on his right.[51]

There are several extant accounts of this flank march of Longstreet's two divisions. McLaws wrote about it in two articles published in the

Philadelphia *Weekly Press* and gave two different speeches to Confederate veterans' groups. Kershaw filed an official report, wrote an article for the "Battles and Leaders" series in *The Century Magazine*, and wrote a very detailed letter to John B. Bachelder. Colonel Alexander wrote an official report of the battle, penned a letter published in the *Southern Historical Society Papers*, and later published his *Military Memoirs of a Confederate*. He also authored a lengthy manuscript for the benefit of his family that was finally published in an edited version in 1989. Alonzo Meyers of the 15th South Carolina wrote an account that appeared in the *National Tribune*. Each of these accounts goes into some detail about Longstreet's flank march before the fighting on July 2.[52]

All of these writings have one very important feature in common—no mention is made of any delay due to skirmish firing at any point during the march. The route of Longstreet's corps would not have made the column visible to Berdan's party when the fighting took place in Pitzer's Woods. In an 1892 letter, Colonel Herbert, after describing the skirmish, remarked that "no other Confederates were in sight."[53] It is quite apparent that the weight of evidence is strongly against Berdan's claim that his men stopped Longstreet and won the battle by giving Sickles time to occupy the Peach Orchard. It should also be noted that Wilcox's brigade was not even a part of Longstreet's corps at Gettysburg, but it appears that several early historians overlooked this elementary piece of evidence.[54]

After examining Sickles' thesis that a Confederate move had been under way since daybreak on July 2, a process the general claimed he was aware of early that morning, and then detailing the actual movement of the Confederate troops on Seminary Ridge, the activities of the skirmish lines, the details of the Pitzer's Woods fighting, and the actual movements of Longstreet's corps, we come to the obvious conclusion that Sickles could not possibly have been aware of these movements.

The report of the skirmish in Pitzer's Woods was indeed the decisive event that influenced Sickles to move forward to the Peach Orchard. He was not happy with the initial position of his command on Cemetery Ridge, a fact he told the Committee on the Conduct of the War and repeated numerous times after the war.[55] A report of enemy troops in the woods to his front gave Sickles the excuse to move forward to seize the commanding ground in his front. In this light, most early historians were correct when they concluded that Sickles was lured forward by high ground. Postbattle hindsight enabled Sickles to fabricate the myth that his forward move prevented Longstreet's flank march and thus saved the Army of the Potomac from defeat, rather than almost lose the battle, as his opponents argued.

The anti-Longstreet bias in the South helped Sickles in this aspect of the defense of his activities and forced Longstreet to ally himself with Sickles, who at times was almost as much of an outcast in the North as his former opponent was in the South. General Sickles was also aided, but probably not consciously, by Colonel Berdan. The colonel had his own interests at stake when he exaggerated the importance of the Pitzer's Woods action to enhance his own tarnished reputation. In fact, very little mention was made of the skirmish until Berdan returned to America in 1886.[56]

The contradictory nature of the sources dealing with this aspect of Sickles' defense of his actions, especially the details of the Pitzer's Woods fighting, makes it very difficult to reconstruct a detailed sequence of events leading up to the opening of the general fighting on July 2. For example, there is no evidence that a report of the skirmish ever reached General Meade. General Birney's statements suggest that he was ordered to move forward soon after his report reached Sickles.[57] Meade and his supporters never mentioned receiving any word of the skirmish. The varying accounts of the participants in the Pitzer's Woods skirmish also leave many questions unanswered. But one fact remains clear—Sickles did not know of Longstreet's flanking march until much later, when criticism had already been directed at him for moving off Cemetery Ridge. Hindsight enabled Sickles to develop part of his defense against such criticism.

Chapter Seven

GENERAL SICKLES AND HIS ORDERS, JULY 2, 1863

oncurrent with the thesis that he knew from early morning that the enemy was preparing to attack the 3d Corps, General Sickles maintained that he never received any orders from General Meade about the position his corps was to occupy in the Federal line of battle. However, as with Sickles' error-filled presentations of Confederate movements against his troops, this thesis is also unfounded. On many occasions, Sickles did admit that he had received orders about his position. A summary of this part of Sickles' defense of his actions at Gettysburg, followed by an analysis of the evidence, will reveal that Sickles did indeed receive orders on July 2 concerning the position of the 3d Corps.

In his testimony before the Committee on the Conduct of the War, Sickles stated: "Not having received any orders in reference to my position, . . . I went in person to headquarters and reported the facts and circumstances which led me to believe that an attack would be made there, and asked for orders. I did not receive any orders."[1] Shortly after the war, in a letter to former aide Henry Tremain, Sickles again repeated that he had no orders until General Meade rode out to the 3d Corps line shortly after three o'clock on July 2.[2]

During the escalation of the controversy in 1886, Sickles mentioned the no-orders thesis several times. He uttered this in the course of the Boston Music Hall speech, and then again during the evening Revere House address, when he quoted from Meade's committee testimony.[3] In

117

his July 2 Gettysburg speech, Sickles mentioned this thesis in point nine and then again in point nineteen, when he stated that "on the 2d of July I had no orders before the battle as to the dispositions of my troops to meet Longstreet's assault, nor did I receive an order of any kind during the battle."[4] As part of his reply to Colonel Benedict's article in the Philadelphia *Weekly Times*, Sickles asserted that he had become "weary of so many visits to headquarters during the day" in search of orders, but he did not receive any orders.[5]

Later, in 1891, in his reply to Carswell McClellan, Sickles again stated that he went all day without orders.[6] Finally, in a letter to the son of a 3d Corps regimental commander, Sickles wrote: "I endeavored to get orders as to my position in the afternoon, but could not obtain them. My advanced position was taken on my own responsibility."[7]

However, in spite of the number of times that Sickles remarked he did not receive orders, he also mentioned, on occasion, that he did indeed receive orders about the position of the 3d Corps. But every time he suggested this, Sickles qualified his statement by contending that he was not sure of the position to be taken by his corps. He first stated this to the Committee on the Conduct of the War:

> At a very early hour on Thursday morning, I received a notification that General Meade's headquarters had been established at Gettysburg, and I was directed by him to relieve a division of the 12th Corps, (General Geary's division, I think) which was massed a little to my left, and which had taken position there during the night. I did so, reporting, however, to General Meade that that division was not in position, but was merely massed in my vicinity; the tenor of his order seemed to indicate a supposition on his part that the division was in position.[8]

In his 1886 Music Hall speech, Sickles alluded to the fact that the 3d Corps went into position on the line of Cemetery Ridge: "when we went into our first position on the 2d of July, on the left at Gettysburg. . . ."[9]

During his Gettysburg speech, Sickles twice referred to his orders:

> I kept Gen. Meade constantly advised of the situation on the left flank. I made personal reports to him at his headquarters. I pointed out to him that Geary's Division, which I had been ordered to relieve, had not been in position, but had been massed near me; that I had not received any definite orders as to the disposition of my command, which was massed to the left of

Hancock, a part of the First Division, extending through the low ground in the direction of Round Top . . . I asked for orders. I had no orders. I did not receive any orders. . . .

The battle of July 2 was fought on the lines I occupied on my own responsibility. The battle was fought, so far as the Third Corps is concerned, without orders of any nature from the Commanding General of the Army of the Potomac. From sunrise on the morning of July 2 until after six o'clock in the afternoon, when I was wounded, I received no order from Gen. Meade relating to the dispositions of my troops or to the conduct of the battle, except that I was to occupy the position Gen. Geary had left, which I at once reported to Gen. Meade was no position at all.[10]

In replying to Colonel Benedict's article, General Sickles said that his instructions from Meade "were all verbal and extremely vague and indefinite. . . . The only definite intimation that reached me from Gen. Meade before the battle opened on July 2 was that I should relieve Geary's division, which he had ordered over to the right." Sickles went on to say that Geary's command was merely massed in his vicinity and had marched off before he received Meade's order to relieve it. Geary further complicated the matter by failing to send any staff officer to indicate his position. But Sickles then remarked that Geary did not send an officer "for obvious reasons, because he was not in position."[11]

And so, in more than one instance, Sickles himself did admit to receiving orders, although he qualified such statements by maintaining that he could not obey Meade's ambiguous order because Geary's troops did not occupy any specific point. Further, Sickles stated that Geary failed to provide any staff officer to point out the division's bivouac area before his troops marched off to Culp's Hill.

Yet General Geary, in his 1870 letter to Meade, wrote that he had indeed sent a staff officer to Sickles to explain where his troops were located. Sickles replied that he would attend to matters in due time, but after waiting for an unspecified period of time, Geary felt he had to obey his orders to move his two brigades to Culp's Hill. His troops then departed the Little Round Top area before Sickles' troops actually relieved his men.[12]

Even though Geary marched off without waiting for Sickles to deploy his units, there is evidence that the bivouacs of the 3d and 12th Corps regiments were not that far apart on the evening of July 1. However, none of the official reports on file include any mention of troops from one corps actually seeing soldiers of the other corps. This lack of detail for locating the actual positions of the units led to a wide variance in interpreting where the troops actually were located. There are several postwar maps that depict the southern half of the battlefield and the troops deployed there on the evening of July 1. One such map was drawn for Henry Hunt's series in *The Century Magazine*, and was later copied by Jesse Bowman Young in his *Battle of Gettysburg*. William R. Livermore included a different deployment map in his series, while James K. P. Scott drew a new map for his *Story of the Battles of Gettysburg*. Finally, Glenn Tucker's *High Tide at Gettysburg* included yet another map. These maps show the 3d Corps brigades as either deployed in front of or massed behind Geary's two brigades. Which version is right, if either?[13]

As mentioned above, there is very little detail in the official reports of Geary's unit commanders. Only the report of Col. John H. Patrick of the 5th Ohio included some details of his regiment's deployment on July 1. Patrick wrote that his regiment, accompanied by the 147th Pennsylvania, was detached from Col. Charles Candy's 1st brigade and ordered to occupy Little Round Top. Patrick deployed both regiments on the hill, with skirmishers thrown forward along Houck's Ridge.[14]

Brig. Gen. George S. Greene commanded Geary's 3d Brigade. There are no reports from the five New York regiments comprising this brigade that include any details about the exact position Greene occupied on July 1. However, in 1867, Capt. Charles P. Horton, Greene's adjutant general, wrote a very detailed letter to John B. Bachelder about the brigade's activities at Gettysburg. Horton wrote that after the 2d Brigade of the division was detached to guard the corps artillery and ordnance train on the Baltimore Pike, Geary marched the other two brigades across the fields toward Little Round Top. Horton continued:

> We came into line in rear of a country road along which a considerable force of our cavalry was now galloping to the left. Here the 3rd Brigade formed in line of battalions en masse and supported by the 1st (Candy's) moved over a small but rocky hill in our front descending the slope on the other side. Knapp's Pa. Battery passed around by some road came up & took position on a knoll on our right. Skirmishers were pushed well to the front, & preparations made for entrenching when the head of a column appeared on our front & left. This was I think between 6 and 7 P.M. It was at first supposed to be the enemy and came near being fired upon by the batteries, but was soon discovered to be the Vermont Brigade of Reynolds' Corps—

Captain Weld of Reynolds' staff riding in from this column about this time gave us our first certain information of the fight of the afternoon. Not long afterwards the 3rd Corps (Sickles) appeared and after dark relieved us, our command however bivouacking on the ground.[15]

In analyzing this letter, we see that it appears Greene's brigade took position in the approximate area where the New Jersey Brigade monument is located today, on a rocky hillock north of Little Round Top. According to Horton, when 3d Corps troops occupied the same area, Greene's New Yorkers moved a short distance to the rear, then encamped for the night. Other postwar accounts written by Greene's men provide little additional information to bolster Horton's recollection. Capt. Jesse H. Jones of the 60th New York revisited the battlefield in 1883. He even managed to locate the very rock beside which he slept that night. "When we slept there it was a fair meadow; since then it has become a wet waste." Otherwise, there are no detailed accounts known to this author that further identify the exact camping area of Greene's men and whether or not they spied 3d Corps troops.[16]

A survey of the extant reports from General Birney's division of the 3d Corps reveals that Graham's brigade bivouacked in the fields on George Weikert's farm; it was apparently these troops who relieved Greene's regiments. In summation, a brief analysis of the official reports and postwar recollections indicates that units from both corps occupied and bivouacked on approximately the same terrain. These regiments could very well have seen each other at some point during the evening of July 1. Sickles claimed that Geary never occupied any specific position, but the evidence strongly suggests otherwise.

An examination of the *Official Records*, as well as other sources, reveals that Sickles was wrong in yet another instance about his claim of not receiving orders, or if he did, that he could not obey them. Maj. Gen. David B. Birney, commanding the 1st Division of the 3d Corps, reported:

> At 7 A.M., under orders from Major-General Sickles, I relieved Geary's division, and formed a line, resting its left on the Sugar Loaf Mountain [Little Round Top] and the right thrown in a direct line toward the cemetery, connecting on the right with the Second Division of this corps.[17]

Birney's testimony to the Committee on the Conduct of the War substantiated his official report, since Birney stated, "Upon the 2d of July I was ordered to relieve Geary's division of the 12th corps, that during the night had bivouacked on my left."[18]

Brig. Gen. Andrew A. Humphreys commanded the 2d Division of the 3d Corps. His official report and committee testimony are also in agreement, both indicating that his division was initially massed where it had bivouacked after arriving on the field about one o'clock in the morning of July 2. Both statements included mention of the ridge running from the cemetery to Little Round Top. In an August 6, 1863, letter to a friend, Humphreys remarked that "Sickles was ordered to take position along a certain crest, but instead of that he went half a mile in front of it, and of the rest of the army." Finally, the letter from Carswell McClellan stated that division headquarters knew where the position was long before noon on July 2.[19]

Two more 3d Corps officers also admitted to receiving orders, or at least taking position on Cemetery Ridge. Capt. Benjamin M. Piatt, assistant adjutant general to Colonel de Trobriand, recalled, "It is well known to any one familiar with the history of the battle that Gen. Sickles was ordered to place his command on the left of General Hancock, on the same general line, which would draw it along the prolongation of Cemetery Ridge, toward the Round Top." Capt. George E. Randolph, commander of the 3d Corps artillery, made an oblique reference to orders in a letter to John B. Bachelder when he wrote that the 3d Corps "was assigned to a plan in continuation of the line direct from the Cemetery to Round Top."[20]

General Hancock, commanding the 2d Corps, also knew of Sickles' orders, since the 3d Corps was next to his corps. Hancock mentioned in his official report that the 3d Corps connected with his left flank, extending the line of battle along the crest of Cemetery Ridge to Round Top Mountain. Hancock was a bit more specific in his committee testimony when he remarked: "General Sickles was directed to connect with my left and the Round Top mountain, thus forming a continuous line from Cemetery Hill to Round Top mountain."[21]

General Meade also stated that he sent specific orders to Sickles. His official report included the following statement in regard to the position assigned to the 3d Corps: "The Second and Third Corps were directed to occupy the continuation of Cemetery Ridge on the left of the Eleventh Corps."[22] In his committee testimony, Meade reported:

I had sent instructions in the morning to General Sickles . . . directing him to form his corps in line of battle on the left of the 2d corps . . . and I had indicated to him in general terms, that his right was to rest upon General Hancock's left; and his left was to extend to the Round Top mountain, plainly visible, if it was practicable to occupy it.[23]

Upon General Meade's death in 1872, his son George took up his father's defense against General Sickles and his supporters. The four written descriptions by Colonel Meade concerning his experience at Gettysburg on July 2, are, with the exception of some minor details, consistent in regard to General Sickles.[24] All four accounts detail Meade's visits to 3d Corps headquarters on the morning of July 2 and his conversation with Captain Randolph, followed by his return to army headquarters to report that Sickles' men were not yet in position. After receiving instructions from General Meade, then-Captain Meade returned to Sickles, finding him mounted and the troops moving out. Meade gave Sickles his father's orders, to which Sickles replied that his troops were then moving into position, then added that Geary did not have any discernible position. Captain Meade also wrote about Sickles' eleven o'clock visit to army headquarters and how his father pointed to the Round Tops as the anchor of the 3d Corps left flank. Meade's accounts also included his father's ride to the rear of the Peach Orchard and the animated conversation with Sickles that afternoon, just as Confederate artillery opened fire on the Yankee position.

We can make certain observations regarding Sickles' orders after studying Colonel Meade's writings. Contrary to Sickles' claim that he kept Meade constantly informed of enemy movements opposite the 3d Corps front and that his messengers asked for orders, Colonel Meade wrote that until Sickles came in person to headquarters around eleven o'clock, nothing was heard from the corps commander regarding enemy movements or his position.[25] This viewpoint is substantiated, or so it appears, by the failure of other army staff officers to mention in their writings any visit by Sickles or members of his staff.

Captain Meade also noted Sickles' manner on July 2. When he visited Sickles for the second time that morning, Meade recalled that "his manner was very polite and affable and showed no signs of any feeling or misunderstanding & I left thinking it was all right."[26] Later, when Captain Meade joined his father and General Sickles near the Peach Orchard, he overheard some of the conversation between the two generals. Meade wrote that "Sickles was very polite & affable & a good deal awed. He expressed great regret at having occupied a position that did not meet with Genl. M's approval, &c."[27] Captain Meade noted that Sickles did not mention anything about not receiving orders while speaking with General Meade at this time, a recollection supported by Maj. James C. Biddle, another staff officer who witnessed the scene."[28]

From an examination of the evidence thus far, especially Sickles' own words, it is evident that he did receive orders about the position of the 3d Corps on the morning of July 2. The reports of his two division commanders, Generals Birney and Humphreys, as well as the writings of other 3d Corps officers, confirm that Sickles received instructions. Generals Meade and Hancock also mentioned orders. Captain Meade's version of events, which is consistent except for minor details, leaves no doubt about the existence of orders. Before closing this chapter, there are two other points connected with Sickles' order that should be reviewed; namely, how the order was originally sent and the time of the order.

In reference to the sending of the order on the morning of the second, there are no definite conclusions reached by the participants in the event. When the storm of criticism began to break against him in 1886, General Sickles asked a former aide to institute a search of War Department records in an effort to find the original written order assigning the 3d Corps to a definite position on Cemetery Ridge. No such order was found.[29]

Col. George Meade also did not know how the first order to Sickles was issued. His narrative of what he witnessed at Gettysburg suggests, as he stated more than once, that when General Meade first sent him to Sickles on July 2, it was merely to verify obedience to previous orders and check whether Sickles had anything to report to headquarters. In regard to these orders, Colonel Meade recalled later that he did not know how they were issued, although he hypothesized that the orders were verbal. He told how his father gave verbal orders to General Gibbon when that general rode up to report the impending arrival of the 2d Corps. After Meade's inspection of the proposed battle line before dawn broke, he returned to the cemetery gatehouse and issued verbal orders to those officers assembled there, including Howard, Slocum, and Sickles.[30]

If General Sickles did receive verbal orders, they were evidently reinforced by later written orders. When Generals Meade, Howard, and Hunt made their predawn reconnaissance of the Federal position at Gettysburg, they were accompanied by Captain Paine of the engineers. Paine later recalled that the movement of the party was slow and that only the most salient terrain features were visible. He seemed to think the generals continued all the way to Big Round Top before doubling back north to proceed to Culp's Hill. As it became lighter, Paine began to sketch the terrain and consequently fell behind the three generals. After the captain finished with his sketch map, General Meade indicated the position to be occupied by each corps. Then, Paine had the base map traced and a copy sent to each corps commander. Concerning Sickles' position, Paine wrote: "I well remember that the Peach Orchard and the fact of a ridge extending along where Gen. Sickles took position was not developed so as to be indicated by me on my sketches until some hours later."[31] However, it appears that not every corps commander received a copy of this map. General Gibbon, acting chief of the 2d Corps until Hancock returned to the field, did not remember ever receiving one, so it is not at all certain that Sickles also obtained a copy.[32]

The approximate time that Meade's verbal order was issued, as well as subsequent follow-up orders, remains somewhat of a controversy. General Geary wrote in his official report that the 3d Corps relieved his division at five o'clock in the morning of July 2. Greene's brigade of this division apparently left its bivouac at 4:00 A.M. to march over to Culp's Hill.[33] Colonel Candy's brigade of Geary's division was deployed over a wider area and thus required more time to concentrate before evacuating its position. Two regiments of Candy's brigade, the 5th Ohio and 147th Pennsylvania, had deployed on Little Round Top with skirmishers located along Houck's Ridge. These regiments rejoined the brigade by five o'clock, and, according to the various times mentioned in the official reports, the brigade marched off sometime between 5:30 and 6:00 A.M.[34]

Geary's division left its position near Little Round Top in time to clear the Taneytown Road for the approach of Gibbon and the 2d Corps shortly after six o'clock. Lt. Frank Haskell recalled that the corps was delayed while it waited for other troops ahead to move on up the road. Although Haskell was not specific about the identity of these troops, it may very well have been Geary's division moving to Culp's Hill.[35]

There are conflicting reports for the time of deployment of the 3d Corps. As mentioned previously, General Birney reported that his division relieved Geary at seven o'clock. Of the regimental reports on file from

Birney's command, only one, that of Lt. Col. Benjamin L. Higgins of the 86th New York, is specific about the time. Higgins wrote that his regiment left camp at six o'clock and took position about 7:30 A.M. For Humphreys' division, there are two reports that include the time; both agree that the division was ordered into line about 8:00 A.M. The regimental historian of the 12th New Hampshire also specified this same time.[36]

Captain Meade added to the conflicting times by failing to be consistent in referring to the same time when he visited 3d Corps headquarters. In *Life and Letters* and his 1886 letter to General Hunt, Meade wrote that he went to see Sickles sometime between 8:00 and 9:00 A.M. However, Meade mentioned a time of 7 to 8:00 A.M. in his 1891 notes to Carswell McClellan. In an 1885 letter to Gen. Alexander S. Webb, he stated that his father was waiting for the arrival of the 5th and 6th Corps when he sent his son to Sickles. Since the 5th Corps arrived at 8:00 A.M., the 1885 letter would indicate a time earlier than eight o'clock.[37]

After reconciling the differences of time and how orders were issued, this material can be included in a summation to refute Sickles' claim that he never received any orders concerning the position of the 3d Corps. General Meade arrived on the field at approximately 1:00 A.M. on July 2. After a consultation with the officers assembled at General Howard's headquarters on Cemetery Hill, Meade, accompanied by Generals Hunt and Howard and Captain Paine, made a reconnaissance of the battle line. This survey began sometime after two o'clock and lasted until probably 4:30 A.M. Once Meade had examined the terrain, he indicated the positions to be occupied by each corps. Captain Paine then used his sketch map to have copies traced for each corps commander. Presumably Sickles received verbal orders when Meade returned to the cemetery after his inspection of the line; if he did not, then he almost certainly received a copy of Paine's map.[38]

In accordance with these early morning orders, General Geary began evacuating his position on Cemetery Ridge and marched off to Culp's Hill sometime between 4:00 and 6:00 A.M., just in time to leave the Taneytown Road open for the arrival of the 2d Corps, which, because of all the traffic on this dirt road, took several hours to reach the field and deploy on Cemetery Ridge.[39]

General Sickles was apparently late in deploying his command, and when Captain Meade first visited 3d Corps headquarters sometime around seven o'clock, the corps was not yet in position. Upon his second arrival, Captain Meade was told that the troops were moving and would soon be in position, although Sickles did tell him that Geary had no position as far as he could determine. And thus by 7:30 A.M. or thereabouts, Sickles had at least partially deployed the 3d Corps along the line that Meade designated he should occupy.[40]

Even if Sickles did not truly know where his command was supposed to be, he did ride to army headquarters about 11:00 A.M. and report that he was unsure of his position. Meade thereupon told him that he was supposed to occupy the general line on which Geary had bivouacked, forming his left flank on Little Round Top if it was practicable to occupy that hill, and connect his right with Hancock's left. When Sickles asked if he was authorized to post his corps as he saw fit, Meade replied, "Certainly, within the limits of the general instructions I have given to you; any ground within those limits you choose to occupy, I leave to you."[41] Meade apparently heard nothing more from Sickles until he learned from Warren that some of the latter's engineer officers had reported that Sickles was not in his assigned position.

As a conclusion to this chapter, there are two more points to be argued. It does seem that General Meade issued a general order rather than a more specific instruction regarding the 3d Corps position, or so General Sickles held. Sickles further maintained that because the order was so vague and ill defined, he could not obey it. However, at least one other corps commander also received a vague order to deploy his command. Instead of vacillating as Sickles did, he obeyed it. Coddington pointed out that General Slocum followed Meade's order concerning the position of the 12th Corps by using the terrain to the best of his advantage rather than following the order to the letter. Sickles could have done much the same.[42]

Finally, in reference to Sickles' claim that he did not receive any order at all, General Gibbon commented that he could not "understand how a corps commander could possibly have been omitted under such circumstances, nor, if he was accidentally omitted how he did not get orders by personal solicitation."[43] Had Sickles not received any orders at all, this would show gross incompetence on General Meade's part, which is not in keeping with his character. This alone should have been enough to refute this part of Sickles' defense.

Chapter Eight

THE WEAK POSITION ON CEMETERY RIDGE

The third major point around which General Sickles based the defense of his actions at Gettysburg was his argument that the original position General Meade intended for the 3d Corps to occupy along Cemetery Ridge was a bad tactical position. The low ground of southern Cemetery Ridge was dominated by the higher ground at the Peach Orchard. Enemy occupation of this elevated terrain would render untenable the 3d Corps line on the ridge. Again, a brief summary of what Sickles used to support this view, followed by a critical analysis of his beliefs, will reveal that this point is probably the weakest link in Sickles' defense of his conduct at Gettysburg.

Sickles first spoke of the low ground on Cemetery Ridge in his testimony before the Committee on the Conduct of the War. The general mentioned how he was favorably impressed by the overall position upon reaching the battlefield on the afternoon of July 1. He even wrote to General Meade to express his opinion. Sickles then spoke of Meade's order for him to relieve Geary's division of the 12th Corps and how he reported to headquarters that Geary's command had no position. After telling the committee of his knowledge of the enemy's intentions to attack the Federal left, Sickles went on to describe his visit to army headquarters. Having failed to receive any orders, he asked for General Hunt to accompany him back to the corps to examine the ground. Meade acquiesced, and Hunt went with Sickles, who said to the committee:

General Hunt accompanied me upon a careful reconnoissance [*sic*] of the whole position on the left, in reference to its topography and the best line for us to occupy, and also with reference to the movements of the enemy. I pointed out to General Hunt the line that on a subsequent part of the day, when the battle opened, I actually occupied; that is, a line from Round Top on the left, perpendicular to the Emmettsburg [*sic*] road, but somewhat en echelon with the line of battle established on Cemetery Ridge. I asked for General Hunt's sanction, in the name of General Meade, for the occupation of that line. He declined to give it, although he said it met with the approval of his own judgment; but he said that I would undoubtedly receive such orders as soon as he reported to General Meade.

Sickles went on to say that while awaiting orders that never came, it became more and more likely that he would be attacked, so he ordered his troops forward to the Peach Orchard line.

I took up that line because it enabled me to hold commanding ground, which, if the enemy had been allowed to take—as they would have taken it if I had not occupied it in force—would have rendered our position on the left untenable; and, in my judgment, would have turned the fortunes of the day hopelessly against us. I think that any general who would look at the topography of the country there would naturally come to the same conclusion.[1]

In a speech at Gettysburg in July 1882, the 3d Corps commander again mentioned General Hunt's reconnaissance of the proposed line and how it met with his approval. He also spoke of the present-day military critics who attacked him for leaving his original position in the low ground north of Little Round Top, "in other words, to have formed in the hollow and given the enemy of the advantage of the hills along our front and to have left Round Top entirely uncovered."[2]

Sickles next mentioned the weak position on Cemetery Ridge in his Boston Music Hall speech in April 1886, followed by the address that evening at the Revere House. In these two speeches, Sickles maintained that Little Round Top was the key to the position at Gettysburg and quoted from Meade's official report to support this statement. Sickles said that, since this hill was unoccupied, he advanced his line to cover that position until reinforcements arrived to prevent the Rebels from seizing the eminence. He did acknowledge the truth of the criticism that the advanced line was far too long for the 3d Corps to occupy. Sickles attempted to refute such criticism by declaring that he commanded only one corps and not the army, implying that a more alert general would have strengthened the left flank. In the Revere House speech, Sickles declared:

> I would like to know how you are going to defend a position unless you get in front of it. If I am going to defend entrenchments, I don't want to get behind them. I don't want to get away from them. I don't want to let the enemy occupy them and then defend them. I put myself in front of them, and that is what we did.

In other words, Sickles contended that he occupied the advanced line to prevent the enemy from seizing Little Round Top, the key to the Union position at Gettysburg.[3]

Later in 1886, during the course of the speech delivered to the 3d Corps reunion at Gettysburg on July 2, Sickles again mentioned Hunt's approval of the line by citing that general's committee testimony. He then told the audience that he had never received any orders about where to take position. Therefore, the line he occupied was by his own authority and echoed the discretion allowed a corps commander. "I advanced my corps, leaving the low, marshy swale, extending from the left of the 2d Corps toward Little Round Top, so as to occupy higher and better fighting ground, throwing my left forward, in advance of Round Top, which was unoccupied."

During this speech, Sickles expounded upon twenty-six alleged errors that had appeared in print since 1863 and now needed correcting. Points fourteen, fifteen, and twenty dealt with his original position and the supposedly better line at the Peach Orchard:

> 14. That if our left had been held only on the line indicated by Gen. Meade as the one he intended Sickles should take, to wit, "the continuation of the Cemetery Ridge" to the left of the Second Corps, the enemy could have seized both Round Tops—the key of the whole position—without resistance; since their occupation was not ordered by Gen. Meade until 5 in the afternoon, when his attention was called to their importance by Gen. Warren, as it had been called much earlier in the day before the battle began, by Gen. Sickles.
> 15. That the 10,000 men of the Third Corps in position on the left of Cemetery Ridge would have been powerless to save our left flank, because the enemy in possession of Round Top and all the commanding ridge adjacent to it would have swept us or any equal number of troops from the field, turning our flank and gaining our rear before the hour when our powerful supports arrived. . . .

20. That I moved out from a very weak position to occupy one naturally stronger, which could have been held with perfect success if I had been supported; that is to say, if half the troops afterward brought up to meet the assault had reinforced me earlier in the action, my lines would have been held intact to the end of the battle; in other words, that a line held by 40,000 men is not proof that a more advanced line held by 10,000 was not a good line. Our good and constant friend, Gen. de Peyster, has shown by ample citations from military history that a salient strongly held has been the salvation of great battles, as it was our salvation at Gettysburg.[4]

Sickles again talked about his advanced position in his reply to Colonel Benedict's letter in the Philadelphia *Weekly Press*. The general told the *New York Times* reporter sent to get his reaction to the publication of Meade's 1870 letter that his original line could not have been held because his command did not have enough men to occupy the line from Hancock's left to the Round Tops. He cited the Count of Paris's statement that the distance his line was to occupy was about twenty-two hundred yards, while the 2d Corps frontage was only twelve hundred yards. Thus, his line "would have been a mere skirmish line utterly incapable of resisting assaulting columns." He went on to say that the direct line from Hancock to the Round Tops "was a line through swale morass, swamp, boulders, and forest and tangled undergrowth, unfit for infantry, impracticable for artillery, and hopelessly dominated by the ridge in front." If the enemy had occupied this position without a fight, Sickles claimed that Lee could have turned the Federal left flank and won the battle.[5]

In the course of the 1891 flare-up of the controversy, Sickles mentioned in his reply to Carswell McClellan's article in the *New York Sun* that General Hunt thought his advanced line was a good position.[6] Also, Sickles wrote about both positions in his section of the article published by the *North American Review*. In this article, Sickles again mentioned the depressed ground north of Little Round Top and how his corps contained too few soldiers to hold that line in sufficient force. He ended his discussion of the left flank by writing that if the left of the line had been entrenched and held by at least two corps, the Confederate assault would have been repulsed as easily as had Burnside's at Fredericksburg.[7]

A brief review of Sickles' claim that the original position designated for the 3d Corps was weak shows that he incorporated five major points in defense of his forward move. First, the general argued that the Peach

Orchard line commanded the lower ground on Cemetery Ridge on which his corps was originally posted. Second, he consistently cited General Hunt's viewpoint about the better position at the Peach Orchard. Third, Sickles claimed that he did not have enough men to occupy properly the line assigned to him. Fourth, since he did not have enough men, he could not occupy Little Round Top, the key to the position at Gettysburg, so he moved forward to occupy the advanced line to prevent enemy occupation of the hill. And fifth, Sickles claimed that by moving forward to the stronger position, he gave General Meade enough time to bring up reinforcements to ensure safety to the left flank. However, as with Sickles' other claims, the argument of the weak position on Cemetery Ridge, when examined closely, also appears fallacious.

The major point around which Sickles built this part of his defense was his claim that the higher ground at the Peach Orchard would enable the enemy to dominate the lower ground where the 3d Corps was posted initially. All other statements he uttered in connection with the weak position theory revolved around this crucial point. And to some extent, this claim was indeed true. The angle at the Peach Orchard, as well as most of the 3d Corps line, was formed along the crests of two low ridges. One, beginning at the Peach Orchard, paralleled the Emmitsburg Road for about a half mile to the northeast of the orchard. The other extended from the orchard to the Devil's Den. The highest point of both ridges was the Peach Orchard knob itself, which was between thirty and forty feet higher than the lower half of Cemetery Ridge. It was this position that captured Sickles' attention.[8]

In order to justify his forward move to the Peach Orchard line, Sickles frequently cited the opinion of professional military officers regarding the sagacity of the move. He especially quoted from Henry Hunt's testimony before the Committee on the Conduct of the War to show that Meade's chief of artillery considered the advanced position the better of the two positions for the 3d Corps to occupy. But when citing Hunt's professional opinion, Sickles failed to include those portions of Hunt's testimony where that officer added his reservations about the advanced line.

In his testimony, Hunt mentioned that when leaving Meade's headquarters in Sickles' company, he asked the general why he was needed. Sickles replied that he wished to move his command from the line it then occupied to the Emmitsburg Road to cover that artery. Hunt surmised that since Sickles had left his corps ammunition train behind, he wished to ensure its safe arrival by occupying the Emmitsburg Road area. Hunt therefore examined this position and told Sickles that if he moved forward, his right flank would not be connected with the 2d Corps. Furthermore, the woods some six hundred yards in front of the proposed line could shield the advance of enemy troops. Hunt suggested a reconnaissance of the terrain to locate any possible Confederate troops.[9]

Then Hunt told Sickles that he would follow the proposed line as far as Little Round Top before reporting its description to General Meade:

> I moved down that road; it was a very good line to occupy, provided it was necessary to watch our left flank and prevent a movement by the enemy, or from which to make an offensive demonstration; but one which exposed both its own flank and the flank of the 2d corps, which would have to move forward to join it, to a cross-fire, if the enemy should take possession of the strip of woods of which I have spoken.[10]

In citing Hunt's testimony, Sickles deleted those portions in which Hunt expressed his reservations about the advanced line.

Later, Hunt wrote in more detail about his survey of the advanced line as part of his Second Day article for *The Century Magazine*. Hunt agreed with Sickles that the Peach Orchard area was commanding ground and would be a favorable position for the enemy to hold. Although Hunt recognized the weakness of a salient, he thought that the ridges were high enough to act as traverses to each other and minimize possible enfilade fire. However, the artillerist also saw that the line with the 2d Corps would be broken and that the advanced line was too long for Sickles' men to hold. Then, when riding back to Cemetery Ridge, Hunt realized how much farther in advance the Peach Orchard was than at first glance.

After summarizing his feelings about Sickles' proposed line, Hunt compared the merits of both lines:

> As to the other two lines, the choice between them would depend on circumstances. The direct short line through the woods, and including the Round Tops, could be occupied, intrenched, and made impregnable to a front attack. But, like that of Culp's Hill, it would be a purely defensive one, from which, owing to the nature of the ground and the enemy's commanding position on the ridges at the angle, an advance in force would be impracticable. The salient line proposed by General Sickles, although much longer, afforded excellent positions for our artillery; its occupation would

cramp the movements of the enemy, bring us nearer his lines, and afford us facilities for taking the offensive. It was in my judgment tactically the better of the two, provided it were strongly occupied, for it was the only one on the field from which we could have passed from the defensive to the offensive with a prospect of decisive results. But General Meade had not, until the arrival of the 6th Corps, a sufficient number of troops at his disposal to risk such an extension of his lines; it would have required both the 3d and 5th corps, and left him without any reserve. Had he known that Lee's attack would be postponed until 4 P.M., he might have occupied this line in the morning; but he did not know this, expected an attack at any moment, and, in view of the vast interests involved, adopted a defensive policy, and ordered the occupation of the safe line.[11]

Thus, Sickles failed to appreciate that although General Hunt thought the advanced line was the better tactical position to occupy, Meade's lack of reserves until the arrival of the 6th Corps made such a position untenable for the safety of the Army of the Potomac.

Many other officers had differing opinions of the strength of the original line on Cemetery Ridge, even though the lower half of the ridge might be commanded by enemy artillery posted at the Peach Orchard. General Humphreys told the Committee on the Conduct of the War that Sickles' advanced position was too far from the main line of battle and results showed that his command was driven from this line but not from the Cemetery Ridge line. Later, in 1869, Humphreys had the opportunity to visit the battlefield and walk over the ground where his division fought on July 2. After doing so, he came to the following conclusions: (1) considering both positions simply as ground to be defended, with no outside considerations, the original line was the better one to defend; (2) the Peach Orchard salient was the most serious defect in the advanced line; (3) Sickles occupied an overextended position for his small command; and (4) this line was too far from the main line to be supported properly.[12]

Another 3d Corps soldier, Capt. Edward R. Bowen of the 114th Pennsylvania, a part of General Graham's brigade of Birney's division, wrote a sketch of his regiment's participation at Gettysburg. He said the following about the original position of his command:

> Here is where we should have been allowed to remain in a naturally strong and defensible position, and where, if the enemy had had the temerity to attack us, we could and would have made a successful resistance.[13]

This sentiment was echoed by Colonel de Trobriand in his *Four Years with the Army of the Potomac.* The French veteran wrote that the first position of the 3d Corps was almost as strong as the Confederate line at Fredericksburg, and he regretted the forward move.[14]

Another linchpin associated with Sickles' claim that his first position was weak and dominated by higher ground to his front was the general's claim that the 3d Corps did not have enough soldiers to occupy with any depth the line on Cemetery Ridge. As an example, he cited Hancock's 2d Corps, which had more men than the 3d Corps but occupied a shorter front. Sickles usually enumerated his command at slightly more than ten thousand men, occupying a line of about twenty-two hundred yards. But again, Sickles erred in presenting this part of his thesis.

The strengths of the contending armies at Gettysburg have always been a subject for debate among historians of the battle. When researching the numbers of men engaged, the student has to be careful to differentiate between several different strength totals. These include "present," "present for duty," "present for duty equipped," and "effectives," not to mention the actual engaged strength of the units in question. Failure of previous researchers to pay close attention to the differences inherent in the headings listed above has led to a wide variety of interpretations for the strengths of the different corps comprising the Army of the Potomac. Even the June 30, 1863, returns for the army contain three different figures. This return includes the following statistics for the 2d and 3d Corps:

	2d Corps	3d Corps
Present	14,373	13,881
Present for duty	13,056	12,630
Present for duty equipped	12,996	11,924

The most accurate figure of the three would probably be the "Present for duty equipped," but even this strength does not account for stragglers, detached guards, and other units that did not reach the battlefield, such as the 84th Pennsylvania of the 3d Corps, which was left behind at Westminster to guard the army supplies accumulated there.[15]

A 1986 study by David G. Martin and John W. Busey, *Regimental Strengths and Losses at Gettysburg,* has sorted out most of the confusion and arrived at a new set of figures for both armies. The authors used individual regimental and battery muster rolls for June 30 as a basis for their research, rather than rely on the commonly used consolidated returns for brigade-sized and larger units. On this basis, the authors computed the June 30 "present for duty" strength of Hancock's corps at 13,631 and Sickles' 3d Corps at 13,009 soldiers.[16] However, the authors did not stop here. They combed every available regimental history, searched out state and local histories, newspaper articles, and manuscript sources to locate as many figures of actual battlefield engaged strengths for as many units as possible. For units for which no such figures could be found, Busey and Martin improved upon a system devised by Thomas L. Livermore and later used by William F. Fox. The authors calculated the engaged strengths of such regiments by using a ratio derived from the engaged strengths of all known regiments in a particular corps versus the June 30 strengths for these same units. The result was a percentage of the June 30 muster roll strength that actually reached the battlefield.[17]

On this basis, Busey and Martin calculated the engaged strength of the 2d Corps at 11,347 officers and men, while the 3d Corps brought 10,675 soldiers onto the battlefield. Hancock's corps was thus 672 men larger than Sickles', a difference that approximated the strength of two infantry regiments.[18]

In addition to claiming that the 3d Corps was small, Sickles also stated that the line he was to occupy was far too long for his command. But again, this is another of Sickles' questionable points. The frontage of Hancock's corps, from Ziegler's Grove south along Cemetery Ridge to Patterson's Woods, was about thirteen hundred yards in length. The distance from Patterson's Woods to the summit of Little Round Top is about fifteen hundred yards.[19] On the surface, it appears that General Sickles had a valid criticism of Meade's decision to allot a longer front to the smaller 3d Corps.

However, a survey of how Sickles used his troops to cover the line assigned to the 3d Corps reveals some very serious shortcomings on Sickles' part. At dusk on July 1, General Birney's 1st Division occupied the lower part of Cemetery Ridge, with Graham's and Ward's brigades, together with two artillery batteries. Graham's brigade bivouacked just south of the George Weikert farm buildings. The brigade remained in column of regiments with pickets to the front. Ward's men camped on Graham's right, in a field sandwiched between two patches of woods.[20] Birney's division was presumably in front of Greene's 12th Corps Brigade, which bivouacked farther in the rear, probably on and around the hillock where the 1st New Jersey Brigade monument is now located.[21] When Humphreys' two brigades reached the field in the early morning hours, they went into camp north of the Weikert Farm in the vicinity of Patterson's Woods.[22]

On the morning of July 2, after Geary's division vacated its position to march over to Culp's Hill, Sickles deployed Birney's command by stretching Ward's regiments from the base of Little Round Top to the north.[23] A veteran of the 20th Indiana recalled that his regiment did not move at all that morning, but remained in camp until the brigade marched forward to Houck's Ridge.[24] Graham deployed his five available regiments by placing three in a front line and two as a support line.[25] When Colonel de Trobriand's brigade arrived from Emmitsburg, Birney placed the colonel's five regiments as a reserve force behind the other two brigades.[26]

Although General Humphreys had his men in line sometime around eight o'clock in the morning, the short space held by his division forced him to keep his two brigades massed in column. Brewster's troops occupied the left and Carr's the right. Burling's 3d Brigade was massed in the rear after it reached the field later in the morning. At noon, Humphreys finally received orders to deploy his division in line of battle. Because of the limited front, the general formed Carr's brigade, reinforced by one of Brewster's regiments, as the front line. The rest of Brewster's men were formed in line of battalions in mass some two hundred yards to the rear of the first line. Burling's regiments were drawn up in mass formation two hundred yards in rear of Brewster's line.[27]

Since there were few good artillery positions, only Capt. A. Judson Clark's Battery B, New Jersey Light Artillery, and Lt. John K. Bucklyn's Battery E, 1st Rhode Island Light Artillery, were unlimbered. Both were stationed near the left of Ward's front. The remaining three batteries of the corps artillery brigade were parked in rear of the infantry.[28]

Thus, by noon, Sickles had deployed only part of the 3d Corps. Birney had two brigades in line, with de Trobriand acting as a reserve. Humphreys was allotted a compact front line and so had two of his three brigades formed as a reserve. Several regiments of the corps, notably Berdan's Sharpshooters, 63rd Pennsylvania, and 4th Maine, were used as pickets along the Emmitsburg Road to provide a screen for the main line. On the surface, it appears that Sickles had wisely deployed his command on the front assigned to him, but he completely ignored the key to the position— Little Round Top. Meade had ordered Sickles to form his command on

Hancock's left and extend the line south to the Round Tops, which were to be occupied if practicable. And Gen. Daniel E. Sickles not only found it impracticable to stretch his corps to the summit of Little Round Top, but he also failed to provide even a skirmish line to cover that hill.

If Sickles claimed that he had too few men to form his line to include Little Round Top, he apparently failed to use any initiative to vary his line somewhat both to cover the terrain to the north of Little Round Top and actually place some troops on the hill. Coddington pointed out that when Slocum received orders where to place his corps—between Rock Creek and the crest of the hill (Culp's) held by Wadsworth's division—he used his own discretion in forming his line. Rather than continue the line across the marshy swale in which Spangler's Spring was located, General Williams covered the approach to this area by deploying his regiments so as to cover that field with a crossfire should the enemy attempt to penetrate what appeared to be a gap in the Federal line.[29] Sickles could have done the same thing. His failure to do so caught Hunt's attention. The artillerist wondered why Sickles did not better deploy his men and thus allot some troops for the defense of Little Round Top.[30]

As a final rebuttal to Sickles' claim that the position on Cemetery Ridge could not have been held against an enemy assault, we must enter the realm of speculative history—the very realm in which Sickles formed a major part of the claim that his initial position was very weak. This claim is one of the major fallacies of this aspect of the general's defense of his conduct at Gettysburg. He relied on repeating that the enemy attack would have broken through his thin line on the ridge. Such a thesis is a major fallacy and is pure supposition, not fact. The enemy under Longstreet *did not* attack while the 3d Corps remained on Cemetery Ridge. Thus, we will never know how the 3d Corps might have fared had the Rebels attacked in the morning. Longstreet might have followed his orders more literally and attacked up the Emmitsburg Road toward Hancock's position, ignoring Sickles' position altogether. The result might have been a crushing Confederate defeat. Then again, had the 3d Corps remained on the ridge, the 5th Corps was closer as reinforcements. Or perhaps Longstreet might have seized Little Round Top.

Thus, it again appears that Sickles, in using the thesis of a weak position on Cemetery Ridge as part of his defense, erred very badly in presenting this argument. In doing so, he tried to cover up some major errors in his generalship that illustrated his lack of experience in battlefield command. In maintaining that the Peach Orchard ridge dominated the lower ground on which his corps was first posted, Sickles did have a valid point. However, there were some steps he could have taken to make the best of his assigned position in line. He could have altered his line to allow occupation of Little Round Top while also maintaining a defensible position on the lower ground to the north. The very fact that Sickles completely ignored Little Round Top and did not fully deploy his corps highlights some grievous errors on his part.

Sickles claimed that he did not have enough troops to defend the line adequately. If so, how was his corps supposed to defend the much longer and more exposed Peach Orchard line? Sickles conveniently ignored this criticism of his forward move, except to remark that his advance, which forced Longstreet into a frontal assault, gave General Meade time to bring up reinforcements to occupy Little Round Top before the enemy could seize it. But here, again, General Sickles overlooked the development of the battle on his front—his line was so far advanced from the rest of the army that the reinforcements arrived piecemeal. Many arriving units became detached from their corps and divisions (and from proper command and control) and were defeated in detail by Longstreet's veterans. The need to rush troops from several parts of the line endangered the entire Federal position at Gettysburg. Fortunately for the Union cause, Lee's command system broke down and his attack plan did not proceed as planned. Thus, weak spots such as the center of the line near Meade's own headquarters and the vacant entrenchments on Culp's Hill were not exploited by the uncoordinated Rebel assaults. And so, yet again, another of Sickles' major defense points appears very unconvincing indeed.

Chapter Nine

THE SUPPOSED RETREAT FROM GETTYSBURG

Not having received any orders in reference to my position, and observing, from the enemy's movements on our left, what I thought to be conclusive indications of a design on their part to attack there, and that seeming to me to be our most assailable point, I went in person to headquarters and reported the facts and circumstances which led me to believe that an attack would be made there, and asked for orders. I did not receive any orders, . . . and I was satisfied, from information which I received, that it was intended to retreat from Gettysburg.[1]

With these words, General Sickles announced to the Committee on the Conduct of the War that General Meade had contemplated retiring from the strong position at Gettysburg to make his stand at Pipe Creek. This supposed retreat plan that Meade had drawn up became one of the four major points around which Sickles defended his advance to the Peach Orchard. Later in his testimony, Sickles did state that Meade undoubtedly planned to fight at Gettysburg on July 1, or else he would not have concentrated the army on that field. However, Sickles then remarked that he had reason to know that the plan of operations had been changed and the commanding general had reverted to his idea of fighting behind Pipe Creek. But Sickles did not, and was not asked, to elaborate on what information led him to believe this.[2]

Sickles expanded further on this statement in many of his postwar speeches. During the course of a July 1882 speech, he told the audience

141

that when he rode to headquarters and asked for orders, he concluded, from General Meade's conversation and manner, that he did not intend to fight at Gettysburg. General Butterfield told Sickles that orders were being prepared at that moment to withdraw the army to Pipe Creek.[3] Here, Sickles began to cite Butterfield's role in preparing the retreat order, something he would rely on many times after the war. For example, Sickles, in his Boston Music Hall address in April 1886, did not mention anything about this supposed retreat except to state that he would defer the matter to General Butterfield, who made a speech at the Revere House that evening. And of course, in that speech, Butterfield mentioned that General Meade directed him to prepare the withdrawal order.[4]

In the course of his most-publicized speech at Gettysburg on July 2, 1886, Sickles again cited Butterfield's committee testimony as alleged proof that Meade was planning to retreat from Gettysburg. Sickles worked Butterfield's statements into a detailed analysis of the purpose of the corps commanders' conference called by General Meade at 3:00 P.M. on July 2. He cited Meade's telegram to Halleck as proof that the withdrawal was about to begin, for Meade informed his superior that if he detected any Confederate attempts to interpose between the Army of the Potomac and Washington, then he would fall back to his supply base at Westminster. To Sickles, this was why Buford was withdrawn. Since the enemy was obviously moving around the left flank,

> it may have been that he [Meade] desired to have the advice of the corps commanders on the question, whether he should accept the battle I had represented to be imminent on his left, or whether he should fall back on his supplies at Westminster, or to Pipe Creek, or to some other position more advantageous to us, in his judgment?

Even though Sickles phrased his remarks so that he was vague on what the purpose of this conference might have been, the purport of his words left no doubt to the audience that Sickles believed his advance had forced the opening of the battle and had prevented a retreat. Later in this same speech, Sickles again mentioned that Meade had determined on July 1 to give battle at Pipe Creek. Reynolds's advance to Gettysburg was designed to cover the army's concentration behind that creek.[5]

Later in 1886, when replying to Colonel Benedict's *Weekly Press* article, Sickles remarked yet again about Meade's reluctance to fight at Gettysburg.

He stated that this is why Geary was withdrawn from the left flank and Buford sent to the rear. The general again used Meade's 3:00 P.M. telegram to Halleck as alleged proof that Meade was considering retreat. Finally, Sickles quoted from a letter General Pleasonton had sent him, stating that on the afternoon of July 2, Meade ordered Pleasonton to gather some artillery and cavalry and prepare to cover the retreat.[6]

After the 1886 outburst in the battle literature, Sickles mentioned the retreat order on two more prominent occasions. First, although he did not use the word "retreat" in his 1891 article in the *North American Review*, Sickles again brought up the subject of why Meade was considering a withdrawal if the enemy threatened either flank. Since Sickles had just previously written in great detail about his knowledge of Rebel activity on his front, together with his inferior position on Cemetery Ridge, it became clear to the reader that Sickles was indeed conveying the notion that Meade was planning to withdraw from Gettysburg.[7] The second instance was his introduction to Helen Longstreet's book, in which Sickles wrote the following:

> General Meade's telegram to Halleck, dated 3 P.M., July 2, does not indicate that Lee was then about to attack him. At the time that dispatch was sent, a council of corps commanders was assembled at General Meade's head-quarters. It was broken up by the sound of Longstreet's artillery. The probability is that Longstreet's attack held the Union army at Gettysburg. If Longstreet had waited until a later hour, the Union army might have been moving towards Pipe Creek, the position chosen by General Meade on June 30.[8]

Sickles was supported in this part of his defense by several other officers, most notably Gen. Daniel Butterfield, one of his close friends. Sickles was instrumental in having Senator Chandler request Butterfield's presence before the Committee on the Conduct of the War after General Halleck had refused Butterfield permission to leave his post to come to Washington. When Butterfield was asked to relate his recollections of Gettysburg, the former chief of staff stated that shortly after his arrival on the battlefield early on July 2, General Meade directed him to prepare an order for the army to retreat. Butterfield spent a great amount of time drawing up this order, and even showed it to some other generals to make sure it was correct. Then, continued Butterfield, the order was passed along to Adj. Gen. Seth Williams' clerks for copying as Meade called a meeting of his corps commanders. However, the opening of the battle on Sickles' front prevented the retreat from starting. Butterfield did mention that the retreat order may only have been a contingency plan in case Lee did not wish to fight at Gettysburg. Even so, Butterfield remarked that it was his sincere opinion that the army would have retreated had not the fighting opened. He related this same tale after the war in his April 1886 address at the Revere House, as mentioned above, and in his part of the 1891 *North American Review* article.[9]

Two other officers also supported Sickles' contention that Meade planned to retreat from Gettysburg. One of these was Abner Doubleday, certainly no admirer of Meade after having been unfairly replaced as commander of the 1st Corps. Meade replaced Doubleday with John Newton after he heard some disparaging remarks about the 1st Corps' fighting ability from Oliver O. Howard, something Doubleday did not ascertain until years after the war. Doubleday wrote the *Chancellorsville and Gettysburg* volume for the Scribner Company's "Campaigns of the Civil War" series. Doubleday wrote that Meade indeed planned a retreat from Gettysburg on July 2.[10]

The publication of Doubleday's book touched off a storm of criticism. Some harsh language emanated from the pen of William Swinton, who objected to Doubleday's aspersions on Meade's generalship. Doubleday's reply to Swinton appeared in the April 1, 1883, edition of the *New York Times*. The general concentrated on the results of the evening council on July 2, but also included some new evidence by reproducing a letter he had received from Alfred Pleasonton, another disgruntled officer who had no liking for General Meade. In this letter, Pleasonton claimed that Meade approached him about five o'clock in the afternoon of July 2 and ordered him to gather what cavalry and artillery he could and prepare to take up a position in the rear to cover the withdrawal of the army. Pleasonton further wrote that he was engaged in this activity until 10:00 P.M., which is why he was not present at the evening council of war.[11]

Pleasonton had mentioned this same story in 1865, when he reappeared before the Committee on the Conduct of the War and made a brief report of his wartime activities. He said the following of July 2 at Gettysburg:

> On the second of July, that portion of the army that was on the field was placed in a defensive position, but General Meade had so little assurance in his own ability to maintain himself, or in the strength of his position,

that when the rebels partially broke our line on the afternoon of the 2d, he directed me to collect what cavalry I could, and prepare to cover the retreat of the army; and I was thus engaged until 12 o'clock that night. I mention this fact now, because when I was before your honorable committee and was asked the question whether General Meade ever had any idea of retreating from Gettysburg, I answered that I did not remember, and it was only afterwards recalled by my staff officers on my return to camp.[12]

As a result of Doubleday's article, in 1883 Col. George Meade published the pamphlet, *Did General Meade Desire to Retreat at the Battle of Gettysburg?*[13] Although most of this pamphlet consisted of Meade's analysis of the results of the council of war on the night of July 2, Meade also answered Doubleday's *New York Times* article by scrutinizing Pleasonton's letter, which is the only evidence that Doubleday had included in his article.

Colonel Meade remarked that Pleasonton had not written anything about his alleged activities during the late afternoon and evening of July 2 in his official report of the Gettysburg Campaign, and had not mentioned the incident in his initial committee testimony. So why, Meade wished to know, did Pleasonton suddenly remember it in 1865, when he made the later report to the committee? Although Meade did not say it in so many words, he clearly insinuated that Pleasonton had perjured himself.[14]

Indeed, Meade could find no contemporary evidence to support Pleasonton's allegations. Only the official report of Capt. James M. Robertson, commander of the 1st Brigade, Horse Artillery, even mentioned any retrograde movement on July 2. Robertson reported that about dark on July 2, he was ordered to move his batteries about two miles to the rear, where he encamped without incident before returning to his original position the next morning. No other official reports of any cavalry or artillery units present on the battlefield included any mention of a retreat. Colonel Meade wrote to Captain Robertson to ask about the withdrawal of his batteries. In reply, Robertson said that at dusk, an officer rode furiously up to him, exclaiming that Pleasonton ordered him to withdraw his guns across Rock Creek and go into position on the Baltimore Pike, since the Rebels had broken through the center of the line and the battle was lost! Meade simply commented on Robertson's answer by wondering how Pleasonton could have stated that Meade was lacking in confidence when Pleasonton himself thought the Rebels were winning the battle on the late afternoon of July 2.[15]

Sickles, Butterfield, Doubleday, and Pleasonton were the only officers who thought that Meade intended to retreat from Gettysburg. Others who testified before the committee vetoed this idea. General Hancock did state that Meade had told him on the morning of July 1 that he had decided to fight the imminent battle at Pipe Creek, even though he had not personally inspected the ground. His engineers were then engaged in surveying the terrain, and their initial reports were favorable. When Hancock departed from the battlefield on the evening of July 1 to report back to Meade at Taneytown, he stated that Meade informed him of the decision to continue the engagement at Gettysburg and that he had ordered the army to concentrate at that place. When asked if he knew of any order that would withdraw the army from the field, Hancock remarked that he had never heard of such an order.[16]

Gen. John Gibbon, another 2d Corps officer, also supported Meade's view of affairs. Gibbon told the committee the story of how Butterfield showed him the contingency retreat order he was preparing, and how, after he himself asked the chief of staff if Meade actually intended to retreat, Butterfield told him the order was merely preparatory in case something of the sort was needed. Gibbon repeated this narrative in his *Personal Recollections*. In his 1891 reply to Sickles, Gibbon wrote that when Meade visited him late in the evening of July 1 as he rode toward Gettysburg, "there could, at that time, have been no doubt in General Meade's mind about Gettysburg being a place in which to fight a battle."[17]

Chief of Artillery Henry J. Hunt also admitted his ignorance of this supposed retreat plan of General Meade's. As stated previously, Hunt noted that he would have been one of the first officers to know of any such movement, because the Artillery Reserve, consisting of over a hundred cannon with their attendant horses, men, and ammunition, together with the general reserve ammunition train, blocked the roads to the rear and would have had to withdraw prior to any general retreat by the infantry corps.[18]

General Sedgwick found the idea that Meade planned to retreat very unusual. He told the committee that if Meade desired to withdraw, why did the 6th Corps make a forced march to reach the battlefield? Sedgwick recalled that he received at least three verbal messages via staff officers urging him to move his troops forward as rapidly as possible. He did realize that Meade was naturally apprehensive that the enemy would attempt to turn his flanks and such a move would force him to change positions.[19]

Finally, Meade's adjutant general, Seth Williams, provided some evidence about the supposed retreat order. Williams admitted that to the best of his recollection and belief, Butterfield had indeed handed to him or a clerk a contingency order if the army needed to retire to a different position. He was not sure whether such an order was ever copied; if so, it was never issued and any copies were destroyed afterward. Williams was convinced that all of Meade's actions at Gettysburg illustrated that he never intended to retreat. If he had, Williams remarked that he would surely have seen evidence of the necessary preparations for such a movement.[20]

Having examined the available evidence pertaining to General Sickles' claim that Meade intended to retreat from Gettysburg on July 2, and that the opening of Longstreet's attack prevented the Union commander from carrying out this plan, we can see clearly that this contention is false. Sickles himself never mentioned specific information about Meade's planned retreat when testifying before the Committee on the Conduct of the War. Instead, he was instrumental in having his friend Dan Butterfield brought to Washington to appear before the committee. The former chief of staff elaborated on how Meade ordered him to prepare a retreat order and how the outbreak of the fighting on Sickles' front prevented the withdrawal.

The basis for this retreat was more fantasy than fact. Except for Pleasonton's 1865 testimony, there is no contemporary evidence to support Sickles' thesis. Several officers who were in a position to know of such an order—Seth Williams, Henry Hunt, John Gibbon—stated that they had never heard of it. Gibbon resolutely maintained that Butterfield told him that the order was a contingency plan, not an absolute retreat order.

Meade's own actions are the strongest refutation of the supposed retreat instructions. It is true that on the morning of July 1 Meade planned to fight the expected battle in the Pipe Creek area, and he thus sent out a circular order to his corps commanders. But this document was obsolete by the time it was issued, for the fighting at Gettysburg had already begun. Once Meade heard of the combat, he sent his trusted friend Hancock to take charge of the troops on the field while alerting the other corps commanders of the possibility of moving to Gettysburg. As the day wore on, Meade decided to risk all by concentrating at Gettysburg even before he received Hancock's favorable report. And once he made this decision, Meade never wavered. He repeatedly urged the troops to move forward as quickly as possible. Sedgwick, whose 6th Corps had to march more than thirty miles to reach the field, recalled at least three messages from headquarters urging him on.

Meade's actions on July 2 show that he was worried about an early Confederate assault on his position before the entire army was assembled on the field. This accounts for his second message to Sickles, via Captain Meade, to place his command in position as quickly as possible. Meade contemplated taking the offensive on the morning of the second, but was dissuaded by Slocum's and Warren's unfavorable terrain reports, as well as the late arrival of the 6th Corps. In summation, Meade's actions at Gettysburg hardly resembled those of a timid, confused soldier who did not want to fight at Gettysburg, as Sickles repeatedly claimed.

In addition to contending that Meade planned to retreat from Gettysburg during the day on July 2, Sickles also hinted that the council of war that evening voted to stay and fight, even though Meade himself was opposed to continuing the battle.[21] Rather than talk about something that he did not witness, Sickles relied on the testimony of other officers, primarily Dan Butterfield, to attack Meade on this occasion. Further committee testimony from Generals Birney and Howe supported Sickles, and it is the contention that Meade had to be persuaded to remain at Gettysburg that proved to be the most damaging to his reputation, since many historians have painted this picture of Meade during the council.[22]

After the fighting was over on July 2, Meade summoned many of his chief subordinates to a discussion of future plans and to find out the condition of the army. In addition to Meade, Warren, and Butterfield, the officers present included the infantry corps commanders plus Generals Gibbon and Williams, since Hancock and Slocum were acting as wing commanders. Pleasonton was absent, as were General Hunt and Gen. Robert O. Tyler of the artillery. The latter two officers were late in arriving and missed the conference. Pleasonton claimed that he was out preparing the cover for a retreat.[23]

The conference began with some general discussion about the results of the battle thus far and the losses to the army. Then followed an exchange of ideas about the strength of the position. During this discussion, General Newton expressed his opinion that Gettysburg was no place to fight a battle. After some heated discussion, he clarified his words by stating that he recommended making some minor corrections to the line, but would not retreat. Then, with Meade's assent, Butterfield put three questions before the gathering:

1. Under existing circumstances, is it advisable for this army to remain in its present position, or to retire to another, nearer its base of supplies?
2. It being determined to remain in present position, shall the army attack or await the attack of the enemy?
3. If we await attack, how long?

Of the nine officers who voted (Warren, slightly wounded during the day, fell asleep and did not vote), all were unanimous in wanting to remain in position, although Gibbon, Newton, and Hancock suggested rectifying the line slightly. Everyone also voted to defend and let the Rebels attack, with a variety of answers as to how long to wait.[24]

What did Meade want to do? Butterfield told the committee Meade said that Gettysburg was no place to fight a battle but would abide by the council's decision to remain and let the enemy attack. General Birney stated that Meade seemed indisposed to fight unless on the most favorable terms. Like Butterfield, Birney also recalled that Meade said he would follow the council's decision. General Howe said that his corps commander, General Sedgwick, told him that a retreat to Westminster was considered at the council and the issue was in doubt for some time.[25] General Slocum, in an 1883 letter to Abner Doubleday, wrote that he remembered Meade saying, "Well, gentlemen, the question is settled. We will remain here, but I wish to say that I consider this no place to fight a battle."[26]

Two Union officers who worked for the secret Bureau of Military Information also somewhat agreed with Butterfield that Meade had planned to retreat. Cols. George H. Sharpe and John C. Babcock reported to Meade's headquarters shortly before the council convened. The two men later recalled that their intelligence work in estimating Lee's strength and losses thus far during the battle seems to have been the deciding factor that kept Meade from abandoning his position at Gettysburg. Their reports indicated that only George Pickett's division was as yet unengaged in the fighting. If Meade still vacillated about what to do, recalled Sharpe and Babcock, their report infused the general with fresh confidence and made the decision to remain on the field much easier for Meade.[27]

In opposition to the statements of Butterfield and those who agreed with him, General Meade told the committee that "the opinion of the council was unanimous, which agreed fully with my own views, that we should maintain our lines as they were then held, and that we should wait the movements of the enemy and see whether he made any further attacks before we assumed the offensive." Later, after reappearing before the committee to refute Butterfield's testimony, Meade declared: "I utterly deny ever having intended or thought, for one instant, to withdraw that army . . . [u]nless the military contingencies which the future should develop during the course of the day might render it a matter of necessity that the army should be withdrawn."[28]

Indeed, Meade's statements about the council agreeing with his own view are substantiated by an 8:00 P.M. telegram that the general sent to Halleck. After summarizing the day's fighting, Meade wrote: "I shall remain in my present position to-morrow, but am not prepared to say, until better advised of the condition of the army, whether my operations will be of an offensive or defensive character." The statement about waiting until better advised of the army's condition clearly shows that Meade sent this telegram before the council, which he convened partially to learn about the army's strength and condition.[29]

The recollections of all the other officers present at the evening council substantiate Meade's verbal testimony that he agreed with the council to stay and fight at Gettysburg. When he first heard of the retreat testimony before the committee, Meade addressed a circular letter to Generals Slocum, Sedgwick, Sykes, Newton, Alpheus S. Williams, and Gibbon, asking for their recollections about the council. With the exception of Slocum, who did not reply, the remaining five officers all responded that to the best of their memory, Meade never uttered any word about wanting to retreat or even gave the appearance of being unsure of what to do.[30] During the hearings before the committee, Hancock, Gibbon, and Sedgwick mentioned that they never heard Meade express the desire to retreat and that he fully agreed with the council's votes.[31]

Postwar recollections of the generals also agreed with Meade's statements. General Newton wrote a newspaper article about Gettysburg that was published in 1887 and also wrote a private letter to General Gibbon. In both accounts, Newton mentioned that he never heard Meade consider a retreat.[32] Gibbon's postwar accounts in his *Personal Recollections* and the *North American Review* article are substantially the same as his committee testimony.[33] General Sykes confirmed his answer to the 1864 circular letter in an 1875 missive to General Gibbon.[34] In replying to a letter from Colonel Meade in 1883, General Howard recalled that he "did not hear your father utter a word which made me think that he then favored a withdrawal of his troops. . . . Certainly when your father announced the decision, which he did after a formal vote, he expressed no dissatisfaction or dissent from our opinions."[35] Finally, in 1879, General Warren talked with Lt. Col. Martin T. McMahon, assistant adjutant general on Sedgwick's staff. McMahon recalled that his superior informed him of the results of the council and said that there would be no retreat, since only Butterfield and Newton advised it.[36]

Thus, with the exception of Butterfield, Birney, and Slocum, every other officer who attended the council of war on the evening of July 2 supported Meade's claim that he never intended to retreat from Gettysburg. The individuals who did say that Meade was inclined to withdraw the army all had some grievance against Meade (or, in the case of intelligence officers Sharpe and Babcock, were not fully aware of preceding communications). Meade had displaced Butterfield as commander of the 5th Corps. Then Meade had superseded his good friend Joe Hooker as commander of the Army of the Potomac. Furthermore, Meade's search for a new chief of staff must certainly have rankled Butterfield. Given Butterfield's friendship with Sickles, it is no wonder that the New Yorker tried to tarnish Meade's reputation whenever possible.

General Birney, an officer in Sickles' 3d Corps, also had occasion to rail against his chief. At Gettysburg on July 2, Meade placed Hancock in temporary command of the 3d Corps after Sickles was wounded. Birney, a major general with seniority over the younger Hancock, later was overheard complaining to Meade about this. The son of a prominent abolitionist, Birney lacked any real military experience before the Civil War, but he became an experienced division commander as the conflict progressed. His cold demeanor and his own self-interest in promotion made him some enemies. Years after the war, General Warren recalled that Birney "had no hesitation at times to tell lies."[37]

General Slocum's failure to respond to Meade's March 1864 letter manifested the general displeasure he was experiencing at the time. Slocum was unhappy with his position ever since the 11th and 12th Corps were sent west under Hooker's overall command. In March 1864, Slocum was in charge of the Vicksburg garrison, refusing to serve under Hooker's direct command. He remained at Vicksburg until Hooker resigned from the army during the Atlanta Campaign. Slocum had also just finished reading Meade's report of the Gettysburg Campaign. In his report, Meade inadvertently failed to give proper credit for several exploits of the 12th

Corps. Slocum protested vehemently, which caused Meade to amend his report. Butterfield, as Hooker's chief of staff, may also have influenced Slocum to change his mind about Meade's generalship.[38]

After examining all the evidence, we can see quite clearly that Meade never did intend to retreat from Gettysburg unless Lee forced him to evacuate the strong defensive position occupied by the Army of the Potomac. Nevertheless, the disparaging statements of Butterfield, Doubleday, Pleasonton, and others did great damage to Meade's reputation. Because of such statements, many writers have portrayed Meade as a weak, indecisive general who owed the victory at Gettysburg to the many able subordinates he commanded.

Butterfield even persuaded prominent artist James E. Kelly to execute a drawing showing the council of war on the night of July 2; it was for inclusion in William Cullen Bryant's forthcoming United States history textbook. Kelly wrote to some of the participants for information about the council, but his letters evoked a storm of criticism. The result was that none of the generals Kelly contacted would cooperate with him. Several wrote to inform the artist that Butterfield was not a man to be trusted. Indeed, General Warren objected to the use of the words "council of war." In his mind, such a phrase indicated a conference that did not want to fight. Warren considered all such "councils" called by Meade more properly as informal gatherings of corps commanders so the generals could exchange information, be briefed on the overall situation, and voice their opinions to Meade.[39] As Warren commented: "I know he [Meade] meant to fight there next day, as long as his troops could stand, decided upon long before the 'council of war' that was held which was one that reaffirmed, and not decided."[40]

Chapter Ten

CONCLUSIONS

By spinning a contrived tale based on four major points, General Sickles attempted to explain the advance of the 3d Corps to the Peach Orchard line. First, Sickles told the Committee on the Conduct of the War that he had never received any orders from General Meade concerning the position of his command on July 2. According to Sickles, Generals Meade and Halleck were mistaken when they both wrote in their official reports that Sickles had misinterpreted his orders. How could he have done so when he did not have any orders to obey? After the war, Sickles developed this part of his defense even further by contending, in answer to those who maintained he did receive positive orders, that any order he did receive was so vague that he was left to his own devices about its interpretation. And so, any line the 3d Corps occupied during the day was taken up within the discretion allowed every corps commander.

However, an analysis of this contention reveals that Sickles did indeed receive an order to prolong the Union line south along Cemetery Ridge to Little Round Top, which was to be occupied if practicable. Defenders of Meade argued that such an order was probably issued verbally, as General Gibbon recalled that Meade told him personally where to place the 2d Corps on the morning of July 2. And if Sickles missed receiving the sketch map that Captain Paine drew and then traced for each corps commander, then he surely received a direct order when Captain Meade visited him for the second time shortly after 8:00 A.M.

Sickles also argued that when he did receive a vague order to relieve General Geary's division of the 12th Corps, he found that Geary had vacated his position before the 3d Corps troops could relieve Geary's soldiers. Thus, he could not obey the order. Even so, Sickles claimed that Geary's command had merely bivouacked on the ground and had not taken any definite position that could be easily discerned. But the available evidence suggests that Geary did indeed occupy a position and even deployed two regiments on Little Round Top. In arguing this point, Sickles resorted to playing semantics with the word "position." When troops camped overnight, they always left evidence of their presence.

Second, Sickles further developed the "no orders" theory by adding that the position he was supposed to occupy on Cemetery Ridge was a weak military position, dominated by the higher ground at the Peach Orchard. The general was correct in maintaining that the Peach Orchard ridge was indeed some forty feet higher in elevation than the lower half of Cemetery Ridge. However, in contending that his initial line was untenable, Sickles committed some very flagrant errors. The line of the 3d Corps, some 650 men weaker than the 2d Corps, was some two hundred yards longer than Hancock's frontage. Based upon these facts alone, Sickles might seem to be correct in maintaining that the line intended for his corps was too long.

However, when Sickles first deployed his corps in obedience to Meade's orders, he failed to utilize properly either the ground or his men. An analysis of the positions occupied by the 3d Corps regiments on the morning of July 2 illustrates that Sickles deployed only a portion of his command in battle formation. And if Sickles did not fully deploy his corps, he committed the even greater error of completely ignoring Little Round Top. It is rather odd that Sickles failed to comprehend the strategic value of this hill. In many of his postwar writings, Sickles argued consistently that Little Round Top was the key to the position at Gettysburg. But he never mentioned why he failed to occupy the hill, except when he stated that he did not have enough men to stretch his line that far south. Rather, Sickles' attention remained focused on the Peach Orchard ridge to his front. Lt. Col. Charles H. Morgan, inspector general on Hancock's staff, theorized that it was unfortunate that Sickles advanced to Gettysburg via the Emmitsburg Road. Morgan wrote that one gets an exaggerated impression of the importance of this ridge and correspondingly underestimates the value of the lower-elevated Cemetery Ridge.[1]

Third, in referring to the higher ground at the Peach Orchard, Sickles developed the thesis that his skirmishers discovered the Confederate advance toward the Union left flank sometime during the morning of July 2. Sickles claimed that by advancing to the Peach Orchard, he prevented General Longstreet's corps from outflanking the Army of the Potomac from its strong natural position and thus saved the battle for the Union. However, it is quite evident that Sickles used hindsight in presenting this part of his defense of his forward move. No sizable enemy units were in his front until shortly before 3:00 P.M., when McLaws' division emerged from the woods in front of the Peach Orchard to discover Sickles' men already in position there.

The historical confusion surrounding this point of Sickles' defense is connected with the Lee-Longstreet controversy on the Confederate side. Until recently, many historians who wrote about Gettysburg, especially Southern historians, tended to blame Longstreet for disobeying Lee's sunrise attack order and thus hold Longstreet responsible for the defeat. Recent studies by Glenn Tucker and Edwin B. Coddington, among others, have shown that Lee did not issue a positive order to Longstreet until 11:00 A.M. on July 2, and thus there was no order to attack at dawn, as many Virginia writers continue to argue. These early writers, as well as General Sickles, claimed that Lee's order to attack "up the Emmitsburg Road" referred to the position that Sickles occupied at the Peach Orchard, for Lee had correctly realized the strategic value of the ridge there.[2]

But research has shown that Lee's attack order was based upon Capt. Samuel R. Johnston's early morning reconnaissance of the Federal left flank. When he reported back to Lee, Johnston stated that the enemy line extended only about halfway south along Cemetery Ridge. Lee planned to use Longstreet's two available divisions to attack northeast from the Peach Orchard while Ewell's divisions assaulted the enemy right at Culp's Hill. If all went according to plan, Lee's attacks would catch the Army of the Potomac in a nutcracker and force a retreat. Sickles naturally followed the old interpretation of Lee's attack order and claimed that his position at the Peach Orchard was much more important to Lee than it actually was.

In continuing with this thesis, Sickles contended that had the Confederate forces occupied the higher ground without a fight, his own position would have been untenable since the Rebel artillery would have commanded the lower ground on Cemetery Ridge. Here Sickles indulged in speculative history that could neither be proven nor disproved, since his statements that he could not have held the original line were based on conjecture, not fact. Perhaps Longstreet would not have attacked had Sickles' troops remained on Cemetery Ridge.[3] Or perhaps the forward move did force the battle since Longstreet launched a frontal attack on the 3d Corps line. The result will never be known, of course, but Dan Sickles did such a magnificent job of stressing this "what if" scenario that many historians have fallen into the same trap and have repeated the same error of reasoning.

Fourth and finally, Sickles claimed that by moving forward and precipitating the battle on July 2, he prevented the Army of the Potomac from retreating from Gettysburg. Although Sickles himself did not mention this line of reasoning very much, the very fact that he intimated this before the Committee on the Conduct of the War led to the charge that Meade did not want to fight at Gettysburg. Meade's critics contended that he wanted to fight at Pipe Creek on July 1 and had sent out his Pipe Creek circular for that reason. However, they claimed, Reynolds' fight led the army to Gettysburg. They further stated that, once Meade arrived, he ordered Butterfield to prepare a retreat order and at 3:00 P.M. called a council of war to issue this order. Thus they said Longstreet's attack on Sickles prevented the withdrawal, and that evening, Meade again summoned a council, which talked him into staying at Gettysburg to fight on July 3.

An examination of Meade's strategy and actions throughout the battle indicates that he did not consider withdrawing unless Lee attempted to outflank him and force a retreat. The Pipe Creek circular was a contingency plan based upon what Lee might do. Meade had decided to concentrate the army at Gettysburg even before receiving Hancock's report of conditions there. The general's repeated messages to Sedgwick reveal clearly his determination to fight at Gettysburg. Meade called a conference of his corps commanders at 3:00 P.M. on July 2 when Sedgwick's corps was seen approaching the battlefield. Meade had not yet had the time to meet with all of his subordinates since being elevated to army command on June 28. And finally, all evidence suggests that Meade did not utter one word in favor of a retreat at the evening council on July 2. Sickles' claim of a retreat never did have anything to do with his position at Gettysburg. The fact that he included some vague statements in his committee testimony illustrates his training as a lawyer. Sickles knew just what to say and how to say it to deflect attention from his own shortcomings and focus them on his superior.

Having examined Sickles' contentions and seen the extent to which they were grounded in faulty reasoning, we must ask, why did Sickles advance to the Peach Orchard? The report of the Berdan-Wilcox skirmish in Pitzer's Woods was the deciding factor that brought about the 3d Corps advance, but Berdan's report was only the pinnacle of the iceberg. There is much evidence that Sickles was very dissatisfied with his initial position on Cemetery Ridge. He was slow in deploying his troops, he did not deploy the entire corps, and finally, he did not occupy Little Round Top. Instead, Sickles seems to have been mesmerized by the Peach Orchard ridge. There is a key statement in Sickles' reply to General Hunt's request for information while the latter was drafting his articles for *The Century Magazine*. In reply to Hunt, Sickles wrote:

> [B]etween Hancock's left and Round Top there was a low, marshy swale and a rocky, wooded belt unfit for artillery & bad front for infantry. Hence my anxiety to get out of the hole where I was & move up to the commanding ground—en echelon to the 2d Corps & covering Round Top as well as the Emmettsburg [*sic*] Road & the intersecting roads leading to our left flank.[4]

What did Sickles mean by his "anxiety to get out of the hole"? As mentioned above, the clinching factor in the advance of the 3d Corps was Berdan's report of Rebels moving south in the woods in front of the Peach Orchard. Sickles was anxious to prevent enemy occupation of the high ground, probably as a result of his experience at Chancellorsville just two months previous. During this former battle, Sickles' corps had occupied Hazel Grove, the commanding ground in the center of Hooker's position near the Chancellor House. After Hooker ordered its abandonment, the Confederates were quick to take advantage of the terrain and placed several artillery batteries in position at Hazel Grove. Their fire added to the many Federal casualties in the May 3 fighting. This experience undoubtedly accounted for much of Sickles' worry over the higher ground at the Peach Orchard. He would not want a repeat performance of Jackson's attack on the 11th Corps at Chancellorsville, where thousands of enemy soldiers suddenly emerged from the woods to rout that hapless Federal corps.

But in moving forward, Sickles jeopardized the entire Federal line. He failed to recognize the importance of Little Round Top, and by isolating himself from immediate support, forced Meade to throw in reinforcements piecemeal as they arrived. Many of these units were defeated in detail by Longstreet's brigades. Meade was fortunate that Lee's command system broke down. Ewell failed to take advantage of the weakened Federal right flank on Culp's Hill. Moreover, several uncoordinated assaults on the center of the position near Meade's own headquarters and against Cemetery Hill failed miserably, in part because of Meade's ability to shift units quickly from one part of the line to another. It is true that Sickles may have forced Longstreet into a frontal assault that weakened his command and forced Lee to attack the center the next day. However, it is also true that any adventure into the realm of speculative history will remain just that—an adventure into a fantasy world.[5]

Thus Sickles advanced his command in part because of his Chancellorsville experience and in part because of Berdan's report of Confederates moving across his front. Was this a disobedience of orders, as some historians claimed? The answer is, very definitely—even had Meade's order been so vague as Sickles claimed, it apparently was definite enough to have been obeyed had Sickles desired to do so. Sickles did claim that he acted within the discretion allowed a corps commander, but even this defense of his advance is too far-fetched to be believed after examining all the evidence available. Sickles disobeyed orders, and even though he thought he was bettering Meade's instructions, the very fact that he moved his command as if acting independently from the rest of the army illustrates this disobedience.

Many postwar historians have not taken Sickles' personality and character into account when writing about his actions in that battle. Understanding Sickles' personal traits is key to understanding some of the motives behind his relentless attacks on the criticism of his Gettysburg performance. Sickles' personality was such that he would not admit to making a mistake, let alone to disobeying orders. Meade was generous enough to write in his official report that Sickles had misinterpreted his orders, but to someone like Daniel Edgar Sickles, this statement reflected upon his judgment as a corps commander. Thus, Sickles attempted, with a great deal

of success, to deflect most of the criticism from his actions by casting aspersions upon Meade's generalship. To Sickles, this was merely playing politics. Yet his action against Meade was not an isolated case in the Army of
the Potomac. The army was continually plagued by malcontents of differing political alignments, such as those who sought to have Burnside
removed from command after the battle of Fredericksburg, and those
many army officers who were opponents of McClellan. Sickles was friendly
with Hooker and Butterfield, and the former officer, who went to Washington to complain about Burnside's generalship, may have influenced
Sickles to some degree.[6] By playing this kind of dirty politics, Sickles damaged Meade's reputation and effectively damaged Gettysburg historiography. General Hunt was keen enough to see this; in writing to the editors
of *The Century Magazine*, he remarked: "In fact the controversy is queer.
With Sickles' friends, it is 'which was the best line to adopt.' The *real* one
is 'Was Sickles justified in departing from his instructions if he understood
them.'"[7]

Sickles' postwar career also fueled the general's continual efforts to
defend his record at Gettysburg. Initially after the war, Sickles was placed
in command of the military district embracing the Carolinas to enforce
Northern reconstruction. However, President Johnson, after receiving
numerous complaints about Sickles' "overzealousness" in the prosecution
of his duties, removed him in 1867. Two years later, Sickles was named
minister to Spain, a position he held until he resigned in 1873. While in
Madrid, Sickles acquired the nickname "Yankee King of Spain" because of
his influence in the Spanish court, especially regarding his relationship
with Queen Isabella. Through his efforts, a short-lived Spanish republic
was established, but its collapse forced Sickles to leave his post.

Back in the United States, Sickles became chairman of the New York
State Monuments Commission in 1886, but he was forced to resign in
1912 amidst rumors of embezzlement. Sickles was also a New York con-
gressman during the 1893–1895 period, during which time his greatest
contribution was to have the Gettysburg battlefield transferred from a private memorial association to the federal government, thus ensuring the
battlefield's preservation as a memorial for future generations of Americans.

Along with his career failures, Sickles had an unfortunate personal
life after the war. After leaving Spain, he married a second time while in
Europe. When he returned to America, his wife refused to join him. They

were reconciled only at his deathbed in 1914. Sickles also squandered the fortune left him by his father, and he constantly sought new sources of capital to pay for his continued extravagant lifestyle. In effect, the continued postwar failures made Sickles more determined than ever to protect what he thought was his greatest achievement—his role in the Battle of Gettysburg.

Sickles never had a problem getting his side of the story into the press. In spite of his dubious personal traits, he had many influential friends. Sickles himself was such a colorful figure because of his military service and escapades in Spain that he was never at a loss for publicity. And with all the opportunities for publicity, Sickles never missed a chance to speak out on what he did at Gettysburg. And, unfortunately, since Sickles outlived all the other actors in this drama, his repeated claims received much more publicity than those of Meade, who died in 1872.

General Meade was a radically different personality type from Sickles. A brief summary of his personality traits goes a long way in upholding the truth of his statements about Gettysburg. As mentioned in Chapter 1, Meade's prewar career was unspectacular but solid. The same can be said of his wartime experience prior to Gettysburg. Meade was absolutely candid, diligent in his duty, and had no aspirations to the high command so suddenly entrusted to him. He refused to participate in the partisan politicking so prevalent in the Army of the Potomac and instead preferred to immerse himself in his duties, the responsibility of which weighed him down at times. While the general had a quick temper, he was conservative in his approach to problems, at times jeopardizing his own career in putting the safety of his soldiers first. On the whole, Meade was a reliable, capable officer whose attention was fixed on his duty, with no concern for posterity or how others saw him.

Meade's character helps explain his silence on the controversy stirred up by General Sickles. As he told Colonel Benedict in 1870, Meade preferred to let his record and his committee testimony speak for him. The bad press Meade received at the time of the committee hearings, coupled with a June 1864 incident with *Philadelphia Inquirer* reporter Edward Cropsey, led him to mistrust newspapermen and thus he never publicized his own version of Gettysburg.[8] But an analysis of his actions during the battle reveals that there is a consistent story told by his son George and by his friends, especially Generals Gibbon, Warren, and Hunt, very much unlike the inconsistent "facts" presented by Sickles and his supporters. Considering Meade's character, this consistency is not surprising at all, and is corroborated by Meade's own personality.

Meade's one major shortcoming, as far as the controversy with Sickles is concerned, is that Meade personally failed to examine the army's left flank until he met with Sickles sometime after 3:00 P.M. He did make a predawn reconnaissance of the entire battle line, but Captain Paine recalled that this survey failed to reveal the Peach Orchard area and the fact that there was a low ridge in that area.

Meade's early order to Sickles to occupy Cemetery Ridge south of Hancock's corps may indeed have been less than precise. But as Coddington has pointed out, Meade's instructions to Slocum were equally vague as to the exact position to be occupied, but Slocum obeyed his order by using his own discretion as to the best way to deploy his troops within the limits of his orders. Sickles could have done the same thing but instead chose to disobey his orders. In 1864, Meade did admit that Cemetery Ridge was not very perceptible where Sickles was supposed to deploy his corps, but that position was clear enough to the observer looking south from Hancock's position.[9]

Meade also ignored Little Round Top. However, this statement presupposes that Meade would know in advance that Sickles did not occupy that hill, as he had been instructed to do. Apparently, Meade did not know of Sickles' vacillation in regard to his original position until Sickles appeared at headquarters at 11:00 A.M., when Meade pointed south to the hills and told Sickles to anchor his left flank there. Thereafter, Meade and his supporters claimed that nothing more was heard about Sickles' actions until some of Warren's aides reported a problem at 3:00 P.M. But the question remains as to why Meade failed to notice that Sickles did not occupy Little Round Top. Glenn Tucker theorized that Meade may have regarded the battle lines of the opposing armies as running generally from east to west, but there is no contemporary evidence to verify this idea.[10] Also, the statement that Meade should have inspected the line personally insinuates that Meade had no confidence in the abilities of his corps commanders, all of whom were West Pointers except Sickles. Only in hindsight can one say that Meade should have checked his position in person.

General Hunt, after conducting the research for his three articles for *The Century Magazine*, came to have a high regard for Meade's generalship at Gettysburg. He later wrote to General Webb:

> Meade was suddenly placed in command. From that moment *all* his acts and intentions, as I can judge them, were just what they *ought* to have been, except perhaps in his order to attack at Falling Waters on the morning of the 13th, and especially on the 14th of July, when his Corps Commanders reported against it; and I was *then* in favor of the attack, so I can't blame him. He was *right* in his orders as to Pipe Creek; *right* in his determination under certain circumstances to fall back to it; *right* in pushing up to Gettysburg after the battle commenced; *right* in remaining there; *right* in making his battle a purely defensive one; *right*, therefore, in taking the line he did; *right* in not attempting a *counter-attack* at *any* stage of the battle; *right* as to his pursuit of Lee. Rarely has more skill, vigor, or wisdom been shown under such circumstances as he was placed in, and it would, I think, belittle his grand record of that campaign by a formal defense against his detractors, who will as surely go under as will this show story.[11]

Unfortunately, General Hunt was mistaken about the harmless and temporary nature of the claims by Sickles and his supporters. Their story of the battle of Gettysburg has survived to the present day and detracts from the actual history of the battle. Much of the reason for its long life stems from the faulty research of most students of the Gettysburg Campaign. The continuing debate over the many controversies of this most famous of all Civil War battles would be helped immensely by a thorough examination of *all* the material. Only then will the historical record be set straight.

NOTES

Notes to Preface

1. "The New Battle of Gettysburg," *New York Tribune*, August 8, 1886.
2. Edwin B. Coddington, "The Strange Reputation of George G. Meade: A Lesson in Historiography," *The Historian* 23 (1962): 147.
3. Harry W. Pfanz, *Gettysburg: The Second Day* (Chapel Hill: University of North Carolina Press, 1988).

Notes to Chapter 1

1. For a concise summary of the Confederate invasion plans, see Edwin B. Coddington, *The Gettysburg Campaign: A Study in Command* (New York: Charles Scribner's Sons, 1968; reprint, Dayton, Ohio: Morningside, 1979), 4–11. For a more wide-ranging approach, see James A. Kegel, *North with Lee and Jackson: The Lost Story of Gettysburg* (Mechanicsburg, Pa.: Stackpole Books, 1996), 219–38. Kegel contends quite persuasively that Stonewall Jackson had first proposed a Northern invasion in late 1861, and that Lee wanted to carry out this plan, but was thwarted by Federal moves until after Chancellorsville.
2. Coddington, *Gettysburg Campaign*, 11–22.
3. Ibid., 373–78; Edward J. Nichols, *Toward Gettysburg: A Biography of General John F. Reynolds* (University Park: The Pennsylvania State University Press, 1958), 182–84, 220–23.
4. See Coddington, *Gettysburg Campaign*, 48–49, 54, for Hooker's reaction to the intelligence reports of enemy movements. For a more detailed analysis and narrative of Union intelligence activities from late May through June 9, see Edwin C. Fishel, *The Secret War for the Union: The Untold Story of Military Intelligence in the Civil War* (Boston: Houghton Mifflin, 1996), 414–32.

5. Coddington, *Gettysburg Campaign*, 52–53, 66–67.

6. See ibid., 38–39, 97–100, for a discussion of the Union enlistment terminations and the reinforcements from Washington to replace these regiments. There is voluminous literature on the strengths of the two armies during the Gettysburg Campaign. The study by John Busey and David G. Martin, *Regimental Strengths and Losses at Gettysburg* (Hightstown, N.J.: Longstreet House, 1986) pulls together all previously published material and also utilizes archival material to arrive at the most accurate battlefield strengths ever computed. This book was originally published in 1982 as *Regimental Strengths at Gettysburg;* the second edition corrected some minor errors, added some new figures, and presented losses for both armies.

7. The most detailed account of the fighting at Winchester is Wilbur S. Nye, *Here Come the Rebels!* (Baton Rouge: Louisiana State University Press, 1965), 66–123.

8. Details of the Confederate invasion of Pennsylvania can be found in Nye, *Here Comes the Rebels!*, 124–62, 212–356; Coddington, *Gettysburg Campaign*, 134–79; and Jacob Hoke, *The Great Invasion of 1863, or, General Lee in Pennsylvania* (Dayton, Ohio: W. J. Shuey, 1887), 89–233.

9. Stuart's role in the Gettysburg Campaign is highly controversial. Many of the Confederate leaders blamed his raid behind Federal lines as part of the reason for the defeat at Gettysburg, while his aide Henry B. McClellan and former partisan ranger John S. Mosby vigorously defended Stuart's honor.

10. See John Bakeless, "James Harrison: Rebel Enigma," *Civil War Times Illustrated* 9 (April 1970): 12–20, for a sketch of Longstreet's agent behind Federal lines and his role in bringing news to Lee during the campaign.

11. On Hooker and Harper's Ferry, see Coddington, *Gettysburg Campaign*, 130–33; and Andrew T. McReynolds, "Maj. Gen. Hooker, " *Washington Sunday Herald*, December 7, 1879.

12. Coddington, *Gettysburg Campaign;* McReynolds, "Maj. Gen. Hooker."

13. Coddington, *Gettysburg Campaign*, 131–33.

14. The biographical information about Sickles is taken from W. A. Swanberg, *Sickles the Incredible* (New York: Charles Scribner's Sons, 1956), 77–198. Swanberg's book is heavily biased in favor of the general, but remains the best sketch of Sickles yet in print. The only other major biography is that by Edgcumb Pinchon, *Dan Sickles: Hero of Gettysburg and "Yankee King of Spain"* (Garden City, N.Y.: Doubleday, Doran, 1945). Pinchon's book is overly laudatory and contains no footnotes for verification of his sources. A more recent biography by Jeanne W. Knoop, *"I Follow the Course, Come What May": Major General Daniel E. Sickles, USA* (New York: Vantage Press, 1998), adds nothing new to the existing literature on Sickles.

15. The usual account relied upon by historians for the details of Meade's appointment to command is that by Charles F. Benjamin, "Hooker's Appointment and Removal," *The Century Magazine* 33 (November 1886): 106–11, reprinted in Robert U. Johnson and Clarence C. Buel, eds., *Battles and Leaders of the Civil War, Based upon "The Century War Series,"* 4 vols. (New York: Century, 1884–89), 3: 239–43 (hereafter, all references to this series are from vol. 3, *Battles and Leaders*).

However, Coddington, *Gettysburg Campaign*, 664–65, notes 30 and 38, convincingly points out some major flaws in Benjamin's story. On Meade's problems with Hooker, see Coddington, *Gettysburg Campaign*, 116–19; and Nichols, *Toward Gettysburg*, 180–82.

16. For Meade's background and personality, I have relied upon Freeman Cleaves, *Meade of Gettysburg* (Norman: University of Oklahoma Press, 1960; reprint, Dayton, Ohio: Press of Morningside, 1980), 3–114. Older biographies include those by Richard M. Bache, *Life of General George Gordon Meade, Commander of the Army of the Potomac* (Philadelphia: Henry T. Coates, 1897); Isaac R. Pennypacker, *General Meade* (New York: D. Appleton, 1901); and a compilation by his son, George Meade, *The Life and Letters of George Gordon Meade*, 2 vols. (New York: Charles Scribner's Sons, 1913; reprint, Baltimore: Butternut & Blue, 1994).

17. United States War Department, *The War of the Rebellion: A Compilation of the Official Records of the Union and Confederate Armies*, 70 vols. in 128 parts (Washington, D.C.: Government Printing Office, 1880–1901), vol. 27, part 1, 61. Hereafter, all references are abbreviated as *O.R.*, with appropriate volume and part.

18. Coddington, *Gettysburg Campaign*, 217–18.

19. *O.R.*, vol. 27, part 1, 61–62.

20. For the locations of the corps, see Coddington, *Gettysburg Campaign*, map between 180 and 181; *O.R.*, vol. 27, part 1, 143.

21. Ibid.

22. Coddington, *Gettysburg Campaign*, 220–21. Kilpatrick's two brigade commanders were Elon J. Farnsworth and George A. Custer. The third new brigadier was Wesley Merritt, who was assigned to command of the Reserve Brigade, 1st Division. Custer and Merritt were both captains prior to their promotions to general.

23. Ibid., 218–19.

24. Ibid., 218; Cleaves, *Meade of Gettysburg*, 124–25; Gouverneur K. Warren to Winfield S. Hancock, October 1, 1879, copy in G. K. Warren Papers, New York State Library, Albany, N.Y.

25. *O.R..*, vol. 27, part 1, 66–67.

26. *O.R..*, vol. 27, part 3, 395–96.

27. Ibid., 398–99.

28. On the bad maps, see Cleaves, *Meade of Gettysburg*, 131; Emily Warren Roebling to G. K. Warren, December 18, 1877, Warren Papers; William H. Paine to George Meade, May 22, 1886, George G. Meade Papers, Historical Society of Pennsylvania, Philadelphia, Pa. Warren sent Lieutenant Washington A. Roebling of his staff to Trenton, New Jersey, because Roebling mentioned that his father had a topographical map of Pennsylvania. He returned to headquarters on July 1. See D. B. Steinman, *Builders of the Bridge: The Story of John Roebling and His Son* (New York: Harcourt, Brace, 1945), 258. See also a message from General Howard to General Reynolds, June 30, 1863, in *O.R.*, vol. 27, part 3, 419, in which Howard asked Reynolds for a map of Adams County, Pennsylvania, as he did not have any at 11th Corps headquarters.

29. The order of march is in *O.R.*, vol. 27, part 3, 402.

30. Ibid., 416.

31. See Meade to Halleck, July 1, 1863, in ibid., vol. 27, part 1, 70–71; and Meade to Mrs. Meade, June 30, 1863, in Meade, *Life and Letters*, 2: 18.

32. For an analysis of the Pipe Creek line, see Frederic S. Klein, "Meade's Pipe Creek Line," *Maryland Historical Magazine* 57 (1962): 133–49.

33. The Pipe Creek circular is in *O.R.*, vol. 27, part 3, 458–59.

34. *O.R.*, vol. 27, part 1, 70–71.

35. For Buford's reports, see *O.R.*, vol. 27, part 1, 923–24.

36. *O.R.*, vol. 27, part 3, 416.

37. Ibid., 460.

38. Meade, *Life and Letters*, 2: 35–36; Cleaves, *Meade of Gettysburg*, 134–35.

39. *O.R.*, vol. 27, part 1, 924.

40. *O.R.*, vol. 27, part 3, 461. This order was timed 12:30 P.M.

41. Ibid., 462.

42. United States Congress, Joint Committee on the Conduct of the War, *Report of the Joint Committee on the Conduct of the War, at the Second Session Thirty–eighth Congress*, vol. 1, *Army of the Potomac, Battle of Petersburg* (Washington, D.C.: Government Printing Office, 1865), 348 (hereafter abbreviated as *C.C.W.*).

43. *O.R.*, vol. 27, part 3, 461.

44. Ibid., 457–58; Coddington, *Gettysburg Campaign*, 283.

45. *O.R.*, vol. 27, part 1, 924–25.

46. *O.R.*, vol. 27, part 3, 465–66; Coddington, *Gettysburg Campaign*, 714, note 9.

47. *O.R.*, vol. 27, part 1, 71–72.

48. Meade, *Life and Letters*, 2: 38.

49. *O.R.*, vol. 27, part 1, 366.

50. Coddington, *Gettysburg Campaign*, 298–99. For Warren's presence on the field, see Warren to Theodore Lyman, June 18, 1877, copy in Warren Papers.

51. *O.R.*, vol. 27, part 3, 420.

52. Ibid., 419, 424–25; Coddington, *Gettysburg Campaign*, 231–32.

53. Swanberg, *Sickles the Incredible*, 202, using Henry E. Tremain, *Two Days of War: A Gettysburg Narrative and Other Excursions* (New York: Bonnell, Silver & Bowers, 1905), 14. Sickles' failure to march the 3d Corps to Gettysburg after receiving Reynolds's suggestion touched off a postwar controversy with members of Reynolds's staff, who asserted that Reynolds ordered Sickles to the front on the morning of July 1 and Sickles disobeyed these instructions. See the following literature: "Another Gettysburg. Col. Norris Charges that Sickles Disobeyed Orders," Philadelphia *Weekly Press*, July 7, 1886; James Beale, "Reynolds and Sickles. Mr. Beale's Important Statement Regarding Gettysburg," *Philadelphia Press*, July 12, 1886; A. Wilson Norris, "The Gettysburg Controversy," *Philadelphia Press*, July 14, 1886; Joseph G. Rosengarten, "Was Sickles Dilatory in Moving to the Front?" *Philadelphia Press*, August 15, 1886; Daniel E. Sickles, "Sickles Defends the Course Pursued by Him at Gettysburg," *National Tribune*, August 26, 1886; Hoke, *Great Invasion*, 558–70.

54. Swanberg, *Sickles the Incredible*, 202.
55. Ibid.; Tremain, *Two Days of War*, 18; *O.R.*, vol. 27, part 3, 463.
56. *O.R.*, vol. 27, part 3, 364–65; *O.R.*, vol. 51, part 1, 1066.
57. *O.R.*, vol. 27, part 3, 466.
58. Ibid., 468. Meade had already left Taneytown for Gettysburg when this message arrived at headquarters.
59. Ibid., 467–68.
60. Andrew A. Humphreys to Archibald Campbell, August 6, 1863; Official Report of Charles Hamlin, August 11, 1863; Humphreys to John Watts De Peyster, July 21, 1869, all in Humphreys Papers, Historical Society of Pennsylvania, Philadelphia, Pa.
61. Coddington, *Gettysburg Campaign*, 324.

Notes to Chapter 2

1. Emerson G. Taylor, *Gouverneur Kemble Warren: The Life and Letters of an American Soldier, 1830–1882* (Boston: Houghton Mifflin, 1932), 122, from the original letter of Warren to Theodore Lyman, June 18, 1877, copy in Warren Papers.
2. William H. Paine to Theodore Lyman, June 27, 1877, copy in Warren Papers. See also Paine's diary entry for July 1 in his 1863 diary, William H. Paine Papers, New York Historical Society, New York, N.Y.
3. John Gibbon, *Personal Recollections of the Civil War* (New York: G. P. Putnam's Sons, 1928; reprint, Dayton, Ohio: Press of Morningside, 1978), 133.
4. George Meade, *With Meade at Gettysburg*, ed. George G. Meade (Philadelphia: John C. Winston, 1930), 95–96; Paine to Lyman, June 27, 1877, copy in Warren Papers. Coddington, *Gettysburg Campaign*, 713–14, note 2, points out the discrepancies in the reporting of the time of Meade's arrival at Gettysburg.
5. For a general description of the Union positions, see John B. Bachelder to Fitzhugh Lee, January 23, 1878, John B. Bachelder Papers, New Hampshire Historical Society, Concord, N.H.
6. Paine to Lyman, June 27, 1877, copy in Warren Papers; Meade, *With Meade at Gettysburg*, 96. Paine was a very quick mapmaker. "His habit was to place a board on the pommel of his saddle and sketch out the topographical features before him while riding. Making use of the lithographical process and having his assistants trained according to his own methods, he would complete in a day a map that other engineers required three weeks to produce." *National Cyclopaedia of American Biography*, 63 vols. (New York: J. T. White, 1898–1984), 21: 242.
7. Meade, *With Meade at Gettysburg*, 96–97; George Meade, "Notes on the 2d Day at Gettysburg," Fitz-John Porter Papers, Library of Congress, Washington, D.C.; Gibbon, *Personal Recollections*, 133–34.
8. Bachelder to Lee, January 27, 1878, Bachelder Papers; Henry J. Hunt, "The Second Day at Gettysburg," *Battles and Leaders*, 3: 294–97; Meade, *With Meade at Gettysburg*, 97–99.
9. Meade, *With Meade at Gettysburg*, 100.

10. For this order, see *O.R.*, vol. 27, part 3, 487. Or at least Meade associated this particular order with the supposed retreat order. See Meade's testimony in *C.C.W.*, 438.
11. Gibbon, *Personal Recollections*, 139.
12. George Meade to Henry J. Hunt, July 22, 1886, Henry J. Hunt Papers, Library of Congress, Washington, D.C.; Meade to Alexander S. Webb, December 7, 1885, Alexander S. Webb Papers, Yale University, copy in Robert Brake Collection, United States Army Military History Institute, Carlisle, Pa. Meade, "Notes on the 2d Day," Porter Papers; Meade, *With Meade at Gettysburg*, 100. General Meade's son George held the rank of captain during the Gettysburg Campaign. Later he rose to the rank of brevet lieutenant colonel. When referring to George's postwar writings, I refer to him as Colonel Meade, and as Captain Meade during the Gettysburg Campaign.
13. Meade to Hunt, July 22, 1886, Hunt Papers; Meade, "Notes on the 2d Day," Porter Papers; Meade, *With Meade at Gettysburg*, 100–101.
14. Meade to Hunt, July 22, 1886, Hunt Papers; Meade, "Notes on the 2d Day," Porter Papers; Meade, *With Meade at Gettysburg*, 101–102.
15. Ibid.
16. *O.R.*, vol. 27, part 1, 482 (General Birney's report).
17. *O.R.*, vol. 27, part 3, 486–87.
18. *O.R.*, vol. 27, part 1, 72; *C.C.W.*, 331.
19. *C.C.W.*, 331. See also George G. Benedict, "General Meade's Letter on Gettysburg," Philadelphia *Weekly Press*, August 14, 1886, reprinted in Meade, *Life and Letters*, 2: 350–54, on 354.
20. Hunt, "Second Day," 297, 301–2; *C.C.W.*, 449 (Hunt's testimony).
21. Hunt, "Second Day," 302; *C.C.W.*, 449–50.
22. On this skirmish, see Colonel Berdan's report in *O.R.*, vol. 27, part 1, 515; Charles A. Stevens, *Berdan's U. S. Sharpshooters in the Army of the Potomac 1861–1865* (St. Paul, Minn.: Price-McGill, 1892; reprint, Dayton, Ohio: Press of Morningside, 1972), 303–15.
23. Coddington, *Gettysburg Campaign*, 360–63; Douglas S. Freeman, *Lee's Lieutenants: A Study in Command*, 3 vols. (New York: Charles Scribner's Sons, 1942–44), 3: 106–10.
24. Coddington, *Gettysburg Campaign*, 363–67.
25. Ibid., 368–70.
26. Ibid., 370–71.
27. Ibid., 371.
28. Ibid., 372–73.
29. Ibid., 374–75; Freeman, *Lee's Lieutenants*, 3: 111–13.
30. Coddington, *Gettysburg Campaign*, 374, 277–78; Freeman, *Lee's Lieutenants*, 3: 113–14. For Lee's battle plan, see his reports in *O.R.*, vol. 27, part 2, 308, 318–19.
31. Coddington, *Gettysburg Campaign*, 375–78; Freeman, *Lee's Lieutenants*, 3: 115, 118; *O.R.*, vol. 27, part 2, 358.

32. Coddington, *Gettysburg Campaign*, 384; Freeman, *Lee's Lieutenants*, 3: 117; *O.R.*, vol. 27, part 2, 613–14 (Anderson's report).
33. Coddington, *Gettysburg Campaign*, 378–79; Freeman, *Lee's Lieutenants*, 3: 116. The Union signalmen did not detect Longstreet's men at this time. Later they did notice the corps as it moved north along Herr Ridge. See the reports of 1:30 P.M. and 2:10 P.M. in *O.R.*, vol. 27, part 3, 488.
34. Coddington, *Gettysburg Campaign*, 379. There is some doubt whether McLaws's division continued in the lead during the countermarch or whether Hood's division led. For differing accounts, see ibid., 379–80; Joseph B. Kershaw, "Kershaw's Brigade at Gettysburg," *Battles and Leaders*, 3: 332; and Lafayette McLaws, "The Battle of Gettysburg," in United Confederate Veterans, Georgia Division, Confederate Veterans' Association, Camp 756, Savannah, *Addresses Delivered before the Confederate Veterans Association of Savannah, Georgia, 1896* (Savannah, Ga: Press of George N. Nichol, 1896), 70.
35. McLaws, "Battle of Gettysburg," 75, quoting from his earlier speech printed as "Gettysburg," *Southern Historical Society Papers* 7 (1879): 69–70.
36. Kershaw, "Kershaw's Brigade at Gettysburg," 332; McLaws, "Battle of Gettysburg," 75–76.
37. McLaws, "Battle of Gettysburg," 77–78.
38. Freeman, *Lee's Lieutenants*, 3: 119–20.
39. Meade, *With Meade at Gettysburg*, 106–7. For the order relieving Buford, see *O.R.*, vol. 27, part 3, 1086, and for the replacements, see ibid., 490. The identity of the regiment from Gregg's command has never been ascertained.
40. On Sickles' advance to the Plum Run Line, see *C.C.W.*, 380 (Humphreys' testimony). See also *O.R.*, vol. 27, part 1, 531 (Humphreys' report).
41. *O.R.*, vol. 27, part 1, 482–83 (Birney's report), 532 (Humphreys' report). On the advance of Humphreys' division, see Gibbon, *Personal Recollections*, 135–36; *C.C.W.*, 406 (Hancock's testimony), 440 (Gibbon's testimony); and Frank A. Haskell, *The Battle of Gettysburg* (Madison: Wisconsin History Commission, 1908), 40–42.
42. See *O.R.*, vol. 27, part 3, 1086, for this circular message to the corps commanders.
43. *O.R.*, vol. 27, part 1, 72.
44. George Meade, "Notes on the 5th Corps & Round Top at Gettysburg," Porter Papers. The exact order of events at the 3:00 P.M. conference and after is almost impossible to ascertain. See Meade, *With Meade at Gettysburg*, 108, for a summary of the conference. See also Warren to Lyman, June 18, 1877, copy in Warren Papers; and *C.C.W.*, 460, where General Sedgwick recalled that Meade had already ridden out to see Sickles when he (Sedgwick) arrived at headquarters.
45. These two paragraphs are based on the following: Meade, "Notes on the 2d Day,"' James C. Biddle to George Meade, August 18, 1880, Meade Papers; William H. Paine to George Meade, May 22, 1886, Meade Papers; and Warren to Lyman, June 18, 1877, copy in Warren Papers. For more information, see James C. Biddle to wife Gertrude, July 8, 1863, Biddle Letters, Historical Society of Pennsylvania,

Philadelphia, Pa; Biddle to George Meade, June 10, 1886, Meade Papers; James Starr to George Meade, September 7, 1880, Meade Papers; Meade, *With Meade at Gettysburg*, 114–15; and Tremain, *Two Days of War*, 63.

46. There is disagreement over how Warren went to the left—by his own suggestion or at Meade's order. Warren, in *C.C.W.*, 377, stated that he went by Meade's direction, but later reversed his story and said he suggested to Meade that he attend to the safety of the left. See Warren to Porter Farley, July 13, 1872, in Oliver W. Norton, *The Attack and Defense of Little Round Top, Gettysburg, July 2, 1863* (New York: Neale, 1913; reprint, Dayton, Ohio: Press of Morningside, 1978), 308–9.

47. Warren to Farley, July 13, 1872, in Norton, *Attack and Defense*, 309; *O.R.*, vol. 27, part 1, 202 (report of Capt. Lemuel B. Norton, Chief Signal Officer); Taylor, *Gouverneur Kemble Warren*, 127.

48. Cleaves, *Meade of Gettysburg*, 149. See also Meade, "Notes on the 5th Corps," Porter Papers; and Norton, *Attack and Defense*, 309. For details of Humphreys' brief movement, see Humphreys to John W. De Peyster, July 21, 1869, Humphreys Papers, Historical Society of Pennsylvania, Philadelphia, Pa.

49. Reese to Warren, March 11, 1886, Warren Papers.

50. Mackenzie to Meade, March 22, 1864, in *O.R.*, vol. 27, part 1, 138.

51. Norton, *Attack and Defense*, 263–64.

52. There is voluminous literature on the battle for Little Round Top. On Vincent's role in getting to the hill, see Warren to Farley, July 24, 1872, in Norton, *Attack and Defense*, 311–12. See ibid., 253–70, for a summary of the fighting.

53. On Sickles' wound, see George E. Randolph to John B. Bachelder, March 4, 1886, Bachelder Papers; and W. H. Bullard to Sickles, September 13, 1897, Sickles Papers, New-York Historical Society, New York, N.Y.

Notes to Chapter 3

1. James F. Rusling, *Men and Things I Saw in Civil War Days* (New York: Eaton & Mains, 1899), 12–14. For Sickles' stay in Washington, see Swanberg, *Sickles the Incredible*, 220–25. Swanberg's text is based on the reminiscences of Rusling and Tremain, plus some New York newspaper accounts. On page 224, Swanberg writes that he is not sure when Sickles first contemplated taking action against General Meade.

2. *O.R.*, vol. 27, part 1, 116. Meade later recalled that when he wrote his report he honestly believed that Sickles had misapprehended his orders. See Benedict, "Meade's Letter on Gettysburg," Philadelphia *Weekly Press*, August 11, 1886.

3. Swanberg, *Sickles the Incredible*, 232, citing John C. Gray and John C. Ropes, *War Letters 1862–1865 of John Chipman Gray and John Codman Ropes* (Cambridge, Mass.: Riverside Press for the Massachusetts Historical Society, 1927), 256 (Gray to Ropes, November 3, 1863). However, this is the only source in which I have seen this rumor stated. It is unknown where or how it began, but if Meade stated in 1870 that he honestly believed that Sickles had misapprehended his orders,

then there is a strong indication that Meade did not start it. Until the committee hearings, Meade seems to have been unaware of the extent of Sickles' animosity toward him.

4. Swanberg, *Sickles the Incredible*, 232–33.
5. *O.R.*, vol. 27, part 1, 16. Halleck's report is dated November 15, 1863.
6. The older article by W. W. Pierson, Jr., "The Committee on the Conduct of the Civil War," *American Historical Review* 23 (1918): 550–76, has been superseded by Bruce Tap, *Over Lincoln's Shoulder: The Committee on the Conduct of the War* (Lawrence: University Press of Kansas, 1998) as the primary overall study of the committee, its members, and its work.
7. Swanberg, *Sickles the Incredible*, 247–48.
8. *C.C.W.*, 295–304 (Sickles' testimony), at 295–97.
9. Ibid., 297.
10. Ibid., 297–98.
11. Ibid., 298.
12. Ibid., 299.
13. Ibid., 299–304.
14. At the time, Doubleday did not know that the reason Meade replaced him was because of a statement made by General Howard, who told Hancock that "Doubleday's command gave way," when commenting on the retreat on July 1. Hancock repeated this statement in his 5:25 P.M. report to Meade. See *O.R.*, vol. 27, part 1, 366, for Hancock's report. Doubleday apparently did not find out about Howard's statement until after the war, when a lively and protracted exchange of views took place between Howard and Doubleday. In 1883, Doubleday did admit that "I was unnecessarily harsh in my language at that time," referring to his committee testimony. See Doubleday's "Meade at Gettysburg," *New York Times*, April 1, 1883, reprinted in Meade, *Life and Letters*, 2: 396–99. For evidence of Meade's opinion of Doubleday, see Coddington, *Gettysburg Campaign*, 690–91, note 82.
15. *C.C.W.*, 311.
16. Ibid., 313–21.
17. Ibid., xix.
18. Meade to Mrs. Margaret Meade, March 6, 1864, in Meade, *Life and Letters*, 2: 169. In the meantime, General Howe had finished his testimony by slandering Meade as army commander, stating that Meade lacked an "earnestness of purpose." Howe also remarked that Meade was a McClellan sympathizer and that the rank and file had no confidence in his ability. *C.C.W.*, 325–29.
19. *C.C.W.*, 329–30.
20. Ibid., 330–31.
21. Ibid., 331.
22. Ibid., 331–32.
23. Ibid., 332–33.
24. Ibid., 334–40.
25. Meade to Mrs. Meade, March 6, 1864, in Meade, *Life and Letters*, 2: 169–70.

26. Meade to Mrs. Meade, March 8, 9, 1864, in Meade, *Life and Letters*, 2: 176. See *C.C.W.*, 359–66, for Pleasonton's remarks, and 366–76, for Birney's.

27. Meade to Mrs. Meade, March 14, 1864, in Meade, *Life and Letters*, 2: 177; *C.C.W.*, 347–58.

28. Meade to Mrs. Meade, March 14, 1864, in Meade, *Life and Letters*, 2: 178. For more details on individual committee members and what they thought of Meade, see Tap, *Over Lincoln's Shoulder*, 177–78, 183, 185–86, 187.

29. Historicus, "The Battle of Gettysburg," *New York Herald*, March 12, 1864; reprinted in *O.R.*, vol. 27, part 1, 128–36; and in Meade, *Life and Letters*, 2: 323–31.

30. *O.R.*, vol. 27, part 1, 127–28. The identity of Historicus has never been proven. Cleaves, in *Meade of Gettysburg*, 229–30, thought that John B. Bachelder was the culprit. Cleaves followed a 1925 letter from 5th Corps veteran Robert G. Carter, who characterized Bachelder as a "loud–mouthed, blatant photographer, artist at Sickles' headquarters, and henchman of Sickles, made people believe by an avalanche of propaganda that Sickles held back Longstreet, and all writers began to believe it and praised Sickles' act [forward move]." Carter's letter can be found in W. A. Graham, *The Custer Myth: A Source Book of Custeriana* (Harrisburg, Pa.: Stackpole, 1953), 318. However, there is no evidence to link Bachelder, the great early historian of the battle, with Sickles. There are no letters from Sickles in Bachelder's Papers that pertain to the conflict with Meade. Bachelder studiously avoided battlefield controversies in his writing on Gettysburg. Carter may have confused Bachelder with Lt. Col. R. N. Batchelder, one of Sickles' staff officers.

31. Halleck to Meade, March 20, 1864; and Meade to Halleck, March 22, 1864, in *O.R.*, vol. 27, part 1, 137–38.

32. Tilton to Barnes, March 14, 1864, James Barnes Papers, New-York Historical Society, New York, N.Y. This letter was published in the *New York Herald* of March 21 as "Letter from Colonel Tilton."

33. Another Eye-Witness, "The Battle of Gettysburg," *New York Herald*, March 16, 1864.

34. Staff Officer of the Fifth Corps, "The Battle of Gettysburg. The Truth of History, &c.," *New York Herald*, March 18, 1864.

35. This is not exactly true. The assault by Hood's division reached Ward's position on Houck's Ridge about 4:15 P.M., then spread to de Trobriand's line in the Wheatfield area by five o'clock. De Trobriand's brigade repulsed the first Confederate attack and by about 5:20 P.M. there was a lull in the fighting there. It was during this lull that Barnes placed his two brigades in line on the stony hill west of the Wheatfield, about 5:30 P.M. Almost immediately another Rebel assault hit this portion of the Federal line. Vincent's brigade of Barnes's division reached Little Round Top about five o'clock and was immediately assailed by portions of Law's and Robertson's brigades, so the fighting had lasted about forty-five minutes before the Fifth Corps became engaged.

36. James Barnes, "The Battle of Gettysburg," *New York Herald*, March 21, 1864.

37. This line was probably three regiments of Col. George C. Burling's brigade, which soon moved into the Wheatfield to fill a gap in the Union line.

38. Historicus, "The Battle of Gettysburg. Historicus in Reply to General Barnes and the Staff Officers of the Second and Fifth Corps. The Evidence Before the Committee on the Conduct of the War, &c.," *New York Herald,* April 4, 1864.

39. The words "the same thing" so puzzled Barnes that he wrote to Colonel Sweitzer, asking what he meant by that phrase. In reply, Sweitzer said he did not know what statements were made by General Birney that night since he did not talk with him, nor did he speak with General Sykes. Sweitzer added that the only conversation he had with Sykes about Gettysburg occurred while the army was near Williamsport, Md. See Barnes to Sweitzer, April 6, 1864, and Sweitzer to Barnes, April 8, 1864, both in Barnes Papers.

40. Swanberg, *Sickles the Incredible,* 253.

41. *C.C.W.,* 417–22.

42. Ibid., 422–23. Butterfield conveniently did not mention the follow-up message to Sedgwick, ordering the 6th Corps to move with all speed to Gettysburg. See *O.R.,* vol. 27, part 3, 467–69.

43. *C.C.W.,* 424.

44. Ibid., 425–35. Mr. Gooch's questions prompted Butterfield to admit the contingency nature of the retreat order. Mr. Odell got him to speculate on the July 1 circular as well, but Butterfield avoided answering the questions directly, instead giving his own opinions of what he considered to be a bad position at Pipe Creek.

45. Ibid., 435–39.

46. Ibid., 377–79.

47. Ibid., 405, 412.

48. Ibid., 440–43.

49. Ibid., 449, 452–53.

50. Ibid., 461.

51. Ibid., 466, 468.

52. Ibid., lv–lxxvii.

53. See Tap, *Over Lincoln's Shoulder,* 184–85, for a brief account of what some of the Northern newspapers reported about the committee's investigation.

Notes to Chapter 4

1. This article was published in *The Volunteer* 1 (1869): 307–12, 322–39, 354–59.

2. Ibid., 322.

3. For example, see ibid., 324–25, and then compare this with the actual sentence in *C.C.W.,* 366 (Birney's testimony).

4. *The Volunteer,* 308–9, 326.

5. "Address of Lieutenant-Colonel Grout," *Proceedings of the Reunion Society of Vermont Officers, 1864–1884, With Addresses Delivered at Its Meetings . . . and a Roster of the Society* (Burlington: Free Press Association, 1885), 124–25. William W. Grout (1836–1902) was a graduate of the Poughkeepsie Law School prior to the war. His military service consisted of his lieutenant colonelcy with the 15th Vermont, which did not see action at Gettysburg. After the war, Grout served as a Vermont

legislator before his election to the Forty-seventh Congress in 1881. Defeated in 1883, he returned again to serve from 1885–1901.

6. See Benedict's introductory remarks in "General Meade's Letter on Gettysburg," Philadelphia *Weekly Press*, August 11, 1886; reprinted in Meade, *Life and Letters*, 2: 350–54, at 350–51. Benedict's editorials were published as an appendix to the second edition of his *Vermont at Gettysburg* (Burlington: Free Press Association, 1870). Benedict was present at Gettysburg as a member of Brig. Gen. George J. Stannard's staff.

7. For Sickles' presence at this reunion, see "On Gettysburg Field," Philadelphia *Weekly Times*, June 17, 1882.

8. See "The Gettysburg Battle. The Part Taken by the Third Corps," *New York Times*, August 14, 1882. A more detailed account is "General Sickles' Story. The Battle of Gettysburg and the Part of the Third Corps," Gettysburg *Star and Sentinel*, August 23, 1882.

9. The account here is based on "Fighting 'Joe.' Reunion of the Third Army Corps. Notable Gathering in Music Hall. Record of the Third Corps Defended," *Boston Herald*, April 9, 1886. Other reports of this reunion are "Hooker's Men, and Brave Dan Sickles and His Crutches at the Old Third Corps Reunion," Boston *Daily Globe*, April 9, 1886; and "The Third Army Corps," Boston *Evening Transcript*, April 9, 1886.

10. This passage is quoted in Samuel Adams Drake, *The Battle of Gettysburg, 1863* (Boston: Lee and Shepard, 1892), 111.

11. For details about this speech, see Henry C. Kendall to Daniel E. Sickles, December 29, 1897, Sickles Papers, New-York Historical Society, New York, N.Y.; and Henry J. Hunt to George Meade, July 21, 1886, Meade Papers.

12. "Gettysburg. Great Speech of General Sickles on the Battlefield July 2," *National Tribune*, July 15, 22, 1886. An excerpted version is "Sickles at Gettysburg. The Fighting on the Second Day. Replying to Criticisms Against the Third Corps," *New York Tribune*, July 3, 1886.

13. James C. Biddle, "Generals Meade and Sickles at Gettysburg," Philadelphia *Weekly Press*, July 14, 1886. A condensed account appeared as "Sickles in Hot Water," Philadelphia *Press*, July 18, 1886.

14. Lafayette McLaws, "The Second Day at Gettysburg. General Sickles Answered by the Commander of the Opposing Force. The Federal Disaster on the Left," Philadelphia *Weekly Press*, August 4, 1886.

15. "The Battle of Gettysburg. Gen. Humphreys' Chief of Staff Contributes Something to the Discussion—A Caustic Criticism of Gen. Sickles," St. Paul *Pioneer Press*, August 15, 1886. A slightly excerpted version appears as "Sickles at Gettysburg. Gen. Meade's Order and How He Executed It," *New York Times*, August 16, 1886. The author was probably Capt. Carswell McClellan, who was indeed one of General Humphreys' staff officers. A letter from McClellan to Mrs. R. H. Humphreys dated December 24, 1886, is postmarked St. Paul. This letter is in the Humphreys Papers.

16. George G. Benedict, "General Meade's Letter on Gettysburg," Philadelphia *Weekly Press*, August 11, 1886; reprinted in Meade, *Life and Letters*, 2: 351–54; and *Battles and Leaders*, 3: 413–14.
17. "General Sickles Speaks Out," *New York Times*, August 14, 1886. This article was reprinted in *Battles and Leaders*, 3: 414–19, with some slight revisions.
18. Henry J. Hunt, "The Second Day at Gettysburg," *The Century Magazine* 23 (December 1886): 278–95; reprinted in *Battles and Leaders*, 3: 290–313.
19. For their replies to Hunt's questions, see Meade to Hunt, July 22, 1886, Hunt Papers; and Sickles to Hunt, 1886, Hunt Papers. Sickles' reply letter is very mutilated with the first several pages missing, but the letter contains enough information to ascertain that it was written sometime after July 1886.
20. Hunt to Century Company, September 26, 1886, Hunt Letters, Century Collection, New York Public Library, New York, N.Y.
21. Hunt to Meade, October 25, 1886, Meade Papers.
22. Philippe Regis de Trobriand, *Four Years with the Army of the Potomac*, trans. George K. Dauchy (Boston, 1889). The original French edition of the book is *Quatre ans de campagnes à l'Armée du potomac*, 2 vols. (Paris: A. Lacroix, 1867, 1874).
23. For example, see his article "The Battle of Gettysburg Once More–The Fog Thicker and Thicker," *New York Herald*, March 29, 1864; and a letter to Sickles, June 5, 1886, in Marie C. Post, *The Life and Memories of Comte Regis de Trobriand, Major-General in the Army of the United States* (New York: E. P. Dutton, 1910), 469. Both letters are favorable to General Sickles.
24. De Trobriand, *Four Years*, 494.
25. Daniel E. Sickles, David M. Gregg, John Newton, and Daniel Butterfield, "Further Recollections of Gettysburg," *North American Review* 152 (March 1891): 257–86.
26. John Gibbon, "Another View of Gettysburg," *North American Review* 152 (June 1891): 704–13.
27. Ibid., 711–12.
28. Carswell McClellan, "The Gettysburg Fight. The Second Day's Battle, and Gen. Sickle's [*sic*] Part in It," *New York Sun*, June 28, 1891.
29. But see William H. Powell, *The Fifth Army Corps (Army of the Potomac). A Record of Operations during the Civil War in the United States of America, 1861–1865* (New York: G. P. Putnam's Sons, 1896), iii, where Powell writes that this material was excluded from the finished book since it had no direct bearing on the corps history. McClellan died before completing the book.
30. See George Meade to McClellan, March 20, 1891, Porter Papers. Meade enclosed with this letter his two papers, "Notes on the 2d Day at Gettysburg" and "Notes on the 5th Corps & Round Top at Gettysburg."
31. "Gen. Sickles Talks Back. Answering the Criticism of Col. McClellan," *New York Times*, July 5, 1891.
32. Helen D. Longstreet, *Lee and Longstreet at High Tide: Gettysburg in the Light of the Official Records* (Philadelphia: J. B. Lippincott, 1904).

33. Ibid., 22.
34. Ibid., 22–28.
35. Henry E. Tremain, *Two Days of War: A Gettysburg Narrative and Other Excursions* (New York: Bonnell, Silver & Bowers, 1905).
36. Ibid., 42–43, 48–49, 52–55, 60–61.
37. George Meade, *The Life and Letters of George Gordon Meade*, 2 vols. (New York: Charles Scribner's Sons, 1913).
38. See ibid., vol. 2, 62–97, for "The Second Day" chapter.
39. Meade, *With Meade at Gettysburg*.
40. John Gibbon, *Personal Recollections of the Civil War* (New York: G. P. Putnam's Sons, 1928). Gibbon had written the manuscript by 1885, as evidenced by his initials and the date on page 426. Much of the Gettysburg material appeared as "Gettysburg," Philadelphia *Weekly Press*, July 6, 13, 1887, and "Meade to Gibbon. Important Letters Relating to the Battle of Gettysburg Hitherto Unpublished," Philadelphia *Weekly Press*, July 20, 1887. The *Weekly Press* material can be found on pages 132–69 and 185–90 of *Personal Recollections*.
41. Gibbon, *Personal Recollections*, 132–40, 184–90.

Notes to Chapter 5

1. Michael Jacobs, *Notes on the Rebel Invasion of Maryland and Pennsylvania and the Battle of Gettysburg, July 1, 2, and 3, 1863, Accompanied by an Explanatory Map* (Philadelphia: J. B. Lippincott, 1864); Samuel M. Schmucker, *A History of the Civil War in the United States*, 2 vols. (Philadelphia: Bradley, 1864–65).
2. Thomas P. Kettell, *History of the Great Rebellion* (Hartford, Conn.: L. Stebbins, 1865); John S. C. Abbott, *The History of the Civil War in America*, 2 vols. (Springfield, Mass.: Gurdon Bill, 1866); James Moore, *A Complete History of the Great Rebellion; Or, The Civil War in the United States, 1861–1865* (New York: Hurst, 1866); Elliott G. Storke and L. P. Brockett, *The Complete History of the Great American Rebellion, Embracing Its Causes, Events and Consequences*, 2 vols. (Auburn, N.Y.: Auburn, 1865), 2: 1000; Joel T. Headley, *The Great Rebellion: A History of the Civil War in the United States*, 2 vols. (Hartford, Conn.: American, 1863–66), 2: 202.
3. Charles C. Chesney, *Campaigns in Virginia, Maryland, etc. etc.*, 2 vols. (London: Elder, 1865), 2: 68–69.
4. Henry C. Fletcher, *History of the American War*, 3 vols. (London: R. Bentley, 1865), 2: 421.
5. W. A. Crafts, *The Southern Rebellion; Being a History of the United States from the Commencement of President Buchanan's Administration through the War for the Suppression of the Rebellion*, 2 vols. (Boston: Samuel Walker, 1867), 2: 434.
6. William Swinton, *Campaigns of the Army of the Potomac: A Critical History of Operations in Virginia, Maryland, and Pennsylvania from the Commencement to the Close of the War, 1861–1865* (New York: Charles B. Richardson, 1866), 343–45.
7. William Swinton, *The Twelve Decisive Battles of the War* (New York: Dick & Fitzgerald, 1867), 335–36.

8. Horace Greeley, *The American Conflict: A History of the Great Rebellion in the United States of America, 1860–65*, 2 vols. (Hartford, Conn.: O. D. Case, 1864–67), 2: 381.

9. Benson J. Lossing, *Pictorial History of the Civil War*, 3 vols. (Hartford, Conn.: T. Belknap, 1866–68), 2: 65.

10. Willard Glazer, *Battles for the Union* (Hartford, Conn.: Gilman, 1878), 262.

11. Asa Mahan, *A Critical History of the Late American War* (New York: A. S. Barnes, 1877), 292.

12. William R. Balch, *The Battle of Gettysburg: An Historical Account* (Philadelphia: Press of McLaughlin Brothers, 1885), 63.

13. John B. Bachelder, *Gettysburg: What to See and How to See It* (Boston: [self-published], 1873); Theodore A. Dodge, *A Bird's-Eye View of Our Civil War* (Boston: James R. Osgood, 1883); John Formby, *The American Civil War* (New York: Charles Scribner's Sons, 1910); James K. Hosmer, *The American Civil War*, 2 vols. (New York: Harper & Brothers, 1913); Vernon Blythe, *A History of the Civil War in the United States* (New York: Neale, 1914); Walter Geer, *Campaigns of the Civil War* (New York: Brentano's, 1926); John B. McMaster, *A History of the People of the United States through Lincoln's Administration* (New York: D. Appleton, 1927).

14. Bachelder's history, compiled by request of the War Department, was never published in his lifetime. Two copies seemed to have survived, one in the Bachelder Papers in the New Hampshire Historical Society, and a typed copy in the library of Gettysburg National Military Park. The book was finally published by David L. and Audrey J. Ladd, eds., *John Bachelder's History of the Battle of Gettysburg* (Dayton, Ohio: Morningside House, 1997). On Bachelder in general, see Richard A. Sauers, "John B. Bachelder: Government Historian of the Battle of Gettysburg," *Gettysburg Magazine*, no. 3 (July 1990): 115–27.

15. John W. Draper, *History of the American Civil War*, 3 vols. (New York: Harper & Brothers, 1870), 3: 143.

16. John L. Wilson, *The Pictorial History of the Great Civil War* (Kansas City: Western Installment Book, 1878), 510.

17. Abner Doubleday, *Chancellorsville and Gettysburg* (New York: Charles Scribner's Sons, 1882), 162–64.

18. Hoke, *Great Invasion*, 317–19, with appendix on pages 570–79.

19. Rossiter Johnson, *A History of the War of Succession, 1861–1865* (Boston: Ticknor, 1888), 260; Cecil Battine, *The Crisis of the Confederacy: A History of Gettysburg and the Wilderness* (London: Longmans, Green, 1905), 212–18; Henry S. Burrage, *Gettysburg and Lincoln, the Battle, the Cemetery, and the National Park* (New York: G. P. Putnam's Sons, 1906), 34, 36–37; William R. Livermore, *The Story of the Civil War: A Concise Account of the War in the United States of America Between 1861 and 1865, in Continuation of the Story by John Codman Ropes*, part 3, book 2, *The Campaigns of 1863 to July 10th, Vicksburg, Port Hudson, Tullahoma and Gettysburg* (New York: G. P. Putnam's Sons, 1913), 441–45.

20. James S. Montgomery, *The Shaping of a Battle, Gettysburg* (Philadelphia: Chilton Book, 1959), 97; James W. Bellah, *Soldiers' Battle, Gettysburg* (New York: David McKay, 1962), 110–18; Shelby Foote, *The Civil War: A Narrative*, 3 vols. (New York: Random House, 1958–74), 2: 493–97.

21. Samuel P. Bates, *The Battle of Gettysburg* (Philadelphia: T. H. Davis, 1875), 108–11.

22. Willis C. Humphrey, *The Great Contest: A History of the Military and Naval Operations during the Civil War in the United States of America, 1861–1865* (Detroit: C. H. Smith, 1886), 125–26.

23. Charles C. Coffin, *Marching to Victory* (New York: Harper & Brothers, 1889), 235. For the speech Coffin cited, see "At Gettysburg. Encampment of the G.A.R. of Pennsylvania," *National Tribune*, July 8, 1886.

24. James H. Stine, *History of the Army of the Potomac* (Philadelphia: J. B. Rodgers Printing, 1892), 495–96.

25. New York Monuments Commission for the Battlefields of Gettysburg and Chattanooga, *Final Report on the Battlefield of Gettysburg*, 3 vols., ed. William F. Fox (Albany, N.Y.: J. B. Lyon, Printers, 1900), 1:28, 41.

26. Ibid., 38–39, 94–95.

27. Francis M. Pierce, *The Battle of Gettysburg, The Crest-Wave of the American Civil War* (New York: Neale, 1914), 140; Gustav J. Fiebeger, *The Campaign and Battle of Gettysburg, From the Official Records of the Union and Confederate Armies* (West Point, N.Y.: U.S. Military Academy Press, 1915), 75.

28. Glenn Tucker, *High Tide at Gettysburg: The Campaign in Pennsylvania* (Indianapolis, IN: Bobbs-Merrill, 1958), 237–40.

29. Louis Philippe Albert d'Orléans, Comte de Paris, *Histoire de la guerre civile en Amérique*, 7 vols. (Paris: Michel Levy, 1874–1890); *History of the Civil War in America*, 4 vols., trans. Louis F. Tasistro, vols. 1 and 2, ed. Henry Coppee; vols. 3 and 4, ed. John P. Nicholson (Philadelphia: Porter & Coates, 1875–88).

30. Paris, *History of the Civil War*, 3: 590–91. However, George Meade later wrote that the Count must have misunderstood him since he had written the Frenchman a letter with his recollections of Gettysburg, in which he said that he did not carry any orders to Sickles on his first visit to 3d Corps headquarters. See Meade, "Notes on the 2d Day," Porter Papers.

31. Ibid., 592, 601–4.

32. Ibid., 601–2, 604–6.

33. Drake, *Battle of Gettysburg 1863*, 103–11.

34. John M. Vanderslice, *Gettysburg: Where and How the Regiments Fought and the Troops They Encountered—An Account of the Battle, Giving Movements, Positions, and Losses of the Commands Engaged* (Philadelphia: J. B. Lippincott, 1895), 70–71.

35. Robert K. Beecham, *Gettysburg: The Pivotal Battle of the Civil War* (Chicago: A. C. McClurg, 1911), 142–43, 146, 155, 157–58.

36. Jesse Bowman Young, *The Battle of Gettysburg: A Comprehensive Narrative* (New York: Harper & Brothers, 1913), 221.

37. Ibid., 222–26.

38. Bruce Catton, *Glory Road* (Garden City, N.Y.: Doubleday, 1952), 286–88.

39. Edward J. Stackpole, *They Met at Gettysburg* (Harrisburg: Eagle Books, 1956), 190–95.

40. Coddington, *Gettysburg Campaign*, 330, 336–56.

41. Harry W. Pfanz, *Gettysburg–The Second Day* (Chapel Hill: University of North Carolina Press, 1988), xv–xvi.

42. Ibid., 82–103, 106–7, 113–14, 140–44.

43. Herman Hattaway, *Shades of Blue and Gray: An Introductory Military History of the Civil War* (Columbia: University of Missouri Press, 1997), 145; Russell F. Weigley, *A Great Civil War: A Military and Political History, 1861–1865* (Bloomington: Indiana University Press, 2000), 248–50; David J. Eicher, *The Longest Night: A Military History of the Civil War* (New York: Simon & Schuster, 2001), 523–26.

44. Bache, *Life of General George Gordon Meade*, 307–31.

45. Pennypacker, *General Meade*, 162–69.

46. Cleaves, *Meade of Gettysburg*, 140–48. General Meade deserves a better biography than Cleaves's effort, which, although the best of Meade's biographies, contains many errors of fact and interpretation.

47. Pinchon, *Dan Sickles*, 193–99.

48. Swanberg, *Sickles the Incredible*, 205–11, 221–24, 230–58.

Notes to Chapter 6

1. *C.C.W.*, 297–98.

2. The two Historicus articles are in the March 12 and April 4, 1864, issues of the *New York Herald*. For a concise analysis of the comparison of Sickles and Historicus, see Coddington, *Gettysburg Campaign*, 721–22, note 98.

3. Sickles, "The Gettysburg Battle," *New York Times*, August 14, 1882.

4. "Fighting 'Joe,'" *Boston Herald*, April 9, 1886.

5. Sickles, "Gettysburg," *National Tribune*, July 15, 22, 1886.

6. Sickles, "Sickles Speaks Out," *New York Times*, August 14, 1886.

7. Sickles et al., "Further Recollections," 263.

8. *O.R.*, vol. 27, part 2, 658 (report of Maj. J. A. Englehard, Pender's division), 665 (report of Brig. Gen. James H. Lane); letter of Kathleen R. Georg to author, May 8, 1981.

9. *O.R.*, vol. 27, part 2, 613 (report of Maj. Gen. Richard H. Anderson), 616–17 (report of Brig. Gen. Cadmus M. Wilcox); Georg letter, May 8, 1981.

10. *O.R.*, vol. 27, part 2, 643 (report of Maj. J. Jones, 26th North Carolina), 649 (report of Brig. Gen. Joseph R. Davis).

11. *O.R.*, vol. 27, part 2, 358 (Longstreet's report).

12. Ibid., 671 (Colonel Lowrance's report).

13. *O.R.*, vol. 27, part 1, 369 (report of General Hancock), 427 (report of Brig. Gen. Alexander S. Webb), 433–34 (report of Lt. Col. William L. Curry, 106th Pennsylvania), 449 (report of Maj. S. W. Curtis, 7th Michigan), 453 (report of Brig. Gen. Alexander Hays), 456–57 (report of Col. Samuel S. Carroll), 458 (report of Col.

John Coons, 14th Indiana), 460 (report of Lt. Col. John W. Carpenter, 4th Ohio), 464 (report of Col. Thomas A. Smyth), 469 (report of Lt. John T. Dent, 1st Delaware), 472 (report of Lt. Col. J. M. Bull, 126th New York).

14. Ibid., 498 (report of Major Danks), 509 (report of Lieutenant Colonel Sawyer), 515 (report of Colonel Berdan), 547 (report of Lt. Col. Clark B. Baldwin, 1st Massachusetts). Later, in May 1865, Baldwin wrote a longer report of the regiment's activities at Gettysburg to John B. Bachelder. Regarding the skirmishing on July 2, Baldwin wrote that his regiment was exposed to a "hot fire from the enemy's sharpshooters." Still, Baldwin's report clearly indicates that the Rebels did not press his line very much until later in the afternoon, when the battle opened. See Baldwin's report in *Supplement to the Official Records of the Union and Confederate Armies,* 100 vols. (Wilmington, N.C.: Broadfoot, 1995–2000), vol. 5, 176–78.

15. *O.R.,* vol. 27, part 1, 927–28 (Buford's report), 939 (Devin's report).

16. Hillman A. Hall and W. B. Besley, *History of the Sixth New York Cavalry, Second Ira Harris Guard, Second Brigade, First Division, Cavalry Corps, Army of the Potomac, 1861–1865* (Worcester, Mass.: Blanchard Press, 1908), 142–43.

17. Newal Cheney, *History of the Ninth Regiment New York Volunteer Cavalry, War of 1861 to 1865* (Jamestown, N.Y.: Martin Merz and Son, 1901), 114–15.

18. *O.R.,* vol. 27, part 1, 522 (report of Lt. Col. Charles B. Merrill, 17th Maine), 523 (report of Lt. Col. Edwin S. Pierce, 3rd Michigan), 587 (report of Capt. George B. Winslow, Battery D, 1st New York).

19. See Martin D. Haynes, *A History of the Second Regiment, New Hampshire Volunteer Infantry in the War of the Rebellion* (Lakeport, 1896), 168; Edwin B. Houghton, *Campaigns of the Seventeenth Maine* (Portland: Short & Loring, 1868), 91; Thomas Rafferty, "Gettysburg," Military Order of the Loyal Legion of the United States, New York Commandery, *Personal Recollections of the War of the Rebellion, First Series* (New York: The Commandery, 1891), 8; George B. Winslow, "On Little Round Top," Philadelphia *Weekly Times,* July 26, 1879; and pages 156–59 of an unpublished manuscript history of the 110th Pennsylvania, by Capt. James C. M. Hamilton, Civil War Library and Museum.

20. De Trobriand, *Four Years,* 493–94; Haynes, *Second New Hampshire,* 167; Winslow, "On Little Round Top."

21. For accounts of this reconnaissance, see Hunt, "Second Day," 301–2; *C.C.W.,* 449 (Hunt's testimony), 298 (Sickles' testimony); Tremain, *Two Days of War,* 43.

22. For the conflicting claims, see *O.R.,* vol. 27, part 1, 482 (Birney's report), 515 (Berdan's report); Hunt, "Second Day," 302; *C.C.W.,* 449 (Hunt's testimony).

23. *O.R.,* vol. 27, part 1, 507 (Lakeman's report), 515 (Berdan's report), 516–17 (Trepp's report).

24. *O.R.,* vol. 27, part 2, 617.

25. Ibid.

26. Undated Wilcox report in the Robert E. Lee Headquarters Papers, Virginia Historical Society, copy in the library of the Gettysburg National Military Park, Gettysburg, Pa.

27. Fleming W. Thompson to sister and mother, July 17, 1863, University of Texas Library, copy in Robert Brake Collection, United States Army Military History Institute.

28. Hilary A. Herbert, "History of the Eighth Alabama Volunteer Regiment, C.S.A." *Alabama Historical Quarterly* 39 (1977): 114–15.

29. Herbert's letters were to J. C. Kelton, July 18, 1892, in National Archives, Record Group 94, Records of the Office of the Adjutant General, F442, VS 1863, Box 222, Hiram Berdan; to John B. Bachelder, July 9, 1884, Bachelder Papers; and to E. P. Alexander, August 18, 1903, Alexander Papers, Southern Historical Collection, Chapel Hill, N.C.

30. Wilcox to H. A. Johnson, February 19, 1880, in H. A. Johnson, "What Regiment Supported Berdan's Sharpshooters?" *National Tribune*, May 16, 1889.

31. George Clark, *A Glance Backward: Or Some Events in the Past History of My Life* (Houston, Tex.: Press of Rein & Sons, 1914), 36.

32. Herbert to Kelton, July 18, 1892, Berdan Service File; Herbert, History of the 8th Alabama," 114; Wilcox's report, Virginia Historical Society; *O.R.*, vol. 27, part 2, 350 (Pendleton's report).

33. *O.R.*, vol. 27, part 1, 482 (Birney's report); *C.C.W.*, 391 (Humphreys' testimony); *O.R.*, vol. 27, part 3, 488 (signal report); Coddington, *Gettysburg Campaign*, 724, note 122; Beecham, *Gettysburg*, 155.

34. *O.R.*, vol. 27, part 1, 515, 517.

35. Nathaniel Sessions and L. Y. Allen, "Berdan Sharpshooters," *National Tribune*, August 12, 1886; H. A. Johnson, *The Sword of Honor: A Story of the Civil War* (Hallowell, Maine: Register Printing House, 1906), 11; Stevens, *Berdan's Sharpshooters*, 303–4.

36. *O.R.*, vol. 27, part 2, 617 (Wilcox's report); Herbert to E. P. Alexander, May 18, 1903, Alexander Papers; Herbert to J. B. Bachelder, July 9, 1884, Bachelder Papers; Herbert to J. C. Kelton, July 18, 1892, Berdan Service File; Wilcox to H. A. Johnson, February 19, 1889, in Johnson, "Gettysburg. What Regiment Supported Berdan's Sharpshooters?" *National Tribune*, May 16, 1889.

37. Stevens, *Berdan's Sharpshooters*, 308.

38. Ibid., 305–7.

39. Lossing, *Pictorial History*, 2: 65; Bates, *Battle of Gettysburg*, 109.

40. Hiram Berdan (1824–1893) was one of the war's "colorful" characters, but very little has been written about his life and Civil War combat record. He has been given credit for recruiting the sharpshooters and obtaining breechloading rifles for his men. Berdan was accused of cowardice more than once, but was always exonerated. After the battle of Gettysburg, Berdan took a recruiting detail to New York City, ostensibly to fill the depleted ranks of his regiments. Once in New York, Berdan dismissed the detail and proceeded to take his family on a four-week vacation in New Hampshire's White Mountains. General Birney attempted to have Berdan court-martialed for this episode, but Berdan used the excuse of a supposed wound incurred at Second Manassas to evade conviction. Prolonged

illness for more than seventy consecutive days caused Berdan to be mustered out of service in January 1864.

After the war, he went to Russia to aid in the manufacture and instruction of a sharpshooting rifle. In 1886, Berdan came back home and sought to blame the government for an alleged patent infringement on his rifle. In 1892, Berdan applied for a Medal of Honor based upon his "discovery" of Longstreet's flank march at Gettysburg, but the medal was denied because no one could find enough supporting evidence to back the colonel's claim. Berdan died suddenly in 1893 and is buried in Arlington National Cemetery.

41. Roy M. Marcot, *Hiram Berdan, Civil War Chief of Sharpshooters, Military Commander and Firearms Inventor* (Irvine, Calif.: Northwood Heritage Press, 1989); Richard A. Sauers, "Colonel Hiram Berdan and the 1st United States Sharpshooters," *Susquehanna University Studies* 12, no. 1 (1983): 26–42; Wiley Sword, *Sharpshooter: Hiram Berdan, His Famous Sharpshooters and Their Sharps Rifles* (Lincoln, R.I.: Andrew Mowbray, 1988).

42. This paragraph is based on four orations given by Berdan. See "At Gettysburg," *National Tribune*, July 8, 1888; "General Berdan and His Famous Sharpshooters at Gettysburg," *National Tribune*, September 9, 1886; an undated, but probably a late July 1888 newspaper clipping from the Washington *Sunday Herald* in Berdan's Volunteer Service File; and his monument dedication speech of July 2, 1889, in *New York at Gettysburg*, 3: 1078–79.

43. "On Gettysburg's Field," *New York Times*, July 2, 1888.

44. This letter is printed in Longstreet, *Lee and Longstreet at High Tide*, 8; and Tremain, *Two Days of War*, 67–68.

45. There is a large body of literature on the Lee-Longstreet controversy. For extended treatment, see Coddington, *Gettysburg Campaign*, 359–84; Freeman, *Lee's Lieutenants*, 3: 106–40, 173–76; and Glenn Tucker, *Lee and Longstreet at Gettysburg* (Indianapolis, Ind.: Bobbs-Merrill, 1968), 1–70.

46. Kershaw, "Kershaw's Brigade at Gettysburg," 331; J. B. Kershaw to John B. Bachelder, March 20, 1876, Bachelder Papers; McLaws, "Battle of Gettysburg," 68–69.

47. McLaws, "Battle of Gettysburg," 69.

48. For Johnston's reconnaissance, see Freeman, *Lee's Lieutenants*, 3: 111, 174–75; McLaws, "Battle of Gettysburg," 71–73, in which McLaws quotes Captain Johnston's letter to him of June 27, 1892. The McLaws Papers, Duke University, contains an unfinished paper by McLaws in which he also quotes from this letter, but the manuscript and the 1896 address are not identical. For Johnston's recollections of his actions on July 2, see Johnston to Fitzhugh Lee, February 16, 1878; Johnston to McLaws, June 27, 1892; and Johnston to George Peterkin, undated, all in Johnston Letters, Virginia Historical Society, Richmond, Va., with copies in the Gettysburg National Military Park Library.

49. For Lee's plan of battle, see *O.R.*, vol. 27, part 2, 308, 318 (reports of General Lee), 358 (report of General Longstreet); E. P. Alexander, *Military Memoirs of a Confederate* (New York: Charles Scribner's Sons, 1907), 391; Coddington, *Gettys-*

burg Campaign, 377–78; Freeman, *Lee's Lieutenants*, 3: 113–18. For the difficulties involved in the morning scouting by Captain Johnston, see Freeman, *Lee's Lieutenants*, 3: 755–56, Appendix 1, Frederick Tilberg and J. W. Coleman, "Reconnaissance on the Confederate Right, July 2, 1863."

50. Gary W. Gallagher, ed., *Fighting for the Confederacy: The Personal Recollections of General Edward Porter Alexander* (Chapel Hill: University of North Carolina Press, 1989), 235–37.

51. Many of the accounts of the flank march are vague as to the exact route taken. For the more detailed memoirs, see Kershaw, "Kershaw's Brigade at Gettysburg," 331–32; Kershaw to Bachelder, March 20, 1876; and McLaws, "Battle of Gettysburg," 69–70.

52. For these accounts, see McLaws, "The Battle of Gettysburg," Philadelphia *Weekly Press*, April 21, 1886; McLaws, "The Second Day at Gettysburg," Philadelphia *Weekly Press*, August 4, 1886; McLaws, "Gettysburg," 68–71; McLaws, "Battle of Gettysburg," 69–77; *O.R.*, vol. 27, part 2, 366–67 (Kershaw's report); Kershaw, "Kershaw's Brigade at Gettysburg," 331–32; Kershaw to Bachelder, March 20, 1876, Bachelder Papers; *O.R.*, vol. 27, part 2, 429, report of Colonel Alexander, dated August 3, 1863, *Southern Historical Society Papers* 4 (1877): 235–39, contains a report dated August 10, 1863; Alexander, *Military Memoirs of a Confederate*; Gallagher, *Fighting for the Confederacy*; Alonzo Meyers, "Kershaw's Brigade at Peach Orchard," *National Tribune*, January 21, 1926.

53. Herbert to Kelton, July 18, 1892, Berdan File, National Archives, Washington, D.C.

54. Wilcox's brigade, as well as Anderson's entire division, was a part of Longstreet's corps until the Army of Northern Virginia was reorganized in late May–early June 1863. Early critics may well have associated Anderson's command with Longstreet until the War Department published the official orders of battle long after the war. For example, Sickles, in his July 2, 1886, speech at Gettysburg, stated that Longstreet had thirteen infantry brigades under his command on July 2, when in fact he had only the eight in McLaws's and Hood's divisions. Thus, even Sickles attached Anderson's five brigades to Longstreet when they actually were a part of A. P. Hill's 3d Corps.

55. *C.C.W.*, 298.

56. Regarding Berdan, Sickles did not mention the skirmish in his committee testimony, although General Birney did (*C.C.W.*, 366). It is extremely difficult to determine where the early historians got their information for their writings on Gettysburg.

57. *O.R.*, vol. 27, part 1, 482; *C.C.W.*, 366.

Notes to Chapter 7

1. *C.C.W.*, 297–98.

2. Sickles to Tremain, June 30, 1867, Sickles Papers, New York Public Library, New York, N.Y.

3. "Fighting 'Joe,'" *Boston Herald*, April 9, 1886.

4. Sickles, "Gettysburg," *National Tribune*, July 22, 1886.

5. Sickles, "Sickles Speaks Out," *New York Times*, August 14, 1886.

6. Sickles, "Sickles Talks Back," *New York Times*, July 5, 1891.

7. Sickles to Richard B. Bartlett, February 19, 1904, Daniel E. Sickles Letterpress Book, Perkins Library, Duke University.

8. *C.C.W.*, 297.

9. "Fighting 'Joe,'" *Boston Herald*, April 9, 1886.

10. Both quotations are from Sickles, "Gettysburg," *National Tribune*, July 15, 22, 1886. The first is on page one, column four, of the July 15 issue; the second, in the July 22 issue, page one, column four.

11. Sickles, "Sickles Speaks Out," *New York Times*, August 14, 1886.

12. Benedict, "Meade's Letter on Gettysburg," Philadelphia *Weekly Press*, August 11, 1886.

13. For these maps, see Hunt, "Second Day," 292, reprinted in Young, *Battle of Gettysburg*, map between 208 and 209; Livermore, *Story of the Civil War*, Map XVII at end of volume; James K. P. Scott, *The Story of the Battles of Gettysburg* (Harrisburg, Pa.: Telegraph Press, 1927), 298; Tucker, *High Tide*, 185.

14. *O.R.*, vol. 27, part 1, 839.

15. Horton to Bachelder, January 23, 1867, Bachelder Papers.

16. Jesse H. Jones, "Saved the Day," *National Tribune*, March 7, 1895.

17. *O.R.*, vol. 27, part 1, 482.

18. *C.C.W.*, 366.

19. *O.R.*, vol. 27, part 1, 531; *C.C.W.*, 390; Humphreys to Archibald Campbell, August 6, 1863, Humphreys Papers; McClellan, "The Battle of Gettysburg," St. Paul *Pioneer Press*, August 15, 1886.

20. Benjamin M. Piatt, "A Battle Picture," Gettysburg *Star and Sentinel*, February 3, 1876; Randolph to Bachelder, June 15, 1880, Bachelder Papers.

21. *O.R.*, vol. 27, part 1, 369; *C.C.W.*, 405–6.

22. *O.R.*, vol. 27, part 1, 116.

23. *C.C.W.*, 331.

24. Colonel Meade's four Gettysburg accounts are: Meade to Alexander S. Webb, December 7, 1885, Webb Papers, Yale University, copy in Brake Collection; Meade to Henry J. Hunt, July 22, 1886, Meade Papers; Meade to Carswell McClellan, March 20, 1891, enclosing his notes on Gettysburg, Porter Papers; and Meade, *Life and Letters*, 2: 66–79, reprinted in Meade, *With Meade at Gettysburg*, 100–15. On the whole, these four accounts are remarkably similar.

25. See Meade to Webb, December 7, 1885, Webb Papers.

26. Meade, "Notes on the 2d Day," Porter Papers.

27. Meade, "Notes on the 5th Corps," Porter Papers.

28. Biddle to Meade, August 18, 1880, and June 10, 1886, Meade Papers.

29. J. W. Clous to Sickles, July 19, 1886, Sickles Papers, New-York Historical Society.

30. Meade to Webb, December 2, 1885, Webb Papers, copy in Brake Collection; Meade to Hunt, July 22, 1886, Hunt Papers; Meade, "Notes on the 2d Day," Porter Papers.

31. Paine to Meade, May 20, 1886, and May 22, 1886, Meade Papers; Paine to Theodore Lyman, June 27, 1877, copy in Warren Papers.

32. Gibbon to Meade, July 24, 1886, Meade Papers.

33. The reports of Greene's brigade are vague as to the time the unit left Cemetery Ridge. Only the report of Col. Henry A. Barnum of the 149th New York (*O.R.*, vol. 27, part 1, 868) mentions the time. Barnum wrote that his regiment moved to the right at four o'clock. All other regimental reports indicate six o'clock as the time they took position on Culp's Hill.

34. For the times mentioned by units of Candy's brigade, see *O.R.*, vol. 27, part 1, 839 (report of Col. John H. Patrick, 5th Ohio), 840 (report of Col. William R. Creighton, 7th Ohio), and 842 (report of Capt. Wilbur F. Stevens, 29th Ohio). In a postwar monument dedication speech, J. A. Moore of the 147th Pennsylvania said that the division vacated its position at 2:00 A.M. See Pennsylvania Gettysburg Battlefield Commission, *Pennsylvania at Gettysburg: Ceremonies at the Dedication of the Monuments Erected by the Commonwealth of Pennsylvania to Mark the Positions of the Pennsylvania Commands Engaged in the Battle*, 2 vols., ed. John P. Nicholson (Harrisburg, Pa.: E. K. Meyers, State Printer, 1893), 2: 702–3.

35. Haskell, *Battle of Gettysburg*, 103. Gibbon reported to Meade at 6:00 A.M. The actual arrival of the Second Corps was sometime later. The reports of the 2d Corps vary in time between 3:00 and 10:00 A.M., making it almost impossible to draw any valid conclusions on arrival times. Only the report of Maj. Leman W. Bradley of the 64th New York (*O.R.*, vol. 27, part 1, 407) mentioned any specific times. Bradley wrote that his regiment awakened at 2:30 A.M., moved out at 4:10 A.M., halted in a wood at 5:45 A.M., marched out of this wood across the Taneytown Road at 6:10 A.M. and formed line of battle at seven o'clock.

36. *O.R.*, vol. 27, part 1, 511 (Birney's report), 551 (report of Capt. Matthew Donovan, 16th Massachusetts), 563 (report of Maj. William H. Hugo, 70th New York); Asa W. Bartlett, *History of the Twelfth Regiment New Hampshire Volunteers in the War of the Rebellion* (Concord, Mass.: Ira C. Evans, 1897), 120.

37. Meade to Webb, December 7, 1885, Webb Papers, copy in Brake Collection; Meade to Hunt, July 22, 1886, Hunt Papers; Meade, "Notes on the 2d Day," Porter Papers; Meade, *Life and Letters*, 2: 66; Meade, *With Meade at Gettysburg*, 100.

38. For the time of the reconnaissance, see Paine to Meade, May 20, 1886, Meade Papers; and Paine to Theodore Lyman, June 27, 1877, copy in Warren Papers. See also *O.R.*, vol. 27, part 1, 349 (report of Brig. Gen. George J. Stannard), where Stannard wrote that he met Generals Meade and Howard about 3:00 A.M., as the generals rode south along Cemetery Ridge.

39. See note 35 above for the arrival times of the 2d Corps.

40. The time of Captain Meade's visit to Sickles' headquarters is my reconstruction of events. Most historians write that Captain Meade visited Sickles between 8:00 and 9:00 A.M. (For example, see Coddington, *Gettysburg Campaign*, 343). However, considering the time that Birney deployed, and Sickles' statement to Meade that his troops were moving, a time after eight o'clock seems too late.

41. *C.C.W.*, 331.
42. Coddington, *Gettysburg Campaign*, 349.
43. Gibbon to Meade, July 24, 1886, Meade Papers.

Chapter 8
1. *C.C.W.*, 297–98.
2. Sickles, "The Gettysburg Battle," *New York Times*, August 14, 1882.
3. "Fighting 'Joe,'" *Boston Herald*, April 9, 1886.
4. Sickles, "Gettysburg," *National Tribune*, July 15, 22, 1886.
5. Sickles, "Sickles Speaks Out," *New York Times*, August 14, 1886.
6. Sickles, "Sickles Talks Back," *New York Times*, July 5, 1891.
7. Sickles et al., "Further Recollections," 263–64, 267.
8. This topographical description is from Hunt, "Second Day," 295–96.
9. *C.C.W.*, 449–50.
10. Ibid., 450.
11. Hunt, "Second Day," 301–3.
12. *C.C.W.*, 393; Andrew A. Humphreys memo dated July 3, 1869, Humphreys Papers.
13. Edward R. Bowen, "Collis' Zouaves: The 114th Pennsylvania Infantry at Gettysburg," Philadelphia *Weekly Press*, June 22, 1887.
14. De Trobriand, *Four Years*, 494.
15. Figures are from *O.R.*, vol. 27, part 1, 151.
16. Busey and Martin, *Regimental Strengths and Losses at Gettysburg*, 16.
17. Ibid., 3–15.
18. Ibid., 16.
19. The frontage measurements were supplied by Kathleen Georg Harrison, using the Warren Survey Map as a base against which to measure.
20. For the positions of Birney's regiments during the evening of July 1, see David Craft, *History of the One Hundred and Forty-first Regiment Pennsylvania Volunteers, 1862–1865* (Towanda, Pa.: Reporter-Journal Printing, 1885), 117–18.
21. For Greene's bivouac, see Charles P. Horton to Bachelder, January 23, 1867, Bachelder Papers.
22. See Craft, *History of the 141st Pennsylvania*, 117, for the location of Humphreys' men.
23. On Ward's deployment, see the following: *O.R.*, vol. 27, part 1, 493 (report of General Ward), 511 (report of Lt. Col. Benjamin L. Higgins, 86th New York), 513 (report of Maj. John W. Moore, 99th Pennsylvania); *New York at Gettysburg*, 2: 868 (for the 124th New York); *Pennsylvania at Gettysburg*, 2: 532 (for the 99th Pennsylvania).
24. N. B. Easton, "The Third Corps at Gettysburg," *National Tribune*, October 8, 1908.
25. On Graham's deployment, see *O.R.*, vol. 27, part 1, 498 (report of Col. Andrew H. Tippin, 68th Pennsylvania), 500 (report of Col. Calvin A. Craig, 105th Pennsylvania), 504 (report of Col. Henry J. Madill, 141st Pennsylvania); Bowen, "114th Pennsylvania."
26. On de Trobriand's position, see Craft, *History of the 141st Pennsylvania*, 118.

27. For Humphreys' deployment, see *O.R.*, vol. 27, part 1, 531–32 (General Humphreys' report), 543 (report of Brig. Gen. Joseph B. Carr), 551 (report of Capt. Matthew Donovan, 16th Massachusetts), 552–53 (report of Col. Robert McAllister, 11th New Jersey), 558 (report of Col. William R. Brewster), 563 (report of Maj. William H. Hugo, 70th New York), 565 (report of Col. John S. Austin, 72d New York), 570 (report of Col. George C. Burling); Bartlett, *12th New Hampshire*, 120–21; *C.C.W.*, 390 (Humphreys' testimony).
28. *O.R.*, vol. 27, part 1, 581 (report of Captain Randolph), 585 (report of Captain Clark), 589 (report of Lt. Benjamin Freeborn, Battery E, 1st Rhode Island).
29. Coddington, *Gettysburg Campaign*, 349.
30. See Hunt to Meade, July 24, 1886, and March 10, 1887, Meade Papers.

Notes to Chapter 9
1. *C.C.W.*, 297–98.
2. Ibid., 299–300.
3. Sickles, "The Gettysburg Battle," *New York Times*, August 14, 1882.
4. "Fighting 'Joe,'" *Boston Herald*, April 9, 1886.
5. Sickles, "Gettysburg," *National Tribune*, July 22, 1886.
6. Sickles, "Sickles Speaks Out," *New York Times*, August 14, 1886.
7. Sickles et al., "Further Recollections," 263–65.
8. Longstreet, *Lee and Longstreet at High Tide*, 22.
9. *C.C.W.*, 424–25, 433; "Fighting 'Joe,'" *Boston Herald*, April 9, 1886; Sickles et al., "Further Recollections," 282, 286.
10. Doubleday, *Chancellorsville and Gettysburg*, 184–85.
11. Doubleday, "Meade at Gettysburg," *New York Times*, April 1, 1883.
12. United States Congress, Joint Committee on the Conduct of the War, *Supplemental Report of the Joint Committee on the Conduct of the War*, 2 vols. (Washington, D.C.: Government Printing Office, 1866), 2: 10.
13. George Meade, *Did General Meade Desire to Retreat at the Battle of Gettysburg?* (Philadelphia: Porter & Coates, 1883); reprinted in Meade, *Life and Letters*, 2: 400–22.
14. Meade, *Life and Letters*, 2: 404–6. At least one of Pleasonton's cavalry officers thought that his chief was a bad character and essentially a humbug and glory seeker. See Worthington C. Ford, ed., *A Cycle of Adams Letters, 1861–1865*, 2 vols. (Boston: Houghton Mifflin, 1920), 2: 8, 44, 111. Col. Charles R. Lowell of the 2d Massachusetts Cavalry thought Pleasonton's reputation and promotions were bolstered by "systematic lying." The latter is quoted in Stephen Z. Starr, *The Union Cavalry in the Civil War*, 3 vols. (Baton Rouge: Louisiana State University Press, 1979–85), 1: 314.
15. Meade, *Life and Letters*, 2: 406; *O.R.*, vol. 27, part 1, 1021 (Robertson's report).
16. *C.C.W.*, 403–5, 412.
17. Ibid., 442; Gibbon, *Personal Recollections*, 139–40; Gibbon, "Another View," 708.
18. *C.C.W.*, 452; Hunt, "Second Day," 300.
19. *C.C.W.*, 461.

20. Ibid., 465–66, 468.
21. Ibid., 302.
22. For the best account of this council, see Coddington, *Gettysburg Campaign*, 449–53. For adverse criticism of Meade, see Tucker, *High Tide*, 307–12, and Hoke, *Great Invasion*, 352–54. On the damage to Meade's reputation, see Coddington, "Strange Reputation of Meade," 145–46.
23. For Hunt's and Tyler's absences, see *C.C.W.*, 451, and Hunt to Warren, October 8, 1879, Warren Papers.
24. *O.R.*, vol. 27, part 1, 73–74; Gibbon, *Personal Recollections*, 142–44.
25. *C.C.W.*, 313 (Howe's testimony), 367–68 (Birney's testimony), 425 (Butterfield's testimony).
26. Slocum to Doubleday, February 19, 1883, in Doubleday, "Meade at Gettysburg," *New York Times*, April 1, 1883.
27. Fishel, *Secret War for the Union*, 526–30. It is quite evident from this text that Fishel agrees with the Sickles view of Meade as a timid and vacillating general until he heard the intelligence report.
28. *C.C.W.*, 350, 436.
29. *O.R..*, vol. 27, part 1, 72.
30. The circular letter and replies can be found in *O.R.*, vol. 27, part 1, 123–27, 139. They were reprinted in Meade, *Life and Letters*, 2: 413–16.
31. *C.C.W.*, 407, 441–43, 460.
32. Newton, "Reminiscences of Gettysburg," *New York Times*, March 13, 1887; Newton to Gibbon, January 5, 1876, in Gibbon, *Personal Recollections*, 197.
33. Gibbon, *Personal Recollections*, 140–45; Gibbon, "Another View," 708–9.
34. Sykes to Gibbon, December 24, 1875, in Gibbon, *Personal Recollections*, 195–96.
35. Howard to Meade, June 9, 1883, in Meade, *Life and Letters*, 2: 418–19. The original letter is in the Meade Papers.
36. See Warren's memo of this conversation, October 1, 1879, Warren Papers.
37. For Birney's complaint to Meade, see Gibbon, *Personal Recollections*, 144. See Warren to Sykes, August 20, 1876, copy in Warren Papers, for Warren's appraisal of Birney. A brief biography highlighting Birney's personal traits appears in Pfanz, *Gettysburg*, 83–86. Birney did not survive the war. He was later promoted to command of the 10th Corps, Army of the James, but died in October 1864 of malaria.
38. For Slocum's grievances, see Coddington, *Gettysburg Campaign*, 772–73, note 57.
39. For the incident concerning James E. Kelly and the engraving of the council of war, see the following, all in the Warren Papers: Kelly to Warren, September 29, 1879; Warren's memos of October 1 and 2, 1879; Warren to Hunt, October 1, 1879 (copy); Warren to Hancock, October 1, 1879 (copy); William G. Mitchell to Warren, October 2, 1879; Hunt to Warren, October 8, 1879; Warren to Kelly, October 17, 1879 (copy); Warren to Meade, October 18 and 24, 1879 (copies). The sketch Kelly made is reproduced in Cleaves, *Meade of Gettysburg*, between pages 148 and 149. This sketch never did appear in Bryant's history.
40. Warren to Hancock, October 1, 1879, copy in Warren Papers.

Notes to Chapter 10

1. Undated account of the movements of the 2d Corps during the Gettysburg Campaign by Charles H. Morgan, Bachelder Papers.
2. For Lee's reports, see *O.R.*, vol. 27, part 2, 308, 318.
3. General McLaws thought that had Sickles remained on Cemetery Ridge and occupied Little Round Top, Longstreet would not have attacked. See McLaws, "Second Day at Gettysburg," Philadelphia *Weekly Press*, August 4, 1886.
4. Sickles to Hunt, undated 1886 letter, Hunt Papers.
5. Col. Edward Porter Alexander, one of Longstreet's artillery officers, thought the Peach Orchard position was not of any benefit to the Rebels after they seized control of it. On the evening of July 2, Longstreet instructed Alexander to arrange the corps artillery to support the projected assault on the Union center the next day. The colonel arranged his cannon and was not happy. "All the vicinity of the Peach Orchard, any how, was very unfavorable ground for us, generally sloping toward the enemy. This exposed all our movements to his view, & our horses, limbers, & caissons to his fire. If any who read [*sic*] this ever go over that ground, & then see the beautiful ridge positions from which the enemy could answer us, with more & bigger guns, & better ammunition, I know we will have their sympathies." See Gary W. Gallagher, ed., *Fighting for the Confederacy: The Personal Recollections of General Edward Porter Alexander* (Chapel Hill: University of North Carolina Press, 1989), 244–45.
6. Sickles and Hooker were friends before Chancellorsville, but there is evidence that Sickles berated Hooker's generalship at the council of war on the night of May 4. See Warren to Biddle, May 26, 1877, copy in Warren Papers, for Warren's statements about this council.
7. Hunt to The Century Company, September 26, 1885, Century Collection.
8. Edward Cropsey, a reporter in the army for the *Philadelphia Inquirer*, acting on a story supplied to him by Rep. Elihu B. Washburne of Illinois, wrote that after the initial fighting in the "Wilderness," Meade had advocated a retreat across the Rappahannock River but was overruled by General Grant. Although the story was untrue, it received wide publicity. Meade's temper got the best of him in this case and he had Cropsey expelled from the army. In retaliation, several reporters banded together and refused to include Meade's name in their stories unless the general's name was coupled with unfavorable reports. See Cleaves, *Meade of Gettysburg*, 252–55, for a more complete view of this incident. For a contemporary view of the situation, see Allan Nevins, ed., *A Diary of Battle: The Personal Journals of Colonel Charles S. Wainwright 1861–1865* (New York: Harcourt, Brace & World, 1962), 409.
9. Ropes to Gray, April 16, 1864, in Gray and Ropes, *War Letters*, 318.
10. Tucker, *High Tide*, 238–39.
11. Hunt to Webb, January 12, 1888, in Powell, *Fifth Corps*, 559.

BIBLIOGRAPHY

Unpublished Primary Sources

Civil War Library and Museum, Philadelphia, Pa. James C. M. Hamilton, manuscript history of the 110th Pennsylvania.

Duke University, William R. Perkins Library, Manuscripts Department, Durham, N.C. Lafayette McLaws Papers. Daniel Edgar Sickles Letterpress Book.

Historical Society of Pennsylvania, Philadelphia, Pa. James Cornell Biddle Letters. Andrew Atkinson Humphreys Papers. George Gordon Meade Papers.

Library of Congress, Manuscripts Department, Washington D.C. Henry Jackson Hunt Papers. Fitz-John Porter Papers.

National Archives, Washington, D.C. Record Group 94, Records of the Office of the Adjutant General. F442, VS 1863, Box 222, Hiram Berdan.

New Hampshire Historical Society, Concord, N.H. John Badger Bachelder Papers.

New-York Historical Society, New York, N.Y. James Barnes Papers. William H. Paine Papers. Daniel Edgar Sickles Papers.

New York Public Library. Astor, Lennox and Tilden Foundation, Rare Books and Manuscripts Department, New York, N.Y. Henry Jackson Hunt Correspondence. In Century Company Records. Daniel Edgar Sickles Papers.

New York State Library, Albany, N.Y. Gouverneur Kemble Warren Papers.

Southern Historical Collection. Wilson Library, University of North Carolina, Chapel Hill, N.C. Edward Porter Alexander Papers.

United States Army Military History Institute, Manuscripts Department, Carlisle Barracks, Pa. Robert L. Brake Collection.

Virginia Historical Society, Division of Archives and Manuscripts, Richmond, Va. Samuel R. Johnston Letters. Robert Edward Lee Headquarters Papers.

Yale University Library, Manuscripts and Archives Division, New Haven, Conn. Alexander Stewart Webb Papers.

Published Primary Sources

Alexander, Edward P. "Colonel E. P. Alexander's Report of the Battle of Gettysburg." *Southern Historical Society Papers* 4 (1877): 235–39.

———. "Letter from General E. P. Alexander." *Southern Historical Society Papers* 4 (1877): 97–111.

———. *Military Memoirs of a Confederate: A Critical Narrative.* New York: Charles Scribner's Sons, 1907.

Another Eye-witness (pseud.). "The Battle of Gettysburg." *New York Herald*, March 16, 1864.

Barnes, James. "The Battle of Gettysburg." *New York Herald*, March 21, 1864.

Benedict, George G. "General Meade's Letter on Gettysburg. A Letter Written by General Meade, Now Published, Concerning General Sickles' Conduct at Gettysburg." Philadelphia *Weekly Press*, August 11, 1886.

Benjamin, Charles F. "Hooker's Appointment and Removal." *The Century Magazine* 23 (November 1886): 106–11. Reprinted in Robert U. Johnson and Clarence C. Buel, eds. *Battles and Leaders of the Civil War, Being for the Most Part Contributions by Union and Confederate Officers, Based Upon "The Century War Series."* 4 vols. New York: The Century, 1884–89, 3: 239–43.

Berdan, Hiram. "General Berdan, and His Famous Sharpshooters at Gettysburg." *National Tribune*, September 9, 1886.

Biddle, James C. "Generals Meade and Sickles at Gettysburg." Philadelphia *Weekly Press*, July 14, 1886.

———. "Sickles in Hot Water." Philadelphia *Press*, July 18, 1886.

Clark, George. *A Glance Backward; Or Some Events in the Past History of My Life.* Houston, Tex.: Press of Rein & Sons, 1914.

De Trobriand, Philippe Regis de Kerendern, Comte. "The Battle of Gettysburg Once More—The Fog Thicker and Thicker." *New York Herald*, March 29, 1864.

———. *Four Years with the Army of the Potomac.* Trans. George K. Dauchy. Boston, Mass., 1889.

Easton, Noble B. "The Third Corps Position at Gettysburg. The Battle Began Later Than Stated. The Corps's Disadvantageous Position." *National Tribune*, October 8, 1908.

Ford, Worthington C., ed. *A Cycle of Adams Letters 1861–1865.* 2 vols. Boston, Mass.: Houghton Mifflin, 1920.

Gallagher, Gary W., ed. *Fighting for the Confederacy: The Personal Recollections of General Edward Porter Alexander.* Chapel Hill: University of North Carolina Press, 1989.

Gibbon, John. *Personal Recollections of the Civil War.* New York: G. P. Putnam's Sons, 1928; reprint edition, Dayton, Ohio: Press of Morningside, 1978.

Gray, John C., and John C. Ropes. *War Letters 1862–1865 of John Chipman Gray and John Codman Ropes.* Cambridge, Mass.: Riverside Press for the Massachusetts Historical Society, 1927.

Haskell, Frank C. *The Battle of Gettysburg.* Madison: Wisconsin History Commission, 1908.

Herbert, Hilary A. "Colonel Hilary A. Herbert's 'History of the Eighth Alabama Volunteer Regiment, C.S.A.'" Ed. Maurice S. Fortin. *Alabama Historical Quarterly* 39 (1977): 5–321.

Historicus (pseud.). "The Battle of Gettysburg. Historicus in Reply to General Barnes and the Staff Officers of the Second and Fifth Corps. The Evidence Before the Committee on the Conduct of the War, &c." *New York Herald*, April 4, 1864.

———. "The Battle of Gettysburg. Important Communication from an Eye-Witness. How the Victory was Won and How Its Advantages were Lost. Generals Halleck's and Meade's Official Reports Refuted." *New York Herald*, March 12, 1864.

Hunt, Henry J. "The Second Day at Gettysburg." *The Century Magazine* 23 (December 1886): 278–95. Reprinted in Robert U. Johnson and Clarence C. Buel, eds. *Battles and Leaders of the Civil War, Being for the Most Part Contributions by Union and Confederate Officers, Based Upon "The Century War Series."* 4 vols. New York: The Century, 1884–89, 3:290–313.

Johnson, H. A. *The Sword of Honor: A Story of the Civil War.* Hallowell, Maine: Register Printing House, 1906.

Johnson, Robert U., and Clarence C. Buel, eds. *Battles and Leaders of the Civil War, Being for the Most Part Contributions by Union and Confederate Officers, Based Upon "The Century War Series."* 4 vols. New York: The Century, 1884–1889.

Jones, Jesse H. "Saved the Day. Greene's Battery [*sic*] Behaves Nobly at Gettysburg." *National Tribune*, March 7, 1895.

Kershaw, Joseph B. "Kershaw's Brigade at Gettysburg." Robert U. Johnson and Clarence C. Buel, eds. *Battles and Leaders of the Civil War, Being for the Most Part Contributions by Union and Confederate Officers, Based Upon "The Century War Series."* 4 vols. New York: The Century, 1884–89, 3:331–38.

McClellan, Carswell. "The Battle of Gettysburg. Gen. Humphreys' Chief of Staff Contributes Something to the Discussion—A Caustic Criticism of Gen. Sickles." St. Paul *Pioneer Press*, August 15, 1886. Reprinted and excerpted as "Sickles at Gettysburg. Gen. Meade's Order and How He Executed It." *New York Times*, August 16, 1886.

McLaws, Lafayette. "The Battle of Gettysburg." Philadelphia *Weekly Press*, April 21, 1886.

———. "The Battle of Gettysburg." In United Confederate Veterans. Georgia Division. Confederate Veterans' Association, Camp 756, Savannah. *Addresses Delivered Before the Confederate Veterans Association of Savannah, Georgia, 1896*, 57–97. Savannah: Press of George N. Nichols, 1896.

———. "Gettysburg." *Southern Historical Society Papers* 7 (1879): 64–90.

———. "The Second Day at Gettysburg. General Sickles Answered by the Commander of the Opposing Force. The Federal Disaster on the Left." Philadelphia *Weekly Press*, August 4, 1886.

McReynolds, Andrew T. "Maj. Gen. Hooker." *Washington Sunday Herald*, December 7, 1879.

Meade, George. *The Life and Letters of George Gordon Meade*. Ed. George G. Meade. 2 vols. New York: Charles Scribner's Sons, 1913.

———. *With Meade at Gettysburg*. Ed. George G. Meade. Philadelphia: John C. Winston, 1930.

Meyers, Alonzo. "Kershaw's Brigade at Peach Orchard." *National Tribune*, January 21, 1926.

Nevins, Allan, ed. *A Diary of Battle: The Personal Journals of Colonel Charles S. Wainwright, 1861–1865*. New York: Harcourt, Brace & World, 1962.

Newton, John. "Reminiscences of Gettysburg." *New York Times*, March 13, 1887.

Piatt, Benjamin M. "A Battle Picture. Thrilling Description of the Great Fight at Gettysburg." Gettysburg *Star and Sentinel*, February 3, 1876.

Rafferty, Thomas. "Gettysburg." In Military Order of the Loyal Legion of the United States, New York Commandery, *Personal Recollections of the War of the Rebellion, First Series*, 1–32. New York: The Commandery, 1891.

Rusling, James F. *Men and Things I Saw in Civil War Days*. New York: Eaton & Mains, 1899.

Sessions, Nathaniel, and L. Y. Allen. "Berdan Sharpshooters. Two Interesting Letters Describing the Important Service They Rendered at Gettysburg." *National Tribune*, August 12, 1886.

Sickles, Daniel E. "Gen. Sickles Speaks Out. A Strong Reply to Gen. Meade's Letter." *New York Times*, August 14, 1886.

———. "Gen. Sickles Talks Back. Answering the Criticisms of Col. McClellan." *New York Times*, July 5, 1891.

———. "Gettysburg. Great Speech of Gen. Sickles on the Battlefield July 2." *National Tribune*, July 15, 22, 1886.

———. "The Gettysburg Battle. The Part Taken by the Third Corps." *New York Times*, August 14, 1882. A more complete account is "General Sickles' Story. The Battle of Gettysburg and the Part of the 3d Corps." Gettysburg *Star and Sentinel*, August 23, 1882.

———. "Sickles Defends the Course Pursued by Him at Gettysburg." *National Tribune*, August 26, 1886.

Sickles, Daniel E., David M. Gregg, John Newton, and Daniel Butterfield. "Further Recollections of Gettysburg." *North American Review* 152 (March 1891): 257–86.

Staff Officer of the Fifth Corps (pseud.). "The Battle of Gettysburg. The Truth of History, &c." *New York Herald*, March 18, 1864.

Tilton, William S. "Letter from Colonel Tilton." *New York Herald*, March 21, 1864.

United States. Congress. Joint Committee on the Conduct of the War. *Report of the Joint Committee on the Conduct of the War, at the Second Session Thirty-eighth Congress*. Vol. 1. *Army of the Potomac. Battle of Petersburg*. Washington: Government Printing Office, 1865.

———. *Supplemental Report of the Joint Committee on the Conduct of the War*. 2 vols. Washington: Government Printing Office, 1866.

United States. War Department. *The War of the Rebellion: A Compilation of the Official Records of the Union and Confederate Armies.* 70 vols. in 128 parts. Washington: Government Printing Office, 1880–1901.

Winslow, George B. "On Little Round Top." Philadelphia *Weekly Times*, July 26, 1879.

Secondary Works

"Another Gettysburg. Colonel Norris Charges that Sickles Disobeyed Orders." Philadelphia *Weekly Press*, July 7, 1886.

"At Gettysburg. Encampment of the G.A.R. of Pennsylvania." *National Tribune*, July 8, 1888.

Bache, Richard M. *Life of General George Gordon Meade, Commander of the Army of the Potomac.* Philadlephia: Henry T. Coates, 1897.

Bachelder, John B. *Gettysburg: What to See and How to See It.* Boston: [self-published], 1873.

Bakeless, John. "James Harrison: Rebel Enigma." *Civil War Times Illustrated* 9 (April 1970): 12–20.

Balch, William R. *The Battle of Gettysburg: An Historical Account.* Philadelphia: Press of McLaughlin Brothers, 1885.

Bates, Samuel P. *The Battle of Gettysburg.* Philadelphia: T. H. Davis, 1875.

Battine, Cecil. *The Crisis of the Confederacy, A History of Gettysburg and the Wilderness.* London: Longmans, Green, 1905.

Beale, James. "Reynolds and Sickles. Mr. James Beale's Important Statement Regarding Gettysburg." *Philadelphia Press*, July 12, 1886.

Beecham, Robert K. *Gettysburg, The Pivotal Battle of the Civil War.* Chicago: A. C. McClurg, 1911.

Bellah, James. *Soldiers' Battle, Gettysburg.* New York: David McKay, 1962.

Benedict, George G. *Vermont at Gettysburgh. A Sketch of the Part Taken by the Vermont Troops in the Battle of Gettysburg.* Burlington, Vt.: Free Press Association, 1870.

Bowen, Edward R. "Collis' Zouaves. The 114th Pennsylvania Infantry at Gettysburg." Philadelphia *Weekly Press*, June 22, 1887.

Burrage, Henry S. *Gettysburg and Lincoln, The Battle, The Cemetery, and the National Park.* New York: G. P. Putnam's Sons, 1906.

Busey, John, and David G. Martin. *Regimental Strengths and Losses at Gettysburg.* Hightstown, N.J.: Longstreet House, 1986.

Cleaves, Freeman. *Meade of Gettysburg.* Norman: University of Oklahoma Press, 1960. Reprint edition, Dayton, Ohio: Press of Morningside, 1980.

Coddington, Edwin B. *The Gettysburg Campaign: A Study in Command.* New York: Charles Scribner's Sons, 1968. Reprint edition, Dayton, Ohio: Press of Morningside, 1979.

———. "The Strange Reputation of George G. Meade: A Lesson in Historiography." *The Historian* 23 (1962): 145–66.

De Peyster, John W. "The Third Corps at Gettysburg, July 2, 1863. General Sickles Vindicated." *The Volunteer* 1 (1869): 307–12, 322–29, 354–59.

Doubleday, Abner. *Chancellorsville and Gettysburg.* New York: Charles Scribner's Sons, 1882.

———. "General Meade at Gettysburg." *New York Times*, April 1, 1883.

Downey, Fairfax. *Clash of Cavalry: The Battle of Brandy Station, June 9, 1863.* New York: David McKay, 1959.

Drake, Samuel A. *The Battle of Gettysburg 1863.* Boston: Lee & Shepard, 1892.

Fiebeger, Gustav J. *The Campaign and Battle of Gettysburg, from the Official Records of the Union and Confederate Armies.* West Point: United States Military Academy Press, 1915.

"Fighting 'Joe.' Reunion of the Third Army Corps. Notable Gathering in Music Hall. Record of the Third Corps Defended." *Boston Herald*, April 9, 1886.

Fishel, Edwin C. *The Secret War for the Union: The Untold Story of Military Intelligence in the Civil War.* Boston: Houghton-Mifflin, 1996.

Freeman, Douglas S. *Lee's Lieutenants: A Study in Command.* 3 vols. New York: Charles Scribner's Sons, 1942–44.

Gibbon, John. "Another View of Gettysburg." *North American Review* 152 (June 1891): 704–13.

Graham, W. A. *The Custer Myth: A Source Book of Custeriana.* Harrisburg, Pa.: The Stackpole, 1953.

Grout, William W. "Address of Lieutenant-Colonel Grout." *Proceedings of the Reunion Society of Vermont Officers, 1864–1884, with Addresses Delivered at Its Meetings . . . and a Roster of the Society,* 114–32. Burlington, Vt.: Free Press Association, 1885.

Hoke, Jacob. *The Great Invasion of 1863; Or, General Lee in Pennsylvania.* Dayton, Ohio: W. J. Shuey, 1887.

"Hooker's Name, and Brave Dan Sickles and His Crutches at the Old Third Corps Reunion." Boston *Daily Globe*, April 9, 1886.

Jacobs, Michael. *Notes on the Rebel Invasion of Maryland and Pennsylvania and the Battle of Gettysburg, July 1, 2 and 3, 1863. Accompanied by an Explanatory Map.* Philadelphia: J. B. Lippincott, 1864.

Johnson, H. A. "What Regiment Supported Berdan's Sharpshooters?" *National Tribune*, May 16, 1889.

Klein, Frederic S. "Meade's Pipe Creek Line." *Maryland Historical Magazine* 57 (1962): 133–49.

Longstreet, Helen D. *Lee and Longstreet at High Tide: Gettysburg in the Light of the Official Records.* Gainesville, Ga.: [self-published], 1904.

Marcot, Roy M. *Hiram Berdan, Civil War Chief of Sharpshooters, Military Commander and Firearms Inventor.* Irvine, Calif.: Northwood Heritage Press, 1989.

McClellan, Carswell. "The Second Day's Battle, and General Sickles's Part in It." *New York Sun*, June 28, 1891.

Meade, George. *Did General Meade Desire to Retreat at the Battle of Gettysburg?* Philadelphia: Porter & Coates, 1883.

Montgomery, James S. *The Shaping of a Battle: Gettysburg.* Philadelphia: Chilton Book, 1959.

National Cyclopaedia of American Biography. 63 vols. New York: J. T. White, 1898–84.

"The New Battle of Gettysburg." *New York Tribune,* August 8, 1886.

New York Monuments Commission for the Battlefields of Gettysburg and Chattanooga. *Final Report on the Battlefield of Gettysburg.* 3 vols. Ed. William F. Fox. Albany, N.Y.: J. B. Lyon, Printers, 1900.

Nichols, Edward J. *Toward Gettysburg: A Biography of General John F. Reynolds.* University Park: The Pennsylvania State University Press, 1960.

Norris, A. Wilson. "The Gettysburg Controversy. A Letter from Colonel Norris, Giving His Authorities for His Statements." *Philadelphia Press,* July 14, 1886.

Norton, Oliver W. *The Attack and Defense of Little Round Top, Gettysburg, July 2, 1863.* New York: Neale, 1913. Reprint edition, Dayton, Ohio: Press of Morningside, 1978.

Nye, Wilbur S. *Here Come the Rebels!* Baton Rouge: Louisiana State University Press, 1965.

"On Gettysburg Field." Philadelphia *Weekly Times,* June 17, 1882.

"On Gettysburg's Field. Auspicious Opening of the Great Reunion." *New York Times,* July 2, 1888.

Pennsylvania. Gettysburg Battlefield Commission. *Pennsylvania at Gettysburg. Ceremonies at the Dedication of the Monuments Erected by the Commonwealth of Pennsylvania to Mark the Positions of the Pennsylvania Commands Engaged in the Battle.* 2 vols. Ed. John P. Nicholson. Harrisburg, Pa.: E. K. Meyers, State Printer, 1893.

Pennypacker, Isaac R. *General Meade.* New York: D. Appleton, 1901.

Pfanz, Harry W. *Gettysburg—The Second Day.* Chapel Hill: University of North Carolina Press, 1988.

Pierce, Francis M. *The Battle of Gettysburg: The Crest Wave of the American Civil War.* New York: Neale, 1914.

Pierson, W. W., Jr. "The Committee on the Conduct of the Civil War." *American Historical Review* 23 (1918): 550–76.

Pinchon, Edgcumb. *Dan Sickles: Hero of Gettysburg and "Yankee King of Spain."* Garden City, N.Y.: Doubleday, Doran, 1945.

Post, Marie C. *The Life and Memories of Comte Regis de Trobriand, Major General in the Army of the United States.* New York: E. P. Dutton, 1910.

Rosengarten, Joseph G. "Rosengarten's Reply. Was Sickles Dilatory in Moving to the Front?" *Philadelphia Press,* August 15, 1886.

Sauers, Richard A. "Colonel Hiram Berdan and the 1st United States Sharpshooters." *Susquehanna University Studies* 12 #1 (1983): 26–42.

Scott, James K. P. *The Story of the Battles of Gettysburg.* Harrisburg, Pa.: Telegraph Press, 1927.

Stackpole, Edward J. *They Met at Gettysburg.* Harrisburg, Pa.: Eagle Books, 1956.

Starr, Stephen Z. *The Union Cavalry in the Civil War.* 3 vols. Baton Rouge: Louisiana State University Press, 1979–85.

Steinman, D. B. *Builders of the Bridge: The Story of John Roebling and His Son.* New York: Harcourt, Brace, 1945.

Swanberg, W. A. *Sickles the Incredible.* New York: Charles Scribner's Sons, 1956.

Sword, Wiley. *Sharpshooter: Hiram Berdan, His Famous Sharpshooters and Their Sharps Rifles.* Lincoln, R.I.: Andrew Mowbray, 1988.

Tap, Bruce. *Over Lincoln's Shoulder: The Committee on the Conduct of the War.* Lawrence: University Press of Kansas, 1998.

Taylor, Emerson G. *Gouverneur Kemble Warren: The Life and Letters of an American Soldier, 1830–1882.* Boston: Houghton Mifflin, 1932.

"The Third Army Corps. Its Reunion in the Music Hall Yesterday. General Sickles Defends Hooker's Cause and His Own. The Dinner at the Revere House." Boston *Evening Transcript*, April 9, 1886.

Tucker, Glenn. *High Tide at Gettysburg: The Campaign in Pennsylvania.* Indianapolis, Ind.: Bobbs-Merrill, 1958. Reprint edition, Dayton, Ohio: Press of Morningside, 1973.

———. *Lee and Longstreet at Gettysburg.* Indianapolis, Ind.: Bobbs-Merrill, 1968.

Vanderslice, John M. *Gettysburg. Where and How the Regiments Fought and the Troops They Encountered. An Account of the Battle, Giving Movements, Positions, and Losses of the Commands Engaged.* Philadelphia: J. B. Lippincott, 1897.

Young, Jesse B. *The Battle of Gettysburg: A Comprehensive Narrative.* New York: Harper & Brothers, 1913. Reprint edition, Dayton, Ohio: Press of Morningside, 1976.

General Civil War Histories Consulted for Chapter 5

Abbott, John S. C. *The History of the Civil War in America.* 2 vols. Springfield, Mass.: Gurdon Bill, 1866.

Blythe, Vernon. *A History of the Civil War in the United States.* New York: Neale, 1914.

Catton, Bruce. *Glory Road.* Garden City, N.Y.: Doubleday, 1952.

Chesney, Charles C. *Campaigns in Virginia, Maryland, etc. etc.* 2 vols. London: Smith, Elder, 1865.

Coffin, Charles C. *Marching to Victory.* New York: Harper & Brothers, 1889.

Crafts, W. A. *The Southern Rebellion: Being a History of the United States from the Commencement of President Buchanan's Administration Through the War for the Suppression of the Rebellion.* 2 vols. Boston: Samuel Walker, 1867.

Dodge, Theodore A. *A Bird's-Eye View of Our Civil War.* Boston: James R. Osgood, 1883.

Draper, John W. *History of the American Civil War.* 3 vols. New York: Harper & Brothers, 1870.

Eicher, David J. *The Longest Night: A Military History of the Civil War.* New York: Simon & Schuster, 2001.

Fletcher, Henry C. *History of the American War.* 3 vols. London: R. Bentley, 1865.

Foote, Shelby. *The Civil War: A Narrative.* 3 vols. New York: Random House, 1958–74.

Formby, John. *The American Civil War.* New York: Charles Scribner's Sons, 1910.

Geer, Walter. *Campaigns of the Civil War.* New York: Brentano's, 1926.

Glazier, Willard. *Battles for the Union.* Hartford, Conn.: Gilman, 1878.

Greeley, Horace. *The American Conflict: A History of the Great Rebellion in the United States of America, 1860–'65.* 2 vols. Hartford, Conn.: O. D. Case, 1864–67.

Hattaway, Herman. *Shades of Blue and Gray: An Introductory Military History of the Civil War.* Columbia: University of Missouri Press, 1997.

Headley, Joel T. *The Great Rebellion: A History of the Civil War in the United States.* 2 vols. Hartford, Conn.: American, 1863–1866.

Hosmer, James K. *The American Civil War.* 2 vols. New York: Harper & Brothers, 1913.

Humphrey, Willis C. *The Great Contest: A History of the Military and Naval Operations during the Civil War in the United States of America, 1861–1865.* Detroit: C. H. Smith, 1886.

Johnson, Rossiter. *A History of the War of Succession, 1861–1865.* Boston: Ticknor, 1888.

Kettell, Thomas P. *History of the Great Rebellion.* Hartford, Conn.: L. Stebbins, 1865.

Livermore, William R. *The Story of the Civil War: A Concise Account of the War in the United States of America Between 1861 and 1865, in Continuation of the Story by John Codman Ropes.* Part 3, book 2: *The Campaigns of 1863 to July 10th, Vicksburg, Port Hudson, Tullahoma and Gettysburg.* New York: G. P. Putnam's Sons, 1913.

Lossing, Benson J. *Pictorial History of the Civil War.* 3 vols. Hartford, Conn.: T. Belknap, 1866–1868.

McMaster, John B. *A History of the People of the United States through Lincoln's Administration.* New York: D. Appleton, 1927.

Mahan, Asa. *A Critical History of the Late American War.* New York: A. S. Barnes, 1877.

Moore, James. *A Complete History of the Great Rebellion; Or, The Civil War in the United States, 1861–1865.* New York: Hurst, 1866.

d'Orléans, Louis Philippe Albert, Comte de Paris. *History of the Civil War in America.* 4 vols. Trans. Louis F. Tasistro. Vols. 1 and 2, ed. Henry Coppee. Vols. 3 and 4, ed. John P. Nicholson. Philadelphia: Porter & Coates, 1875–88.

Schmucker, Samuel M. *A History of the Civil War in the United States.* 2 vols. Philadelphia: Bradley, 1864–65.

Storke, Elliott G., and L. P. Brockett. *The Complete History of the Great American Rebellion, Embracing Its Causes and Events and Consequences.* 2 vols. Auburn, N.Y.: Auburn, 1865.

Swinton, William. *Campaigns of the Army of the Potomac: A Critical History of Operations in Virginia, Maryland, and Pennsylvania from the Commencement to the Close of the War, 1861–1865.* New York: Charles B. Richardson, 1866.

———. *The Twelve Decisive Battles of the War.* New York: Dick & Fitzgerald, 1867.

Weigley, Russell F. *A Great Civil War: A Military and Political History, 1861–1865.* Bloomington: Indiana University Press, 2000.

Wilson, John L. *The Pictorial History of the Great Civil War.* Kansas City: Western Installment Book, 1878.

INDEX

ABOUT THE AUTHOR

RICHARD A. SAUERS, PH.D., is a military historian whose previous books include *Advance the Colors! Pennsylvania Civil War Battleflags, The Civil War Journal of Colonel William J. Bolton,* and *How to Do Civil War Research.* Dr. Sauers holds a master's degree and doctorate in American history from Pennsylvania State University.